THE UGLY HISTORY OF BEAUTIFUL THINGS

ESSAYS ON DESIRE AND CONSUMPTION

KATY KELLEHER

SIMON & SCHUSTER
New York   London   Toronto   Sydney   New Delhi

SIMON & SCHUSTER
1230 Avenue of the Americas
New York, NY 10020

First Simon & Schuster hardcover edition April 2023

SIMON & SCHUSTER and colophon are registered trademarks of Simon & Schuster, Inc.

For information about special discounts for bulk purchases, please contact Simon & Schuster Special Sales at 1-866-506-1949 or business@simonandschuster.com.

The Simon & Schuster Speakers Bureau can bring authors to your live event. For more information or to book an event, contact the Simon & Schuster Speakers Bureau at 1-866-248-3049 or visit our website at www.simonspeakers.com.

Manufactured in the United States of America

10 9 8 7 6 5 4 3 2 1

Library of Congress Control Number: 2023930363

ISBN 978-1-9821-7935-9
ISBN 978-1-9821-7937-3 (ebook)

For Juniper

It is as though beautiful things have been placed here and there throughout the world to serve as small wake-up calls to perception, spurring lapsed alertness back to its most acute level. Through its beauty, the world continually recommits us to a rigorous standard of perceptual care: if we do not search it out, it comes and finds us.
ELAINE SCARRY, *On Beauty and Being Just*

This world is empty to him alone who does not understand how to direct his libido towards objects, and to render them alive and beautiful for himself, for Beauty does not indeed lie in things, but in the feeling that we give to them.
CARL JUNG, *Psychology of the Unconscious*

CONTENTS

CONTENTS

INTRODUCTION

Once, years ago, when I was in therapy for chronic depression, my doctor asked me a simple question. I had just expressed, for what must have been the thousandth time, my ambiguous relationship to survival. I wasn't particularly interested in living, and she knew this. But I also wasn't particularly interested in dying, so we talked around the issue of suicide and focused instead on my general existential dread, my near-constant state of disappointment with the universe. In this particular session, my not-very-good therapist finally asked me a question that mattered.

"What makes you keep getting up and out of bed if you're so bored of everything?" She may have phrased it more sensitively than that, but this is what I remember. I thought about it for a bit, and then I said something that surprised us both. "Beauty," I told her. "I get up because I might see or hold something beautiful." She tented her fingers and hummed. "That's unusual," she said.

Is it unusual? Perhaps. But over the years, I've come to realize just how important beauty is to my life, and to the lives of the people around me. The hope for beauty makes me leave my bed each morning rather than moldering in the sheets until I develop bedsores. The desire for beauty keeps me going to work so I can make money to buy plane tickets to beautiful places, buy beautiful objects, and support people who make beautiful work. The need to share beauty compels me to write, to create, to interact with others.

Beauty and depression are two central factors of my life. Beauty gives light to the darkness; it gives me hope and a sense of purpose. But beauty isn't all rainbows and sunshine. Beauty is also dark. Beauty is ugly. In all my beauty-seeking, I've never found an object that was untouched by the depravity of human greed or unblemished by the chemical undoings of time. There are no pure things in this world: everything that lives does harm; everything that exists degrades. Yet many of us are drawn to these pretty, depraved things. We want to possess and caress the very things that frighten us.

The attraction-repulsion dynamic is something that has interested me since I was an emo teen reading too much Edgar Allan Poe and contemplating suicide in my mother's sunroom. Like many of my stoner friends, I was drawn to the seedier aspects of music culture and more than a little obsessed with the figure of the tragic, starving, alcoholic artist. I believed, like many angsty adolescents do, that my suffering marked me as unique, that my pain (and my obsession with pain) granted me some form of dark glamour. As I grew up, I found that adults lack patience for this sort of morbid posturing, so I became rather more private about my ongoing struggle with depression. I stopped dropping casual references to my family history of suicide into party chitchat and I covered my self-harm scars with floral tattoos.

In my twenties, I found work as a home and design writer, where I was encouraged to write about sun-drenched kitchens and engineered-stone countertops—work I enjoyed, but all the focus on prettiness left me feeling a bit empty (and rather like a tool of the capitalist machine). Publicly, I wrote about beautiful things and their various charms, encouraging readers to spend their money on hand-thrown pottery and naturally dyed linen sheets. (I still think these are nice to own, to be clear.) But in my alone time, I enjoyed reading stories of poison and madness, ritual suffering and animal exploitation. I kept returning to dwell on the ugliness of the world. It was seductive and familiar. I was a rubbernecker, I admit it, but I was also looking for evidence of something I believed to be true. I felt that aesthetic experiences, both positive and negative, were more vital than our culture seemed willing to admit, that beauty and ugliness were deeply intertwined, and that our sensory experiences were slowly being eroded and degraded, replaced with virtual reality and sanitized digital representations.

Then in 2018, my dream column was accepted at *Longreads*. I called it the Ugly History of Beautiful Things, and it was in those pieces that I finally found a way to combine my various interests and pet projects. I began spending all my spare time sifting through histories and collecting stories, devoting hours to reading about perfume mixology, vintage makeup formulations, and the German obsession with uber-white porcelain. I listened to radio shows about cursed jewels and visited botanical gardens to catch a glimpse of historically maligned tropical blossoms. I learned about the quiet, complicated lives of mollusks and the dangerous work of cutting countertops. In researching these objects, I came to see how skillfully we've papered over the crimes of the past, how thoroughly we've hidden evidence of our ugliness behind beautiful facades, and how quickly we can forget the pain of others if it means increasing our own pleasure. I became disgusted by my own complacency and my ability to justify the harm I'd inflicted through my lifestyle. I began to realize how thoroughly brainwashed I'd been by years of consumerist propaganda, by the constant messaging that I needed to buy more things, to be more beautiful, to spend more money. I came to see my own desire for consumer goods as a form of sickness. While desire can feel good, as life-affirming as sex, it can also feel terrible, a constant reminder of lack. Unfulfilled, this kind of wanting can make you long for an end, any end at all.

3

It took years, but I came to accept that desire and repulsion exist in tandem and that the most poignant beauties are interthreaded with ugliness. There is no life without suffering. There is no way to live without causing harm. But despite all that, we keep trying. At least, I do.

Even though my lifestyle causes harm to the natural world, it keeps feeding me miraculous scenes, sounds, scents. It's not quite accurate to say that beauty saved my life, because there were also other therapists, various types of medication, and many different people involved in getting me to this point, where I no longer dream of dying. Certainly, there is more to life than aesthetics. But I do believe that beauty is a necessary part of life, something that thrills and inspires. Wanting beauty is not a shallow impulse. The aesthetic experience can give us awe. It can bring peace. An encounter with a beautiful thing can shift your way of thinking, your way of moving through the world. It can reinforce a sense of connection with the endlessly entangled matter of the universe and it can help ground us within our bodies, creating an anchor tied to the present moment. While I believe we have a moral imperative to change how we consume and experience objects in the twenty-first century, I also don't think we are evil or weak for loving beauty and wanting to be closer to it. It is natural to desire the high that an encounter with the beautiful brings. It is normal.

It's also a highly personal thing. Beauty happens in our minds; it's an experience that we have when using our senses and our critical faculties together. We perceive the qualities of a physical object and then we judge it beautiful. Generally, this feels good. But what pleases your senses is different from what pleases mine. We like different scents, sounds, colors, and textures. Our likes and dislikes aren't innate. They come from individual experience and cultural values.

In this book, I examine a number of objects that have burned brightly for me, kindling covetous desires and sparking lifelong devotion. Although I'm rarely organized—my desk is a bed and my bed is a

THE UGLY HISTORY OF BEAUTIFUL THINGS

mess—this book does have an organizational principle. I've placed my beautiful things in order of when I began to desire them, from my infantile mirror-stage gawking to my more recent obsession with marble. You may notice the oversized shadow cast by Victorian tastes over this book, which is due in part to the glut of new luxury goods that arose during these years as well as the cultural emphasis placed on ornate, pretty, pilfered things. People were delirious over orchids, titillated by cursed rocks, fanatical for porcelain, and drunk on sentiment. I'm no Victorian, but I understand why, in times of swift social change, one might find refuge in the seemingly solid world of things. I'm a fairly typical American middle-class woman, which means that I have feathered my nest with a number of useless objects and jammed my closet full with far too many cheap clothes. Since we're all influenced by marketing and magazines, my desires will likely run along lines that feel familiar to you, though I'm certain we all have our strange loves too. The beauty I crave started small and grew and grew. I went from wanting shiny trinkets to obsessing over vintage glass goblets and hand-painted porcelain plates. I went from scoffing at diamonds to begging for a little sparkle for my left hand.

I was born and raised in America during the last decades of the twentieth century, and this book has been heavily shaped by these facts. During childhood, I picked wildflowers and collected rocks in my dusty New Mexico backyard. Later, once I moved to Massachusetts, I combed the cold beaches for white seashells. As I grew older, my beauties became more complicated and, often, more manufactured. I wore them closer to the skin. As a young teenager with an after-school job at the grocery store, I used my discount to purchase items intended to beautify my face and body. It was the 2000s and I was thin, blond, depressed, and starving. I wanted to look like Kate Moss or Fiona Apple or maybe even Amy Winehouse. I wanted to look frail and bruised, with eyes glazed from late nights. I wanted to find my signature scent, to create an iconic look, to become an object of desire that others could deem beautiful. I wanted what the media told me I should want.

Eventually, I grew out of that phase, though I still wear makeup and perfume, and I still shop for the perfect silk dress, the one that will transform my flawed body into Aphrodite's ethereal form. But my newest desires tend to fall within the realm of the home. As I've grown from girl to teen to woman, I've come to finally appreciate the beauties of domestic life and community rituals. The things I took for granted as a child, mocked as a teenager—white porcelain dishes, expensive countertops, glass chandeliers—now ring with sonorous meaning. The pandemic of 2020 trapped me (and everyone else) inside. I continued to work as a home and design writer from afar, doing video tours of houses that were far fancier than my own, seeing how the wealthy have feathered their nests. I began to feel deeply envious but also deeply fortunate—for my safety, my family, my shelter. Fine dishes, I learned, weren't just for display. They were for gathering, feeding, and sharing. Marble wasn't just for museum sculpture; it was also for tombstones, modest memorials to the unfathomable loss of young life. Those soft stones gave shape to the pain of shared grief, but they also pointed to something deeper. Every piece of stone gestured toward the bedrock of our country, the systems of oppression that undergird our lives in twenty-first-century America.

Sometimes, I admit, these stories can get heavy. Nazi factories and empty oceans don't make for easy reading. Some of these crimes are a thing of the past, but many of them are present. The global fashion industry still employs children to clean silkworm cocoons in vats of scalding liquid, and there are young men right now in Colorado fighting for healthcare treatment for their workplace-induced silicosis.

Not every object is ugly because of how it was made, however. Some beautiful things have been used for nefarious means, even seemingly innocuous things like flowers and river rocks. I'll explain how glass, a miracle material that allows me to see the world clearly, was once used to conjure up wispy, wailing ghosts for audiences of sophisticated Parisians. In my chapter on makeup, I'll reveal the one product I can't live without and discuss the still relevant phenomenon of "slashed beauties." Some of the ugliness found within this book is literal, some is symbolic, some is moral, some is political. Some of the darkness is even quite personal.

This book is shaded, tainted, and colored by my emotions. There's gratitude, pride, and love in these pages. There's also guilt, discomfort, frustration, and fear. I feel guilty because of how much I enjoy contributing to the wide world of garbage, how much I enjoy purchasing things wrapped in plastic, how much I like having stones ripped from the earth adorning my hand. I feel discomforted by my desire for more, always more, even when I know I already have enough. I feel frustrated by how socially constructed my tastes have always been, how conventional. And I'm afraid that my efforts to be better won't matter in the long run, that I will always backslide, that the world will not change, and that I will someday simply stop caring.

By examining the things I find beautiful and interrogating the qualities that create a beautiful object, I hope to expand your capability to find beauty in your own life, as well as your ability to savor it. I don't want to ruin your beloved objects or steal your happiness. Nor do I want to make you feel judged; these desires are mine and these stories are mine. Ideally, I want to help you see the world more clearly, and more generously. Over the years, I've written about many things that I felt ambivalent about at first, like silk. When I started researching this odd animal-made fabric, I didn't find it all that appealing. I wore silk to prom, but without an office job or many parties to attend, silk felt overly fussy, not something that would fit into my life. But at some point, during those months of reading and writing, I slowly fell in love. I found myself enchanted by the subtle iridescence of the weave, the way it drapes around breasts or over a hip. I wanted to lounge around in silk robes, to luxuriate in silk pajamas, to buy an evening gown and wear it somewhere fabulous. I eventually bought a secondhand silk dress, which I wear over a bathing suit on my frequent trips to the beach. It's not how I should treat a nice piece of clothing, but I believe it needs to be worn and, truly, I have few other places to wear it.

Fortunately for my bank account, those quiet months spent in isolation with my immediate family, reading and researching, shifted my relationship with the natural world even more radically than they affected my consumerist desires. I've stopped treating daily walks like chores and instead approach them with hope. Maybe on this walk by the shore, I'll spot the tender head of a seal bobbing above the waves. Maybe on this walk through the field, I'll see a monarch flash its vivid orange wings. Maybe a trip to the bog will leave me suffused with bliss. Small pink orchids, white tufts of bog cotton, the blazing crimson of a blueberry barren—now these ordinary sights can stop me in my tracks, break me free of anxiety spirals, and give me a brief flash of awe and gratitude.

For thousands of years, philosophers and poets have been trying to describe the way that beauty can make us feel with varying degrees of success. From Plato to Kant, there's a deep well of writing about beauty that can, at times, seem impenetrably dense and outdated. Although I don't cover the philosophy of aesthetics in this book, my writing has been informed by my education (both formal and self-directed) and by an ongoing engagement with these historic texts. I've also found great joy in reading the works of contemporary authors who grapple with the problems of beauty. My writing is informed by the likes of Umberto Eco, Ursula K. Le Guin, Chloé Cooper Jones, Elaine Scarry, and Crispin Sartwell. All of these authors have published lucid and thoughtful explorations into aesthetics, and I've found their work helpful in shaping my own.

In his *History of Beauty*, Eco writes of the nineteenth-century artists and poets who privileged beauty above all else, seeking "the ecstasy within things" and the "epiphanic vision" that can appear during an encounter with the beautiful. Eco summarizes the philosophy: "life is worth living only in order to accumulate such experiences." Admittedly, I'm a little old-fashioned. I, too, am drawn to the Romantic understanding of beautiful objects as potential sources of revelation. I live for the moments when beauty breaks me out of my own anxious brain. Drawing on the work of philosopher and novelist Iris Murdoch, writer Chloé Cooper Jones highlights the "unselfing" power of aesthetics in her memoir *Easy Beauty*. According to this framework, beauty is a mental experience, one so intense that it quiets the needs of the ego and the concerns of the social self. For Cooper Jones, beauty offers an opportunity to open our minds, to shift first our perceptions, then our actions. Unselfing can happen in an Italian art museum, surrounded by millennia-old marbles or in a screaming crowd at a Beyoncé concert. Murdoch saw this idea embodied in a kestrel, swooping and diving by her window.

Yet we always must fall back down to Earth. The life-giving, thrilling highs aren't sustainable; nor are they the only things that make life worth living. This book is, like my life, about a lot more than just buying beautiful objects. It's also about seeking them, sharing them, releasing them, and sometimes refusing them. It's about living in a world that is both immensely lovely and, at times, almost unbearably sad. It's about recognizing that desire, a fundamental part of beauty, will always exist. When it comes to beauty, I can never have enough (which, of course, means I already do have enough). "We do not only want to be satisfied; we also want to want," writes Sartwell in *Six Names of Beauty*. "To desire is to feel intensely the life within yourself."

Understanding beauty begets beauty, I have found. It's like love, in that way. Identifying the mundane qualities of sensory pleasure has enabled me to find so much more of it, just as recognizing the specific quirks of my family has given me greater appreciation for our tightly sewn bonds. I've poured my love for beauty into this book, as well as my tendency toward darkness. I want you to become more aware consumers, certainly, but that's not my only end goal. Ideally, reading this book will help you open your eyes to the beauty that already surrounds you, beauty that already exists in your cities and homes and backyards. I want you to understand how that beauty came to be, what price was paid and by whom, and how you can most ethically partake in the beauty of the world, whether it is by visiting a museum, walking on a beach, or commissioning a painting. I want you to feel as though your relationship with beauty has been expanded and deepened. That you not only know more about beautiful objects, but that you know more about your personal tastes, desires, needs. I want you to move through the moral and physical disgust that comes with witnessing suffering and staring into the abyss and toward a sense of acceptance—maybe even revitalization.

1.

THE MERCURIAL CHARMS OF THE MIRROR

On seeing and being seen

I like to look in the mirror. I don't like to watch myself on video, hear my voice on a recording, or see my face in a photograph. This may seem contradictory, but I don't think it is. I'm not that interested in what a camera can capture, though I do recognize the value of having mementos of earlier times and well-done author photos. When it comes to looking at myself, I simply prefer to see my face in real time, in reverse. I've become accustomed to the slick, shiny surface of a mirror. That's where my truest face resides, where I look most beautiful, most unguarded, most myself. It's where I'm able to drop my guard, alone in the bathroom, and where I can practice putting the mask I wear for others back on.

Perhaps I should feel some guilt admitting all this, but I don't. I used to feel bad about how much I enjoyed mirrors. There was a time in my life when I hid my own fascination with the mirror, when I denied how much time I spent in front of them, when I didn't have a pocket mirror or a vintage mirror in a burled wood frame or a magnifying mirror for my bedside table. Now there are mirrors all over my house. The silvery surfaces are made of glass and plastic, materials old and new. I have one surrounded by stained-glass panels, one surrounded by a tacky gilt frame, and one encased in a carved wood latticework, imported from India. I inherited a small mirror in a gold case with my great-grandmother's initials etched on the front. I have a large mirror that used to hang at our family camp in the Adirondacks, back when we had a family house, before my grandfather got sick and died. I have a mirror from a junk shop in northern Maine, an old mirror, with real mercury coating on the back of the glass. That mirror might be my favorite. It's the kind that could make you go mad, were you to lick the glass until the backing peeled off in glittery, poisonous fragments (something I've perversely daydreamed about doing). In this mirror, my face is distorted and discolored. I look watery, unformed, and dreamlike. I love it.

I can't remember when I first looked in a mirror. My life has never been mirror-free; my conception of myself has been shaped by the mirror. According to at least one philosopher, the development of the ego during childhood happens when we look into a mirror and realize that we are people, not fragments of emotions or impulses, but contained people with boundaries to our bodies. French psychoanalyst Jacques Lacan called this the "mirror stage" of human development. He suggested that the symbolic moment of recognition creates a minor crisis inside our tiny brains. We realize we're not infinite, we're not in control, we're not very good at moving our limbs or meeting our own needs. I've always found Lacan's model of the mind rather enticing because it puts the broken, needy, wanting self at the forefront. Even when I feel contained and self-possessed, I also always feel a little of those emotions too.

These mirrors bring me complicated pleasure. Mixed in with the simple, childlike admiration for glimmer and sparkle are swirls of frustration (with my appearance and my lack of body neutrality) and grief (for the hours I've lost to self-loathing and recriminations). And yet, there's joy in seeing light move and wink across a silvery surface, so much like water, so much like the heavens. That's a simple thing, the beauty of reflection and refraction. Light is perhaps the first element of beauty. Even as infants, before we can see color, we can see light.

Some scientists have theorized that our attraction to reflections has an evolutionary purpose. Supposedly, we like gemstones that sparkle and objects that reflect because they remind us of life-giving water. This is just one theory, but I find it interesting. It explains, in part, the seemingly global allure of glitter, polished metals, and atoms arranged in a crystalline structure. Even infants are more likely to shower attention on shiny plates (which they show by picking them up and mouthing them) than on dull ones. Even cultures that never had to compete with their neighbors for resources hoarded gold and gems, although they had no need to accumulate symbols of wealth or worry about trading. For these people, gold should have been just another rock. But it wasn't, because we like shiny things.

We also like looking at images of ourselves. A mirror can be any reflective surface created for the purpose of seeing oneself. The name is taken from the Latin "mirare" and "mirari" ("to look at" and "to wonder at, admire," respectively), They can be made of stone, metal, glass, plastic, or even water.

It's impossible to know exactly when humans first discovered our reflections, though many have tried to imagine the moment. In his 2003 book *Mirror, Mirror*, Mark Pendergrast paints a wavering, dreamlike picture of a hominid drinking from a pool of water. "The scene: an African savanna after a torrential seasonal rain," he writes. With brow furrowed in curiosity, the unnamed figure expresses puzzlement at the "fellow creature looking back at him." First, he is cautious. "Is it an enemy?" he wonders. Then, he is playful. The man winks at himself, touches his nose, and bares his teeth. "He understands, on one level, at least," Pendergrast concludes. "They are the same, yet they are different."

Sure, this could have happened. One by one, they could have slowly fallen in love with their reflections, as the Greeks imagined in the story of Narcissus. They could have drowned gazing into their own eyes, so dark, so mysterious.

Or they could have acted like dolphins do, or elephants, or magpies. According to animal psychologist Diana Reiss, animals go through several stages of mirror self-recognition. Animals first try to look behind the mirror, and then often go through a "Groucho stage," where they repeat odd movements to figure out the relationship between the motions of their bodies and the reflections. Upon realizing what they're seeing, many animals begin using the mirror to see previously unobserved parts of themselves.

Maybe rather than falling in love with his twin, Narcissus showed the pool his butt, peering over his beautiful shoulder to get the view from behind. Yet we prefer to think of Narcissus gazing at his ravishing face for hours, wasting away (or drowning, depending on your mythological source) because he needs to be punished for his self-love. It's a story with a moral, one that cautions against vanity and beauty. It's also a story about the power of reflection, and we keep telling it because it keeps being relatable. We love mirrors, yet we're loath to admit it. We've all been drawn to our own reflection. We've all felt fascinated by the image of our own selves, captured in silver or water or glass. The way we look matters, whether we want it to or not: Our appearance alters our job and mating prospects, contributes to our quality of life (a phenomenon sometimes called "erotic capital"). We value different human bodies differently, and the ugly truth is that the ones that fit the prevailing culture's definition of beautiful are evaluated at a higher worth. There's both a power and a survival necessity in seeing yourself the way the world sees you.

Perhaps this is why mirrors have long been associated with magic. If they can let you see something you normally can't—yourself—maybe they can permit you to see other things beyond your vision. Spirits, perhaps, or ghosts, or maybe even visions of the future. Cultures across the globe have, independently of one another, built their own mythologies around reflective surfaces. Often, these beliefs focused on the light-bending powers of mirrors and their use as fire-starters. For many ancient cultures, mirrors were linked to the sun deity, thus making them symbols of warmth, hope, and protection. The earliest known mirrors were made from polished pieces of obsidian and decorated with painted plaster. These eight-thousand-year-old artifacts were found in the burial chambers of several different women from the ancient Turkish settlement of Çatalhöyük. The clay-walled Neolithic village has been described as an ancient "utopia" due to the equal distribution of resources, and many believe that it holds the secrets to human social development, maybe even the "origin of home" as a concept. Former excavation director and archeologist Ian Hodder has had the chance to examine several of the mirrors found on-site. Over the phone, he refers to them as "beautiful things," adding, "Nobody really expected there would be things like mirrors in those early days. These are the first sort of settlements after people have been living as hunters and gatherers. In many ways, these were quite simple societies, so it is odd." While researchers have also found evidence of cosmetics and face paint in the same tombs, leading some to believe they were used much in the same way we use mirrors today, it's also possible that the dark, glassy surfaces had spiritual significance for members of the Neolithic society. It could be, Hodder says, that "they're something to do with predicting the future or understanding the spirit world through reading images in the mirrors."

The Wiccan's Dictionary of Prophecy and Omens features a listing for "catoptromancy," defined as the "art and practice of divination by means of a special lens or magic mirror." According to this text, the ancient Greeks used a mirror to catch the light of the moon and, peering into it, were able to see visions of the future. (Another kind of divination practiced during the same era involved looking at birds—"ornis," a word that birthed our modern term "omen.") The Roman "blindfolded boys" were special diviners who could call forth images of the future from a thin haze of condensation on the surface of a mirror; one legend has a blindfolded boy predicting the death of Didius Julianus after gazing in a reflective surface, performing incantations, exhaling deeply, and watching as visions of the emperor's untimely end appeared in the moisture.

Nostradamus, the sixteenth-century French astrologer and seer was famous for his scrying abilities. According to legend, the gout-ridden oracle used either a black mirror or a pool of dark water as one of several methods for gathering occult knowledge. Modern mystics claim that Nostradamus correctly predicted a number of our current troubles, from the invasion of Ukraine to the astronomical rise of Elon Musk. While mirrors are no longer a common addition to tombs, people do still use them in feng shui, and there are plenty of socially acceptable ways to practice scrying. Like Victorian ladies begging the mirror to reveal their one true love, people all over America are still gazing into mirrors with the hopes that they'll fast-track success.

Today, you can buy a simple polished obsidian mirror online for less than $30. You can also book an appointment to learn how to scry with a black mirror from a New Orleans witch for just $50. If you haven't the pocket money, you can always watch tutorials on YouTube and DIY scry with your own polished black stone. All you need is the desire to look, long and hard, into the depths.

The first great glass mirrors came from the Italian island of Murano, in the Venetian Lagoon. Venice had been the place for glassmakers since the thirteenth century, and the city drew talent from throughout Europe, all pulled to Venice by the promise of a better life. "The Venetian Republic nurtured them and treated them more like artists than artisans," writes

THE UGLY HISTORY OF BEAUTIFUL THINGS

Sabine Melchior-Bonnet in *The Mirror: A History*. Although this government protection could be stifling, it also granted them more upward social mobility than other craftspeople. They were allowed to marry daughters of nobles, and some of the wealthier glassmaking families ascended to celebrity status. Venetians were proud of their industry and the gold it brought to their city, and that shine rubbed off on the industrious glassmakers.

It's not entirely clear who came up with the formula for Venice's famed translucent glass, nor is it known who first applied a mixture of molten metals to the back of the panes to make the first modern mirror. The glassmakers at Murano jealously guarded the tricks of their trade, as did the Venetian government. Spilling trade secrets was punishable by death, and if a glassmaker dared to leave Murano, their family was sometimes held hostage in an attempt to hasten their return. But even within the reticent community of craftspeople, there was collaboration and experimentation. The mirror makers were always looking for ways to enhance the beauty of their objects, as well as formulas for creating larger and more impressive mirrors. Some added lead to their glass; others embedded glimmering bits of gold leaf within the surface. They lined their mirrors with silver, which had been polished and flattened, or with a tin-mercury amalgam. These materials weren't safe to work with; mercury, in particular, is highly toxic. Workers who inhaled mercury fumes might develop behavioral and personality changes. Their kidneys might fail; their hands might begin to shake. They might begin to experience memory loss, insomnia, depression, and sometimes even delirium and hallucination. If you've heard of "mad hatters," you know about these symptoms, which were just as prevalent in mirror makers as milliners. And they knew precisely what was causing their pain, yet often lacked the economic mobility to make other choices. In 1713, Bernardino Ramazzini documented the ailments of mirror makers: "Those who make the mirrors become palsied and asthmatic from handling

17

mercury. At Venice, on the island called Murano, where huge mirrors are made, you may see these workmen . . . scowling at the reflection of their own suffering in their mirrors and cursing the trade they have chosen."

It was not an easy job to quit, however. The demand for their product remained absurdly high, for Venetian mirrors were considered the height of luxury. Nobles in Germany, Iran, and France installed Venetian mirrors in their palaces, and it became fashionable for upper-class ladies to have a "chamber of mirrors" in their private rooms, following the example of Catherine de' Medici. Naturally, everyone in Paris wanted one. According to receipts from the time, a Venetian mirror framed in silver sold for more than a painting by Raphael. King Henry IV of France tried to hire mirror makers, but he proved unsuccessful in starting his own glass workshop. By the time Louis XIV took the throne, nobles had been scheming for years, trying to concoct new ways to get that valuable glass-rolling technology out of Italy and into their studios, factories, and shops.

In the early 1660s, Louis XIV's finance minister, Jean-Baptiste Colbert, successfully lured a handful of glassmakers away from Murano to start a competing factory. But in 1667, fear gripped the workshop as rumors spread of Italian retribution. Several top artisans died, and there were whispers that they had been poisoned. One got sick with a sudden fever and died after several days of suffering. Another experienced mysterious stomach pains before perishing. They were working with heavy metals and toxic gases, yet their deaths weren't blamed on the workplace conditions. Dread began to permeate the air, polluting the fume-addled minds of the surviving mirror makers. The head of the factory requested an investigation. He blamed the Venetian Republic for the deaths, and he wasn't alone.

This wasn't the beginning of the mirror-based cruelty or the end of it. Two Venetian workers had been assassinated in 1547 after they attempted to emigrate to Germany, and others had seen family members condemned to work on galleys for their choice to leave the country (a sort of punishment by proxy, though it was more common to fine families or seize their property than to jail them). The volley of violence and intrigue went on for the better part of a decade. Italy sent spies to France; France sent spies to Italy. France attempted to bring over the workers' wives, and Italy tried to thwart this tactic (France won the battle in the end, thanks to the malingering of Venetian women, who were all too ready to feign illness if it meant they could escape under the cover of darkness to new lives abroad). Both countries suspected the other of murdering glassmakers, who were well compensated but shackled to the whims of autocratic rulers.

In 1670, the French royally backed company finally figured out how to blow, flatten, coat, and polish large panes of glass. The cat was out of the bag, and Colbert's workers soon began spreading that knowledge to French craftsmen. And in 1684, with the unveiling of the Hall of Mirrors at Versailles, it became obvious to everyone that the closely held secrets of mirror making had truly and irrevocably escaped from Murano.

The history of mirrors is ugly not just because of the poisonous mercury that lined their backsides, or because of the purported murders that ran like a bloody thread through seventeenth-century Europe. Though these things are certainly hideous, the slow, quiet suffering caused by our cultural obsession with looks—and our disavowal of those who fail to measure up—feels even more insidious.

When mirrors were associated with magic, we had more reverence for the power of the object. When they were nearly priceless, mirrors were recognized for what they were—objects of beauty, tools of projection. Today, magic is relegated to the fringes and mirrors have become simple symbols of vanity. Instead of seeking a deeper self or a connection

19

to ancestors or a link to higher powers, a woman looking in the mirror is commonly understood as seeking one thing: the image of herself. Once hoarded by kings, mirrors are now seen as primarily feminine items, despite the fact that everyone uses them. Mirrors, when stripped of their magic, become nothing more than shiny surfaces, which makes it even easier to deride women for their mirror-gazing habits.

This isn't exactly groundbreaking—any student of art history will stumble across hundreds of images of women peering lovingly into mirrors. Titian, Degas, Courbet, Manet, and likely a thousand other painters have used their skills to show feminine bodies doubled in a silvered surface. Some have even gone so far as to title their pieces *Vanity* or *Allegory of Vanity*, failing to see the significance of mirror-gazing for women; it was (and still is) a survival technique. In reality, a woman at the mirror is practicing. She's seeing herself how men see her, how society sees her. She's assessing her value and figuring out how to enhance her worth, her power.

While these masculine painters were creating lovely paintings of supposedly shallow objects, many of them were also using the mirror in their compositions to show themselves, to reveal the creator behind the piece. These painters used mirrors to cheekily insert themselves into a scene while also showing their technical prowess. Yet that same object, when paired with a woman's body, takes on a belittling power. Women aren't shown working in their mirrored reflections, like male artists often were, but simply looking. Art critic John Berger once famously wrote, "You painted a naked woman because you enjoyed looking at her, put a mirror in her hand and you called the painting *Vanity*, thus morally condemning the woman whose nakedness you had depicted for you own pleasure." The two subjects (reflections and women) have been linked so frequently, and depicted with such scorn, it's almost hardwired into our collective consciousness.

We don't often speak of the control a mirror can exert over a person. Instead, we allow this force to alter our perceptions, to diminish our happiness, while denying its power. Looking in a mirror is just something you do—just something *women* do. We're so used to seeing this impulse as vanity that most of us have forgotten the innate sense of awe that comes with looking. We've forgotten how to face our reflections not with judgment or fear but with a sense of joyful discovery, a sense of hope. Instead, we face the mirror with a certain amount of suspicion, as though desiring knowledge of how the world sees you is somehow wrong.

In contemporary culture, there has been some motion toward rewriting the visual symbolism and reclaiming the act of looking in the mirror, primarily through embracing and supporting the art and power of makeup. Young YouTubers frequently show themselves staring into mirrors, carefully applying winged eyeliner, rainbow eye shadow, ombre lips, or mermaid makeup. For them, the mirror is a necessity, and their makeup isn't a way to conceal so-called flaws but rather is an income-generating art form. Unlike the artists of old, who used their mirrors to more realistically depict the human face, these artists are using mirrors to transform the self into whimsical, fantastical creations. One of my favorite trends of recent years has been the "ugly makeup" movement, which encourages surreal makeup looks, like seed pearls glued to eyelids like opalescent warts or baby's breath used as false, fluffy eyebrows or eyelids painted sinister blood red. Browsing through the "ugly makeup" hashtag, it is immediately obvious that no one is trying to look hot. They're trying to look feverish, or old, or strange, or like fairies. They're using cosmetics to embody something other than beauty, something more interesting than so-called conventional beauty. They're often rather disconcerting to look at, but these mirror-made faces have a form of whimsical power. They allow a childlike playfulness to return to the space of the mirror, stripping the reflection of its seriousness, its potency. Seeing so many of these "ugly" creations inspired me to mess around with glitter and paint. Pulling faces in the mirror, painting my eyebrows green—it was good quarantine fun. It reminded me of playing with my baby in front of the big mirror at my mother's house, three generations of women sticking out our tongues and waggling our eyebrows.

I think this is the best way to approach a mirror: not with suspicion but with curiosity and openness. Not seeking flaws or great truths but looking for the quirks of one's face, the shifts of expression, the image of oneself whole and in motion. But it's also important to remember that mirrors, even full-length mirrors, show only a part of the story. It's so easy to forget this, to get swept up in the mythologies of modern life, like that misleading adage, "What you see is what you get." What you see is limited; sight does not equal knowledge. Mirrors have been used to create false realities, to trick people into believing in ghosts and spirits. Too often, we act as though what we see in the mirror is complete—a self fully formed and rendered truly. But the mirror is capable only of showing what others see. Mirrors can reinforce the idea that a person's value lies on the outside of their body, that it's possible to learn our value by examining (and altering) our appearance. Mirrors remind us of the significance of our looks, and even though it may feel good to collect likes and compliments on a selfie, it still reinforces a system in which some physical features are more valuable than others. I know this logically, yet I am not exempt from the desire to be granted a market price, to be visually appraised by relative strangers and found acceptable, attractive, worthy. I look at my face in a mirror and I don't see myself—I see how others might see me, how others might know me, want me. Sometimes, I find myself substituting a camera for a mirror. I turn my iPhone toward my face and use its small screen to check my teeth before a meeting. In the screen, I am flattened and compressed, smaller than myself. I glean information from this likeness, but I can also get lost in it, or overwhelmed by it. I can begin to believe that this version of myself, 2-D and frozen in a picture, is all there is.

Stripped of magic and removed from scenes of worship, the image of the public-facing self is becoming even flatter and more compressed, and the space between the private person and the public image is narrowing. There's something claustrophobic about this. Everything is visible, but nothing really matters. We know the mirror is a trick and a trap, but we also know it's a tool to succeed in a system that is broken, a world that assigns value arbitrarily and penalizes those who can't adequately perform or conform. Perhaps that's the ugliest thing about mirrors. They reveal more about society than they do about individuals.

2.

MOUTH FULL OF PETALS, VEINS FULL OF WAX

On stealing, eating, praying, and playing with flowers

I've been eating flowers for as long as I can remember. I don't recall who taught me that violets and wood sorrel were edible, but I can picture myself, barefoot on my childhood lawn in Massachusetts, picking dog violets from the place where the woods met the grass, and popping them into my mouth. I remember collecting big bunches of them, handfuls of purple, fragrant little flowers, their stems juicy like pea shoots. I spent hours picking violets, stopping only when my hands were too full to fit another transparent stem. I presented them to my mother, who put them in a squat glass tumbler by the sink. When I felt I had done my daughterly duty, I would switch to collecting flowers for myself.

As a little girl, I played at several violet-based crafts. I pressed them and candied them. I tried to make perfume, which resulted in a bottle of murky, foul-smelling water dotted with slimy plant matter. Years later, I made violet-scented syrup, which I poured into fizzy gin cocktails, garnished with white violets. I made this girly, frothy drink for

myself, to celebrate my thirty-second birthday. It amazes me sometimes, how little my tastes have changed in the past few decades.

Eating flowers is a pleasure I rarely deny myself. A forager friend
once showed me her trick for entertaining guests—she likes to roll a log
of goat cheese in nocturnum, dandelion, and marigold petals collected
from her backyard and serve it on a piece of cabbage with crackers. I've
adopted this practice as my own. Like her, I also eat daylily buds before
they open, throwing them into stir fries or adding them to soup. I love
lavender ice cream, particularly when it's sweetened with honey, and I
never say no to a piece of rose-scented Turkish pastry. Once, at a restaurant in Mexico City, I ordered a bowl of soup that was supposedly made
with over thirty different kinds of flowers. It was creamy and luscious,
an orange bowl of savory sunshine.

I've begun to see bouquets of edible flowers sold at outdoor markets. Edible flowers pop up most often on social media, often catego-
rized under the "cottagecore" aesthetic. For adherents of this cutesy,
nostalgic, outdoorsy lifestyle, edible flowers are a staple. While it hasn't
quite caught on with the masses, there is a name for people like me:
we're called lotus-eaters or lotophagi. The nickname was popularized by
The Odyssey, which was translated into English for the first time in the
early seventeenth century, and not long after, the phrase "lotus-eaters"
started popping up in the works of poets and playwrights. In this story,
the hero's ship has been blown off course by some rogue, god-sent winds,
and he has to drop anchor on a pretty little island, covered with greenery
and laden with fresh fruit and water. The island is also home to a group
of natives who don't do much except eat flowers and fruit and bask in
the sun. Odysseus discovers that the natives have shared their delicious
botanical sustenance with his men, and that it's making them a little too
mellow. They've forgotten their lives and duties. He stomps his feet and
shouts and drags his crew back to the ships, where they can labor long
and hard to get the hero home.

Ancient Greek historians, including Herodotus, the so-called father of history, believed that the island of the lotus-eaters was a real place. There were several different locations given for the slothful paradise, but typically lotus-eaters lived in North Africa. Although their lives sound lovely and wholesome to me—a tribe of peaceful vegan stoners napping contentedly in the sun—English and American writers tended to agree with Odysseus's assessment. They were lazy, and according to the dominant Christian culture, laziness wasn't just a vice. It was a sin.

Calling someone a "lotus-eater" is never a compliment. Poets and authors, including Alfred, Lord Tennyson, W. Somerset Maugham, and James Joyce drew inspiration from the episode of the lotus-eaters, as did a number of musicians and filmmakers. While the works differ greatly, their message is the same: lotus-eaters aren't to be emulated, even if you might be tempted by their relaxed lifestyle. In Tennyson's famous poem "The Lotos-Eaters," the poet makes it clear why one might want to linger among the "dark faces" of the "mild-eyed melancholy Lotos-eaters" but also why an upstanding Greek mariner would not. They may look like a contented, liberated, and peaceable group, but their island life was "hollow." In nearly every work of fiction or poetry, it's implied that the lotus-eaters were both purposeless and godless. Unholy and unambitious; I don't know which was seen as worse.

While the moniker appears more often in fiction referring to drug-addled foreigners than to actual petal-crunchers, its very existence speaks to the tendency to censor, eroticize, and exoticize non-white cultures and their practices. And while it's unlikely the actual flower described in Homer's epic was a lotus, I think it's significant that English-speakers chose to assign such negative connotations to a flower that is held sacred in many non-white cultures. "Of all the flowers that have inflamed human societies, the lotus has to come first," writes horticultural historian Jennifer Potter in *Seven Flowers: And How They Shaped Our World*. The lotus, she argues, has played a larger role in religious and cultural symbolism than any other blossom on Earth for the greatest number of people. From Egypt to India to Japan to China, these aquatic blossoms reign supreme.

Blue lotus was central in the creation myths and burial rites of ancient Egyptian peoples. The flowers, which open in the morning and close around noon, were seen as symbolic of regeneration and were linked in one creation myth to the birth of the sun god, Ra. They were also baked into the secular life of the populace. People wore blue lotus crowns to parties, ate blue lotus petals and roots, distilled the blue lotus flowers into perfume, and decorated their houses with bowls of fresh blue lotus flowers. In the burial chamber of King Tutankhamun, archaeologists found blue lotus–inspired art and dried flower petals, including a striking lotus-shaped chalice carved from a single piece of alabaster and a set of silver lotus-shaped trumpets.

In South Asia, it was the pink-tinged "sacred lotus" that captured the minds of storytellers and artists. Compared to the spiky, elongated petals of the blue lotus, the sacred lotus is a round, blushy, soft-looking thing with a yolk-bright yellow center. It has a distinctive paddle-shaped seed head that contains edible, nutrient-rich seeds (also known as lotus nuts) inside its unevenly spaced holes. Sacred lotuses are native to the warmer regions of Asia, but these days they can be found all over the world, from Australia to Russia to South America. Its image is just as widespread, and once you start looking for a lotus, you'll spot them everywhere (particularly if you practice yoga or frequent your local vegetarian restaurants). But before they were adopted as shorthand by hippies and wellness types, lotuses were used by artists to convey devotion.

As the name might suggest, English-speakers have long known that the sacred lotus plays an important role in the cuisine, mythology, art, and religion of many cultures. As a lapsed Catholic, I can't help but compare the lotus to the cross. I used to wear a small gold crucifix necklace everywhere I went, because those simple lines were a reminder that I loved my religion. To me, the cross meant faith, protection, and striving toward goodness. Wearing the necklace was a way to reconnect with my values. Although the iconography is very different, the lotus shape that appears so often in Buddhist and Hindu art and adornment seems to fulfill a similar function for many people. Often shown in profile, the flower is sometimes just an abstraction—an upward crescent of spiked petals. According to *Floriography* by Sally Coulthard, the lotus is a "symbol of purity" in Buddhism. Thanks to something called the lotus effect, the petals of the flower are highly hydrophobic—meaning they are naturally water-resistant and self-cleaning. Dewdrops and mud both slide with ease off the surface of the flower. In Hinduism, these flowers represent the ideal of beauty and the rejection of material attachments. In both religions, its unfurling petals are used as an allegory for the blossoming of the human soul. To see a lotus is to be reminded of the potential for goodness, the possibility of transcendence, the hope for growth.

While this knowledge has greatly increased my appreciation for all water lilies, it also casts a shadow on the lotus jewelry, stickers, candles, and statues that I see in boutiques. I don't wear my cross anymore, because it no longer makes me feel connected to the symbolic realm. It no longer aligns with my values, and although the lotus seems a closer fit, I don't want to wear that symbol either. The subtle power of iconography isn't something I take lightly. Even commonly used symbols are important; I try to choose mine carefully. (I've come to the same realization about cowrie shells, but we'll get to that later.)

I do understand why flower-eating feels like such a rich metaphor, but it's also something people do every single day, all around the globe, often without even thinking about it. Alongside being quite plainly disparaging, this metaphor also reveals an ugly tendency to denigrate those of us who love beauty so much we just want to consume it, from stem to stamen. It's not a phrase you hear very often anymore—we have plenty of newer, harsher words that shame the pleasure-hungry even more effectively—but it's one worth remembering as you're traipsing down the aisles of floral history. Instead of connecting over the very human desire for blossoms, we've turned flowers into symbols for how we are different and transformed the desire to enjoy physical pleasure into a source of shame.

When it comes to blossoms, I'm a glutton in more ways than one. In the spring, I like to buy unopened bunches of daffodils from the grocery store and arrange them in vases and jars throughout my house. I wait eagerly for each one to blossom and spread its strange perfume. In the summer, I gather big bunches of wildflowers from alongside the road, cups of lupines and daisies. In the fall, there are asters, and in the winter, I buy dried flower bouquets from the farm up the road.

I have no problem admitting to this type of behavior. Loving flowers is a very human trait; some evolutionary biologists even theorize that flowers and people evolved together. Following a study on the natural joys brought on by receiving a gift of cut flowers, Jeannette Haviland-Jones, a professor emeritus at Rutgers University suggested that the evolution of flowers could have been akin to the domestication of dogs. Maybe they're another example of "non-species emotional support." In other words, maybe flowers evolved to be beautiful because we love beauty.

We also love sex, though I find it can be hard to talk about sexual desire in such plain terms. I understand entirely why one might use a flower as a stand-in for their sexual organs or as a way to vaguely gesture toward the hidden folds of the human body. Flowers allow plausible deniability—they can put a veneer of scientific innocence on smutty talk. I find it easier to vocally admire the lush purple petals of Georgia O'Keeffe's iris paintings than to admit that I sometimes find other women's vulvas downright remarkable. It's still traditional to throw red rose petals on the bed of a newly married couple, scarlet harbingers for the juicy action to come, and we still consider flowers a part of the human mating ritual. We wear floral scents; we give flowers to lovers. Some people even still use the phrase "deflowering" to describe one's first encounter with the sexual act.

It makes sense that we reach for blossoms during times of transition. The Victorian era was a time of great social upheaval, and during these strange decades, people went absolutely mad for flowers, particularly orchids. Members of the orchid family grow everywhere—on every inhabited continent, which just means they haven't figured out a way to thrive in Antarctica yet. They live in the temperate woodlands of Sweden and in the arid, rocky soil of Arizona. They hang from trees in humid tropical jungles and decorate the mountains of the Middle East. Yet when most people close their eyes and imagine an orchid, they picture a tropical variety. Perhaps the moth orchid, which you can buy in almost any grocery store or gift shop. These orchids have big fuchsia or white petals and sepals surrounding a delicately proportioned "lip" and "throat" (i.e., the flower's sex organs). Or maybe they picture the pale and eerie ghost orchid, the subject of Susan Orlean's *The Orchid Thief*, a book that served as source material for the Academy Award–nominated movie *Adaptation*. You may have seen pictures of the monkey-faced Dracula orchid, whose flowers resemble little simian faces, or the Italian orchid, which looks like a big-dicked stick figure (thus earning the nickname the "naked man orchid"). There are plenty more orchids that you wouldn't even know are orchids, like spiky green bog orchids and plain-jane ladies' tresses. But while North American and English native orchids are important to their ecosystems, they're not the ones that caught Charles Darwin's eye.

Darwin's admiration for fauna is well documented, but people often forget about his devotion to flora. In a later publication devoted to the orchid, Darwin argued that "every trifling detail" of their structure was the result of centuries of wooing insects into their hairy parts. Although orchids have both "male" and "female" organs (stamens and pistils) contained within one flower, they don't pollinate their own ovary. Instead, they work with insects to get the job done, ensuring intercrossing rather than inbreeding. Darwin may have had a personal stake in his argument; he felt quite a lot of guilt over marrying his first cousin, an act that he thought may have contributed to some of the deaths of what one writer called his "rather sickly" children.

Other orchids lure in insects with colors and shapes that mimic those of more nutritious flowers. Orchids pollinated by flies or carrion beetles are often brown and reek of rotting flesh. Slipper orchids are some of the most devious; they use their big, bucket-shaped labellum to trap bees and bugs. The bugs fly in, thinking they're going to get some nice, sweet nectar, and find themselves stuck in an empty cavity. The only way out is through a hairy hole, just big enough for the insect to sneak through. As the still-hungry insects climb out, they brush against the pollen-covered hairs and leave decorated with the orchid version of semen.

These adaptations have compelled Michael Pollan to call orchids "the inflatable love dolls of the floral kingdom," skilled practitioners of "sexual deception." Orchids are, according to Pollan, rather fantastic liars that evolved alongside insects, luring them in time and again with the promise of "very weird sex."

It wouldn't have been possible for Darwin to examine orchids so closely without access to them. While his other works had him trotting around the globe, he researched his little orchid book while hanging out with his family in England. At this time, growing tropical orchids in backyard greenhouses was an incredibly popular pastime for upper- and middle-class men.

The high expense of orchid-rearing didn't much deter the rise of floral madness. Those who couldn't participate firsthand were able to live vicariously through the legendary antics of plant poachers. People were hungry for exotic flowers, and equally hungry for stories of their capture. Scores of orchid hunters died abroad, killed by illness, accident, or foul play. In 1891, an Englishman named Albert Millican published a memoir of his time spent orchid hunting, *Travels and Adventures of an Orchid Hunter in the Northern Andes*. As he travels through the mountains, he meets Native men and women whom he disparages and lusts after, respectively. He sees his companions pierced with poison arrows and doesn't seem particularly bothered by their passing. He also doesn't seem to love orchids all that much: They were a means to an end.

In *The Orchid Thief*, Orlean details one particularly hazardous expedition to the Philippines that took place a decade after Millican's book hit the shelves. Eight men set out to seek their fortunes, but within a few short weeks, there was only one little poacher left standing. "Within a month," Orlean writes, "one of them had been eaten by a tiger; another had been drenched with oil and burned alive; five had vanished into thin air; and one had managed to stay alive." The lucky fellow walked out of the jungle with either 47,000 or 7,000 orchids, depending on the source. This type of botanical gluttony was typical; poachers would harvest as many specimens as they could, leaving no tubers left to regrow the population. Some orchid hunters cared about scientific advancements, certainly, but most were after more money and fame. They could come back with both high-priced stock and tales of wild panthers and wild women, cannibals and conquests.

As the nineteenth century came to a close, orchids and death became more explicitly associated. It wasn't just that people died in their quests to procure them; orchids themselves were also seen as deadly. Stories circulated about orchids found growing in graveyards and on human remains. One tells of an English traveler to New Guinea who, upon finding a new variety of orchid blooming in a cemetery, unceremoniously exhumed the bodies and left with the shoots and roots. (He gave the people of the nearby town a few glass beads to pay for his desecration of their ancestors.) Another orchid hunter sent home plants attached to shin bones and ribs, and still another brought a flower growing from a human skull. This last find was auctioned off at Protheroe's of London, sparking a series of think pieces on these gothic curiosities, these bloody orchids.

As in life so in fiction, and nineteenth- and twentieth-century pulp literature is awash with dangerous flowers. My favorite entry into this highly specific canon is *The Flowering of the Strange Orchid* by H. G. Wells. First published in 1894, it tells of a short, nebbish orchid collector named Mr. Winter-Wedderburn, who laments to his housekeeper, "Nothing ever happens to me." Later that day, he goes into London and returns with several orchid roots. Most of them are identified by the sellers, but one is not. "I don't like the look of it," says his housekeeper, comparing it to a "a spider shamming dead" or "fingers trying to get at you," before defensively telling her boss (who is also her cousin), "I can't help my likes and dislikes." But to Wedderburn, this root is an opportunity. Something, he hopes, might happen.

Of course, something does happen. After time in his overly hot greenhouse, the orchid blossoms. The "rich, intensely sweet" scent of the flowers makes him dizzy; it overpowers all other smells in the greenhouse. It also overpowers Wedderburn, who passes out, to be found later by his trusty housekeeper. He is alive, but barely: Fingerlike aerial roots have swarmed over his body, "a tangle of grey ropes, stretched tight" attached by "leech-like suckers." The housekeeper saves poor Wedderburn by breaking the windows and dragging him outside. The bloodthirsty orchid is left to die in the cold with all of Wedderburn's other plants.

Once he recovers, Wedderburn finds himself thrilled by his little adventure. He's had a brush with the exotic, hypermasculine world of orchid hunting, and he came out on top. What a feat for such a quiet, milquetoast little man.

At the age of seven, I became an orchid mangler. I suppose I could claim I was struck by orchidelirium, but that's not quite true. I had flower delirium in general; I picked flowers from my neighbors' gardens and stole branches of bleeding hearts from my mother's prized plants. I stole flowerheads from grocery-store bouquets. I liked the colors. I wanted to keep them all, even the dyed carnations wrapped in cellophane, even the jewelweed that grew in the swampy parts of our neighborhood. I didn't know that orchids were rare, but I don't know if that would have stopped me in the moment. I was a child, and I felt entitled to a certain amount of prettiness. I wanted one of those pink, bulbous flowers—a pale ballet pink, like the inside of a seashell or my mother's fingernails—so I picked it. When my mother found out, she sat me down and explained protected species and extinction rates. Afraid of disappointing her, I never picked another lady's slipper.

Looking back, it shouldn't have been hard to resist the call of the lady's slipper. Lady's slippers are kind of ugly. Our New England variety reminds me of human testicles, covered in spiderlike veins, more fleshy than flashy.

This isn't a terribly imaginative comparison; orchids have been associated with balls since ancient times. The word "orchid" comes from the Greek word for testicle, "órkhis." The Greeks were inspired by the plant's rounded tubers, which often grow in a pair, one larger and one smaller. Ancient physicians believed that these roots could both cause erections and stop them, depending on which tuber you picked. (The aphrodisiac and the boner killer followed similar recipes: Stew in either goat's milk or water, drink hot root broth, wait. The big one would make the organ swell, the slightly smaller and harder one would quell lust.) In medieval Europe, orchids often went by folk names, like fox stones, hares-bollocks, sweet cullions, dogstones, and goat's stones. (In case further clarification is required, "stones," "bollocks," and "cullions" are all vulgar synonyms for the family jewels.)

35

Despite their associations with certain parts of the male anatomy, during the height of orchid mania, these flowers were often understood as somehow intrinsically feminine. This makes some visual sense: Aside from the roots, orchids tend to look more vaginal than phallic. But it's not really about what the flower looks like. It's about how they were collected, harvested, conquered, bred. And (as usual) it's about sexism. Flowers were, like women, passive players in procreation. A nineteenth-century growing manual would deem orchids "marvelously docile . . . as with women and chameleons, their life is the reflection of what is around them."

When orchids were given some magical agency, it was never very nice. Their sweet scent could lure you in, their beauty might trick you into doing something foolhardy, their silent presence was enough to drive a man wild. Orchids were the femmes fatales of the flower world and like femmes fatales, they could be masculine and feminine, passive and aggressive (sometimes all at once). Popular short stories like "The Purple Terror" by Fred M. White (1898) and "The Orchid Horror" by John Blunt (1911), as well as novels like *Woman of Orchids* by Marvin Hill Dana (1901) blur the line between blossom and woman. In each of these narratives, the reader is cast in the role of the male explorer who is seduced by both the promise of fabulous flowers and the hope to get closer to an alluring, exotic woman. For Jim Endersby, author of *Orchid: A Cultural History,* these stories show not only the fear of women's shifting societal roles but also the fear of (and desire for) the tropics, "ripe with sickness and scheming natives, embodied in seductive exotic women." He goes on to suggest that dangerous orchids like Wedderburn's "seem to imbue women with qualities that were simultaneously repellant and seductive."

The role of the orchid collector, then, was to tame the dangerous woman. To own her, to coax forth her beauty in a safe, contained space. To take her out of her natural habitat and show her how to live; growing orchids as wish-fulfillment. It allowed these men to feel virile and manly, as though they had imposed their will on nature itself. Inside the tidy walls of a steel-reinforced greenhouse, they could be masters of their own little harem. If Hugh Hefner had been born a hundred years earlier, I imagine he would have kept orchids.

In the twentieth century, the orchid fell out of public favor. It's still an object of adoration for many collectors, but it's no longer the chicest bloom to display. The crown was passed, not to a single floral beauty but to a category of consumption. Instead of growing in a greenhouse, it became far more common to buy, give, and arrange cut flowers.

Cut flowers aren't a modern invention. We have evidence from ancient art that people in Egypt, China, and the Middle East were all placing flowers in vases, bringing them indoors. There's even a passage from a popular Middle Ages book that refers to flowers being brought to King Solomon. It was a mixture of fresh-cut flowers and fake blossoms. The Queen of Sheba had tasked him with finding the real among the faux, and with the help of a bee, he located the scentless imposters. For centuries, artists have painted blooms in vases, mainly ones they had gathered from nearby gardens and fields. Few genres please me as much as the floral still life, particularly when you get to see the drooping, dripping, wilting blooms past their prime (a favorite of the Dutch memento mori genre). Flowers have always had a place in our homes, but it wasn't until we had massive greenhouses, refrigerated freight ships, and advanced genetic modification that we began to see alstroemeria and carnations available year-round, even in the depths of winter. And it wasn't until the 1960s and 1970s that people began to buy roses by the dozen in the chilly depths of February.

Valentine's Day is when American rose consumption peaks, but in the entertainment industry, roses are always en vogue. I've been watching *The Bachelor* and its related television shows on and off for over a decade. I'm unwilling to tally up the number of hours of my life that I've given to ABC's premier reality dating show, but it's a lot. I've seen hundreds of rose ceremonies, where people in evening wear with nice hair give other nice-haired people long-stemmed red roses as a token of their affection, or as a way of saying, "I'm not dumping you—yet." These dramatic scenes vary in location. Production has even set a rose ceremony in a freezing cold airplane hangar. Sometimes, the lead will give out their roses to sweating contestants on tropical beaches. While so much is changeable, one thing is always the same: the rigid conformity of the American Spirit.

"American Spirit" is the name of the floral varietal chosen by the show's production team to represent romance, according to a 2016 article in the *New York Post*. Writer Kase Wickman interviewed the show's production designer to find out how the roses are primped, fluffed, and trimmed for the cameras. She finds that each early season episode requires the purchase of around 100 stems. Out of this big bouquet, fewer than 20 are granted screentime. (The rest, we must assume, get thrown out or, best-case scenario, maybe some are salvaged and regifted by members of the crew.) When the show is filming in another country, production sometimes needs to fly in emergency roses on charter planes. Using another type of flower—say, a daisy or a tulip—is simply not an option.

Like many long-stemmed red roses, American Spirit belongs to a group informally known as the "hybrid teas." Most cut roses sold by florists fall into this grouping, as do most supermarket roses. Although you can buy red, pink, orange, and yellow hybrid tea roses, most consumers go for the lipstick-red varieties. In the flower industry, these blooms go by a number of different names, all deeply corny (Red Paris, Grand Prix, Chrysler Imperial, Deep Secret). I know these are biologically distinct breeds, but I have trouble seeing any difference between them. They're not like tomatoes, where a Roma is oblong and a beefsteak is round and any home cook can tell them apart. The distinction is both more specialized and less meaningful than that.

A portion of these red, red roses are grown in California, but the majority come from abroad. They're fertilized, watered, and harvested in Ecuador or Colombia before being shipped (typically by cargo plane) to Miami. Then, they're unloaded into huge, refrigerated hangars, inspected by Customs and Border Protection, and placed into refrigerated trucks. They travel to flower markets, where a florist buys them, brings them to their shop, and places them into a bucket of water. The details of this journey vary, but the basic structure is generally the same. It can take weeks for a rose to get from the farm to your kitchen, sometimes even longer.

As a result, cut roses have been forcefully shaped by demands of the market. Over the past fifty years, they have been bred for international travel. The most popular rose varieties all have long stems, big flowers, tight petals, and not a lot of scent. Some of these have been created using old-fashioned breeding techniques, while others have been shaped through genetic engineering. Like many other crops, our contemporary roses have benefited from the discovery of nuclear radiation. In the 1950s and 1960s, a craze for so-called atomic gardens or gamma gardens swept across America. Inspired by President Eisenhower's 1953 speech "Atoms for Peace," these research gardens were part of an effort to promote the use of nuclear technology in nonmilitary industries. By bombarding plants with gamma rays from radioactive isotopes, we were able to change their DNA. Some of the resulting mutations proved tasty or useful, and so we continued using those varieties. While it's no longer considered wise to advertise the use of radiation in agriculture, the technique is still in use. Furthermore, it's not clear which varietals came from gamma gardening and which were created through old-fashioned cross-pollination. You might even buy a packet of supposedly "heirloom" seeds that spawned from the gamma garden. That designation, like most in agriculture, is not terribly precise.

While flowers grown from irradiated ancestors will not harm you, they might disappoint you. In creating roses that last long enough for shipment, we've created roses that smell like nothing. They may be easy to grow, and they may be easy to ship, but they are lacking in an essential element. Years ago, I attended a conference for floral companies that took place over the course of three days in an upscale hotel. In the main ballroom, there were a half dozen movable walls decorated with flowers to resemble the Wynwood murals. Roses were by far the most common bloom, and one panel was made entirely of South American hybrid tea roses—the crème de la crème, explained a marketing executive. In brilliant red and shocking pink, the roses spelled out a simple message: LOVE. Although there were hundreds upon hundreds of flowers in that room, as fresh as could be and meticulously arranged, the air smelled only of chlorine, a faint whiff emanating from the nearby roof-deck pool.

In some ways, this trip was glamorous, filled with big-headed roses, endless glasses of Champagne, sunset cruises, and fireworks over the city skyline. But it was all so rigidly controlled and purposefully manufactured, as basic as the string of emojis I used to caption the photographs. You could argue that these things are iconic or classic, but I think there's something sinister about all these red blossoms hung up on a wall. They're so obviously consumer products, shaped by global trade, grown by underpaid workers, and flown to wealthy colonizer countries on fuel-guzzling jets. Then, we buy them to give them away, mindlessly enacting a mating ritual that has been codified by marketing, movies, and television.

While the Bachelor franchise no longer uses American Spirits—these days they have another hybrid tea on set, the "American Beauties"—I do understand why producers picked this symbol for their wildly successful show about ill-fated whirlwind romances and backstabbing friend-ships. When you're watching, you're not supposed to pay attention to the specifics of the flower, nor to the specifics of the contestants. You're supposed to be swept up in the general feeling of love, the vague outlines of beauty, the fantasy of attainable luxury, the soft lighting, the red car-pets, the sparkly dresses, the white teeth, the pillar candles, the red roses. Across the franchise, roses are everywhere. They're in the mouths of leads posing coyly for billboards, they're piled high on tables around the "*Bachelor* mansion," and they appear sometimes in vases, just because. For years, the television show branded itself by aligning with red roses and white people. This is changing somewhat—we're seeing more di-verse contestants and leads on the show and its spin-offs—but it's still a very homogenous fantasy. No matter their racial or ethnic background, the women cast on the show are always united in prettiness. They're mostly Christian and mostly thin. They tend to wear similar dresses and intimidatingly high heels on their pedicured feet. The roses, I assume, will always remain red.

I have nothing terribly nice to say about American Spirits or Ameri-can Beauties, but I will say this: at least they're alive. They may have been bred to be boring, but they still have the ability to die. I'm less cer-tain about the roses that sit on my bedside table right now. Technically, they are roses. They look like roses, except they're a bright, garish tur-quoise. They don't smell like roses, nor do they feel like roses. The petals aren't soft enough—they're too papery and lack the velvet plushness of a living flower. I don't know if they taste like roses, because I haven't tried nibbling a petal. Rose petals are edible, but these aren't because their veins are full of wax.

The "eternity rose" (also known as an "infinity rose") is a consumer trend that began picking up steam in the early 2020s. Although there's a company called the Forever Rose that has been selling preserved roses since the late 1990s, their glass-encased "*Beauty and the Beast*" roses never quite took off. The Forever Rose didn't have TikTok or Instagram to speed their company's growth. These roses are made for social media, a place where two-dimensional perfection matters far more than the simple pleasures of taste, touch, and smell.

When I first heard of these flowers, I was intrigued. I assumed these roses had somehow been bred to last a long time, genetically engineered to stay fresh, without water, for a year. But that's impossible. Cell death comes for us all, even roses. It wasn't really my fault that I assumed the roses were some sort of zombie breed of plant; they've been cleverly marketed to obscure the nature of the product. Not one company comes right out and calls them preserved roses or embalmed roses—instead they talk about concepts like "eternity" and use suede-textured boxes, gold embossing, and French words to make their product seem chic and luxurious. Magazine writers have had a hand in promoting the con. In 2018, *House Beautiful* published an article titled "6 Real, Live Flowers That Will Last All Year and Don't Require Watering." The list included bouquets and boxes from brands like Venus et Fleur, Prêt-à-Fleur, and Fleurs de Paris (none of which are based in France). I ordered mine from Le Jardin Infini (also not a French company) because they were having a sale. According to the marketing copy and *House Beautiful* editors, I shouldn't have been able to tell the difference between the preserved rose heads sitting in their blue suede box and the still-living blooms I'd bought from a florist. But I could. Anyone could.

They may be "real," but these flowers were clearly not "live." They look like dried roses, their petals papery thin and ever-so-slightly shriveled. The edges of the petals curl unnaturally. They lack the bounce and heft of live flowers, and they smell faintly of plastic. From a distance, they look like living roses, but so do flowers made of paper, plastic, or silk. And unlike those imitation flowers, which have an inherent artistry that bolsters their appeal, everlasting roses exist in a botanical uncanny valley. They are neither alive nor visibly dead. They're neither real nor fake. They can be displayed for up to a year because, like some cursed princess in a fairy tale, they won't die. Decaying flowers have a certain dignity to them; I've always thought there was no tulip more beautiful than a wilting one, open to the world and lolling around in its vase. These eternity roses will never have a petal drift tragically from their loosening heads, they'll never get that cloying, intense, pleasurable smell of nectar rot. They have no greenery, no thorns, no *meat*. They look like roses, from a distance, but who wants to experience flowers at such a remove?

Amy Stewart, author of *Flower Confidential*, admits to a "smutty" love for flowers that leads her to an almost fatalistic acceptance of the flower industry. In the first chapter of her book, she expresses some disdain for the journalists who queue up every Valentine's Day to write the annual "blood and roses" story. These paint-by-numbers pieces warn the reader that "behind every Latin American or African rose is an exploited worker and a poisoned river." Yet her reporting around the globe reveals that while some flowers are produced under humane circumstances, most are not. Workers are exposed to pesticides and fungicides. They are paid very little for their labor. The agricultural runoff kills wildlife and wrecks ecosystems. "On one hand," Stewart writes, "work on the flower farms was low paying, exhausting and hazardous. All this to produce a short-lived luxury product for Americans who demand ever lower prices for a better and better flower. On the other hand, people need jobs." It's a depressing summary of the agricultural industry, and one that lacks imagination. Wage slavery exists but so does reform. Workers' rights movements can place pressure on local governments to enact laws protecting the individual—this has happened before and it can happen again. The global free market isn't serving the vast majority of people. It works well for those at the top of the wealth pyramid, but those who live on the least are suffering. It's not a humane system, and anyone who says otherwise is lying. While we can do little to change the practices of companies in other countries, it still matters who you vote for locally. Politicians who support unions will always be a fairer choice than those who support business owners, and politicians who scorn the very people they serve should never be trusted. We've seen how unregulated, globalized capitalism works. It's not pretty.

A world where people are paid fairly isn't impossible, but it will require work, sacrifice, and time to get there. Nihilism serves no one, nor does continued acceptance of the status quo. The larger systems of production won't be changed by a few people buying from local farms, but these choices still matter. They add up. Every small farm that thrives is a step in the right direction. You can choose not to buy flowers from the supermarket that were grown under suspicious conditions in places far away. There are greener ways to get flowers into your home. I live down the street from a family owned farm that sells wreaths of dried, Maine-grown flowers. Every fall, I buy a new one, and my walls are filling up with circlets of blossoms, spiky dried dahlias and bushy yellow yarrow. I have a friend who works for an organic flower farm—a business that wouldn't survive without their loyal CSA members. Even city-dwellers can choose to use locavore florists, buy paper flowers, or cultivate flowering potted plants. Personally, I've found a lot of joy in figuring out how to artfully arrange vases full of weeds and boughs of foraged greenery. I use a trick an interiors stylist once taught me: two branches, one short, one long, set in a ceramic vase with a narrow mouth. The elegance of this wild arrangement serves as an evergreen reminder that one doesn't need long-stemmed red roses to live a beautiful life.

Never again will I buy a forever rose, and these days, I grow most of my own flowers. Outside, in my backyard, sits a thorny, two-foot-tall "swamp rose" bush I bought at a local nursery. I chose it because we have poor, waterlogged soil. This scraggly plant blooms in late summer. The flowers are wimpy things, with a single layer of frail pink petals that are prone to ripping. They quickly turn brown, and their fruits are small, hard red hips. And yet, growing this bush has been far more satisfying than my long-lasting luxury roses. The swamp rose participates in the landscape; it struggles and thrives with the ecosystem, just as I do. The forever roses? They won't last forever. Not as a trend, nor as an object I own. Like all flowers, they have an expiration date. In a year, I'll throw them out. In a year, the swamp rose will bloom again, the aphids will come back to feast, and the bees will emerge from their nests, drawn toward the pink petals, the ephemeral perfume. Maybe this year I'll pluck some petals to candy, preserving them briefly, beautifully in a coating of sparkly sugar. I could keep them, but I know I never will. They'll be gone long before the first frost.

3.

BRIGHT BLUES, CURSED CUTS

On gemstones, worry stones, and
her majesty the diamond

Once, almost three decades ago, I found buried treasure. I was playing in the backyard of our home in Los Alamos, kicking my feet in the dirt under the swing set while my younger brother played with some sticks nearby. I saw something in the brown dirt, something that winked sky blue at me before disappearing again under a cloud of dust. I remember getting down on all fours and searching. My older brother came over, and together we dug all around the swing set until our hands were filthy and our nails were hurting. We found two small pieces of turquoise stone—one vivid blue, one teal flecked with bits of brown.

My mother let us believe that we had stumbled across some naturally occurring turquoise, that we had pulled rocks from the earth just like miners did. Looking back, I don't think that was true. Someone probably dropped these pieces, and we simply came along and picked them up. Yet we spent the next year periodically returning to the spot to dig and sift, dig and sift. After all, most mines gave up more than one prize, we knew that from our visits to the garnet mine in New York, as well as the turquoise mines near Santa Fe. Maybe, we thought, we'd struck gold (or at the very least, copper).

Our parents were practical and rather left-brained people, and so we spent a lot of time visiting caves, mines, arboretums, botanical gardens, planetariums, and science museums. In these spaces, beauty was present, but it was a secondary benefit. We weren't seeing stones and trees and constellations because they were awe-inspiring but because they were instructional. My nuclear physicist father wanted me to understand how things worked, from rock formation to the atomic bomb. I remember sitting on the rug in our living room in New Mexico while he demonstrated the mechanisms of a gyroscope. The small metal device spun in the air, hovering above a piece of plywood onto which he had glued strong black magnets. He had many of these gyroscopes in his office, and he used the flying toys to explain concepts far beyond the reach of my young mind—the quarks and protons that made up my body, for instance, or the way tiny pieces of spinning metal could be used to control the trajectory of the Hubble telescope or a missile. I didn't understand then how the pieces fit together, but I knew the gyroscopes were related to his job, which was related to his years of Cold War service on a nuclear submarine, which was, somehow, related to the earlier devastation of Hiroshima, an event I had learned about from picture books and my parents. I also knew there were elements of his work that I could never ask about, things that my mom didn't get to hear about, things that were government secrets. His job was to make weapons fly more efficiently and hit their target more precisely, which he claimed was a good thing, something that could bring about world peace. As a result of this informal indoctrination, I've always known our scientific advances can be deadly, terrible things. I've always known science wasn't just about typing rocks but also undoing them in great displays of fire and smoke.

When I wasn't worried about the end of the world, I was free to explore it. From New York to New Mexico to Massachusetts, each of our homes was surrounded by nature, and my parents had a Montessori attitude toward education and discovery. If we showed an interest in any one subject—like, say, rocks—they would try to nurture that. As a result, I've always had a robust collection of gemstones and crystals, rocks big and small, smooth and jagged. The intention was that I'd learn their names, understand the mechanisms of their formation, and ideally become so inspired that I, too, might pursue a career in STEM. It didn't work, much to the disappointment of my father. I didn't want to undo stones, or even to make my own. The hard sciences were always too rigid for me, and those grow-your-own crystal kits never worked anyway.

Instead, I wanted to make magic from stones, something that myths and legends assured me was possible. I wasn't looking for power over others but control over my own inner world. I wanted to fix my anxiety, heal my psychic wounds, and maybe even grab the ear of some higher power.

Even though I've long known about the destructive powers of our weapons, I didn't fully understand the level of control we've been able to exert over the material stuff of our planet. For too long, I retained a childlike reverence for crystals and jewels and pretty rocks of all stripes. On some level, I thought they were evidence of a world beyond us. Now I know. We can blast the earth apart searching for gemstones and the power they signify. We can make gemstones in a lab, we can build diamonds from ashes, and we can bombard dull brown rocks with radiation until they glow purple and blue. After this is done, we can create a system of value that prices one stone above another, regardless of its rarity, its use, its innate attractions. We have so much power over these hard, glittering things. Without our laboratories, without our kilns and our chisels and our saws, most of them wouldn't even shine.

"Gemstone" is not a scientific term but a capitalist one. A gemstone is a valuable, hard substance that can be used in jewelry. Included in the category of "gemstone" are various types of organic material that aren't stone at all, like ivory, coral, and pearl. Fossilized or petrified organic materials that we deem attractive enough can also be considered gemstones. The real question isn't whether an item is a mineral but whether it is worth money, and how much. Stones that are worth the most money (rubies, diamonds, emeralds, sapphires) are deemed "precious," while all the rest get lumped under "semiprecious," even though some high-grade semiprecious stones are worth more than precious ones. If this sounds like bullshit, that's okay. Markets are like that.

The appearance of a gemstone varies greatly depending on where it was made (in the Earth's crust or in the mantle) and how (some gems grow, others are squeezed, while some are harvested from living creatures). Although I've never scored a pearl, I've pried open oyster shells looking for those iridescent gemstones, and while I've never found anything bigger than a grain of rice, I've sifted through buckets of sand and stone looking for tourmaline pebbles. Once, at a tourist trap outside Acadia National Park, I bought a box of whole "break open" geodes. They were lumpy, round gray rocks, and when I finally mustered up the courage to hit them properly with my hammer, they shattered into dozens of dull pieces. Instead of being rewarded with a secret cavern of glittering crystals (as was advertised), I saw only plain, off-white quartz growths mixed with splotches of brown.

For $40, I had bought myself a chance to play treasure hunter with inferior rocks. At the time, I felt ripped off, but now I realize the product I purchased wasn't the stone—it was the hope for beauty, the opportunity for childlike discovery. I paid for an intangible thing, but that's not unusual. We're constantly spending our hard-earned cash on flimsy premises or trumped-up claims ("forever roses," anyone?). When it comes to valuing a gemstone, the number-one factor that drives the dollar signs

up is *perceived* desire. What are people willing to pay for the substance? The more attractive it is, the higher the price. "Attractive" isn't a scientific term, nor am I using it to mean "beautiful." The bulk of naturally formed gemstones aren't all that pretty or colorful, particularly when they're first pulled from the ground or plucked from the sea. Yet we put these various small, beloved objects into the same rough category because we use them in similar ways, as objects of adornment. We make them desirable through human intervention; we cut them, polish them, grow them, dye them, drill holes in them, string them, set them. Yet because of their supposed "natural" traits, we treat them as though they've earned our lust and faith. I own something called *The Crystal Bible*, a big, fat book devoted to gemstone magic, a thing I do not believe in yet practice regardless. I have a piece of opal that winks tangerine orange and lime green when you hold it up to the sun, and on writing days when I feel particularly stuck, I like to hold this stone and roll it around in my hands. Opal, according to believers, promotes creativity. My blue lace agate is for calm, and my rose quartz is (of course) for love. Once, on a particularly bright winter night, I took several of my rocks outside and let them bask in the light of the full Snow Moon. In the frigid February morning, I brought them back into my house and laid them on my bed. The irregularly shaped agates sat in a little line, cold as ice, moon-washed but otherwise unchanged.

These pretty things haven't fixed all my problems (yet), but the right gemstone can change everything. Up until the late nineteenth century, before women were allowed to own property, upper class women in Europe collected jewelry as a pseudo-financial safety net. If your husband ran off to India, leaving you bereft, at least you might be able to hawk some diamonds and pay for a small, simply furnished room where you could live out your Miss Havisham future. Gems still change everything for some people; a diamond engagement ring isn't going to make much on the secondhand market, but it does signal an impending shift in your legal status and possibly an upcoming tax break.

We put a lot of faith in our stones; we turn to them for salvation and we fear their wrath. There are stories of cursed gems from around the globe, but the haunted-gem genre really took off during the Victorian era, when suddenly every blue carbuncle and yellow moonstone became suspect. Many of these stories were marketing ploys, including the supposed curse of the Hope Diamond. Some were popular works of fiction; Wilkie Collins, Sir Arthur Conan Doyle, and Agatha Christie all wrote stories of cursed gems. These tales follow a fairly rigid pattern: rock is stolen from a temple or a shrine in "the Colonies"; rock is brought back to England; rock's owners die; rock gets stolen; rock gets found; mystery is solved. I love these stories, partially because they stink of thinly disguised guilt. There's a sense that the only honestly procured stone is one that you pulled from the ground with your own two hands. All other rocks are suspicious; you never know whose shrine was desecrated, whose tomb was raided, or whose blood was spilled on that shiny surface before it fell into your hands.

To me, there's something eerie about all large, faceted jewels, from the diamond tiaras of the British monarchy to the honking engagement rings worn by Hollywood starlets. It's too much wealth located in such a small space. Wearing such a thing could get you killed. It seems like hubris, to walk around with millions of dollars displayed on your person. Not that those who have been attacked for their jewels deserve it. I remember feeling strangely moved to read about Kim Kardashian's 2016 attack, though I knew little about her as a public figure and had never connected with her work. Yet the details were terrible. During Paris Fashion Week, the reality superstar was held captive at gunpoint inside her hotel room while thieves ransacked her luggage. She was tied up and forced into a bathroom. She told her sisters after the ordeal that she thought she was going to die if she tried to escape, worrying that she was about to be shot in the back. The intruders, who were dressed in police vests and came in while she was in bed, left with about $10 million worth of jewelry, including her emerald-cut second engagement ring (valued at $4 million). The experience was violent and violating, and it reportedly left her traumatized—and unwilling to wear her fine jewelry in public. I wouldn't wish that on anyone, no matter how much wealth they'd been hoarding.

My perspective on gemstones has been formed by movies, gossip columns, museums, and books. This isn't uncommon; we learn what to desire from our media. In her memoir *Diamond Doris*, career criminal Doris Payne explains how she climbed and clawed her way to stability and wealth during a time when Black women had neither. She was a self-taught jewelry thief who stole millions of dollars' worth of gemstones and jewelry from stores around the world. She started taking jewelry from shops in the 1950s, back when she was a young mother living with her family and children in Ohio. Although Payne was chronically broke, she was able to con jewelry shops into believing she was someone with a different life—a glamorous, moneyed existence. She learned to crave sparkle and to mimic wealth, Payne explains in her memoir, by reading women's magazines.

As a girl, Payne read her mother's magazines, paging through copies of *Town & Country* and *Harper's Bazaar* to find out what movie stars and socialites were wearing, how they were doing their hair, what jewels they were buying. "I didn't feel any less than any of the young women in the magazines," she writes. "Style was style, and made for allure, and magnetism, and envy, and I loved fashion, beautiful hairdos, and a look of class. How was I supposed to know as a child that the world imposed a difference between some women and others?" Payne documents the racism she experienced throughout her life, yet her primary focus isn't on her obstacles but the fruits of her victories. Payne loved diamonds because of what they represented. Diamonds bought her house. Diamonds transformed her life. For a short time, she lived the cushy life of a white woman in a ladies' magazine. She traveled first class, took rich lovers and discarded them, cycled through cinched-waist outfits, and did it all with clear cut carats sparkling from her fingers.

While our lives are very different and I have no desire to become a jewel thief, I do relate to Payne's obsession with glossy magazines. We both used them as guidebooks on how to be a certain kind of woman. Through magazines, Payne learned how to project enough status and wealth that jewelry-store clerks wouldn't think twice about letting her try on their most expensive items. As I read, I found myself agreeing with Payne's justifications for her thievery, her Robin Hood–esque exploits. At one point, she tells her mother that she's not stealing, she's "taking." The diamonds were taken from mines in Africa. Why can't she take them back? The stores, she later argues, are running a con on insurance companies and their customers, overpricing rocks and lying about the value of these pretty things. Why shouldn't she cheat them when they're cheating everyone else?

In economics, there's a phenomenon called the diamond-water paradox or more commonly, the paradox of value. While philosophers have tried to describe the disparity, it was most elegantly summarized by the father of economics, Adam Smith, in 1776. "Nothing is more useful than water: but it will purchase scarce anything; scarce anything can be had in exchange for it. A diamond, on the contrary, has scarcely any value in use; but a very great quantity of other goods may frequently be had in exchange for it," he wrote. One could argue that diamonds are valuable not because they are useful but because they are beautiful or hard or exotic, that diamonds have other intrinsic qualities that make them desirable. But none of these factors fully explains why people are willing to pay so much for diamonds. The answer is a combination of physical traits, combined with the power of storytelling, the allure of advertising, and the glitter and shine of group worship. Diamonds are valuable because the people who already have diamonds decided that they are valuable. Their beauty (as well as their hardness, their scarcity, their clarity, and so on) has never mattered nearly as much as that. It behooves the diamond-havers to continue repeating stories about their bits of carbon because it keeps their wealth intact. As a species, we're marvelously skilled at inciting desire.

I never thought of myself as a diamond-ring kind of woman. Before our engagement, I told my husband not to buy me a diamond ring and to use that money for something else. (He used it to build a teardrop trailer for our annual camping trips to Nova Scotia.) When we got married at the courthouse, we exchanged fragile wooden rings we had carved from a dowel the night before. Our wedding was a sudden decision, inspired by my recent loss of health insurance, and our rings were equally practical, thrifty things. We got married because I needed to see my psychiatrist; we exchanged wooden rings because it was what we had. Yet it was still terribly romantic. (A snowy March evening in Portland, a fistful of white ranunculus and baby's breath, glasses of Champagne at a hotel bar, friends and toasts—even when I'm frugal, I find glamour.)

After we were married and our lives had stabilized a little, I found myself wanting a traditional band, one complete with gemstones, hints of glitter. When friends got engaged, I felt envious of the obvious pride they took in their rings, not to mention that careful moment of attention that women ritually bestow upon the bride-to-be's outstretched hand, the gentle holding of fingers and admiring coos. I wanted to have my hand held, my love acknowledged, my happiness spread and shared around a lunch table. I wanted to look at my own hand and be reminded of the commitment I'd made—it wasn't easy, deciding to share my life so wholeheartedly with someone else. I had to give up elements of my autonomy (we always do, whenever we let other people in) and I wanted external evidence of this huge interior shift. My desire rose until I couldn't ignore it any longer. I caved. I asked for what I really wanted, what I thought I would never want, a thing I had said I didn't want, something I genuinely believed I didn't want. Together, we found a band that would suit my lifestyle, our budget, and my taste for wintery beauty. Now, on the ring finger of my left hand, I wear a slim white gold band with seven "salt-and-pepper" (that is, gray) diamonds embedded on one side. They're small and impure, little specks of carbon—mining by-products, really. It pleases me, how they twinkle like stars. You have to know they're there in order to appreciate them. I like that.

The elevation of the diamond ring is a recent and well-documented invention. It's also an ongoing project that has nimbly adapted to our information age. Many people know, logically, that diamonds aren't the only way to show love or wear sparkle. But we continue to turn to the familiar symbol because it feels safe, in an odd way. Diamonds allow us to perform our emotions legibly on the public stage. They are legible as symbols. They communicate our relationship status and our social standing. And while I think that I would have been equally happy with sapphires or topaz, it is much harder to find a wedding band in my price range with those gemstones embedded. Diamonds are more plentiful. They are the standard stone when it comes to contemporary romance, the default choice for most consumers, which means they're the default for most jewelers. While they are the most highly valued of the four "precious stones" (a category that also includes sapphires, rubies, and emeralds), diamonds are the most common and least complicated. Yet many people scrimp and save to acquire the biggest possible rock for their beloved. As Victoria Finlay wryly notes in *Jewels: A Secret History*, "They are often bought by men at exactly the point when they can least afford them." She goes on to explain how diamonds lose their value immediately after purchase. From the moment you step out of the jewelry store (or from the moment the diamond leaves the jeweler's) it has lost over 50 percent of its value. While some brides do opt for other stones (cubic zirconia or moissanite are both popular alternatives), there's a social stigma attached to these rocks. Even lab-grown diamonds, which are chemically indistinguishable from those yanked from the bowels of the Earth, carry a stigma. Diamonds remain, for better or worse, the ultimate consumer symbol of commitment in American culture.

But diamonds were not always beloved for their beauty. At first, people prized them primarily for their hardness. This is even reflected in the name; the English word comes from the Greek "adamas," meaning "indominable." Since diamonds are so very hard, early people couldn't cut or shape them, which means they were interacting with the stone in its raw form. Rough diamonds aren't ugly, but they're not exactly the flaming light-catchers we see today. They look rather like beach glass or quartz crystal, semi-translucent stones with little color and hardly any natural shine.

There is evidence that people have been using diamonds to polish ceremonial burial axes in ancient China from as early as 2500 BCE. However, most of our diamond knowledge begins to accumulate around the year zero. Trade with the Greeks and Romans brought diamonds from Asia and North Africa to Europe in the first century CE, where they were put to use on bow drills and whetstones. Bead-making workshops used diamonds to engrave and carve holes in colorful pieces of glass, shells, and stones, while knife-makers used them to hone the edges of blades. For millennia, diamonds were enhancers; they made pretty things prettier and deadly things deadlier. Their role wasn't yet ornamental. They could engrave, shape, and polish more colorful gemstones, but it tended to be those other rocks (rubies, topaz, emeralds) that got set in metal and worn around town.

Like mirrors and porcelain cups, diamonds were sometimes revered as magical objects, protective tools that could make the owner stronger, heartier, impenetrable to disease and violence and other misfortunes, and as such they were sometimes set into shields and armor. Looking at examples of these early diamonds, it's easy to see why royals throughout

Europe and Asia seemed to prefer wearing pearls or rubies or just plain, shining gold. Compared to the other gemstones, diamonds are dull and dirty, gray little lumps.

This changed in the late Middle Ages when a Flemish jeweler and gem cutter invented a polishing wheel capable of faceting diamonds. That invention opened up a whole new level of appreciation for the stone, and the value of diamonds rose accordingly. Suddenly, you could see into a diamond, and you could watch as light bounced around inside the rigidly arranged carbon atoms. Like graphite, diamonds are made of pure carbon. The thing that makes diamonds special is how these carbon atoms are arranged tetrahedrally, which makes them both resistant to compression and great at scattering rays of light. When you cut and polish a diamond, you unlock this potential, turning what was once a hard pebble into a twinkling rainbow star, a tiny handheld flame.

From the fifteenth to the mid-eighteenth century, the world's best diamonds came from the mines in the Golconda sultanate (located in present-day Hyderabad, India). The fourteenth-century Deccan sultanate was world renowned for their exceedingly clear diamonds, caused by a complete absence of nitrogen (an impurity that gives stones a yellowish tinge). These stones were so prized that the name Golconda is still evoked among gem dealers and auction houses as a high-water mark of quality. In the eighteenth century, Portuguese colonists began mining diamonds in Brazil using slave labor, a practice that would continue well into the next century. It was a brutal, horrifying chapter of history. Tens of thousands of slaves were brought from Africa to Brazil. Indigenous people were captured and forced to work underground in dangerous tunnels. They were beaten, imprisoned, and routinely abused. They dug for diamonds as well as other gemstones, precious metals, and useful ores. The fruits of their labor were then sent abroad to be turned into more wealth for the Portuguese government. While the liberation of Brazil in 1822 put a stop to some of these exploitations, the practice of slavery continued for another sixty years (at least). A report from 2021 revealed that over three hundred people have been rescued from what was deemed "slave-labor conditions" in illegal Brazilian mines since 2008. But they weren't digging for diamonds—that's mostly gone, now. They were sent underground to seek other precious things: gold, amethyst, kaolin (used in making porcelain), and tin.

The diamond stores of Brazil have been depleted, but that doesn't mean we're running out of them. There are plenty of diamonds in the Earth's crust. There are diamonds in Arkansas, diamonds in Canada, diamonds in Russia, and perhaps most important, there are lots of diamonds in Africa.

The first South African diamond was found in the late 1860s by a fifteen-year-old farm boy, just off the banks of the Orange River. Later, this rock became known as "Eureka," though a more apt name might have been "Janus," for this was a two-faced blessing for the country and its people. In the short term, the rural colonists living in the region benefited from these finds, but as time wore on, it became clear that the wealth ripped from the land wasn't going to stay in the region, much less benefit the original (and already oppressed) inhabitants of the country. The first few alluvial rocks found in the area sparked the Kimberley diamond rush, and British prospectors rushed in to buy the land around the "kimberlite pipes."

At first, there were a few different British men vying for diamond dominance, but in 1888, one came out on top: Cecil John Rhodes. He merged his mine holdings with another local mining magnate to create De Beers Consolidated Mines, which effectively created a monopoly. The Kimberley mines were far more productive than any competing ventures, thanks in part to the use of bonded labor. By this point Rhodes had almost two decades of experience overseeing diamond mines—he arrived in South Africa in 1871—plus a "ruthless" edge. The De Beers company started using convicts in their mines after Rhodes negotiated a contract with the government in 1884. According to historian Martin Meredith, the De Beers convict camps were "grim" places. The miners were treated cruelly, deprived of all family life, and, from the sounds of it, stripped of their basic human dignity. Every night, they would be chained naked in small cells. When their term was over, they would be placed in solitary confinement, naked, with their hands bound in leather gloves. This was all done to ensure they didn't swallow any diamonds or otherwise hide them on their bodies. When it came to workplace safety, "the Kimberley mines had the worst record of any in South Africa," writes Finlay. Hundreds of workers died from sickness, fire, and suffocation in the De Beers camps.

While most people know Rhodes from his famed scholarship, he wasn't a benevolent man. He was a staunch imperialist and firmly believed in the righteousness of British rule on the African continent. For a while there, a territory was even named after him (Rhodesia), which has since been liberated and split into Zimbabwe and Zambia. While some people still defend Rhodes, arguing that he wasn't a "biological racist," as proven by his friendly relations with individual African people, it doesn't really matter what he felt in his heart. He worked throughout his life to uphold and expand a system of colonial rule, and diamonds were a part of that equation. With his diamond-derived wealth, he funded military operations to seize control of more and more land, which he then tried to mine, thus leading to more wealth, more power, more bloodshed.

The new flush of diamonds entering the market led to a decrease in value. While people had learned to love the flash and sparkle of the stones, and while lapidary artists had become quite good at faceting them to show off their light-bending assets, a diamond was still just one pretty gemstone among many. But Rhodes's cartel was already strong, not to mention nimble. Since the late 1800s, the company has used many of the same tactics to stay profitable, including the consolidation of resources (De Beers bought all the mines), uniformly high pricing (De

Beers doesn't do sales), and creating an illusion of scarcity (De Beers patiently hoards diamonds whenever the price falls too low). Rhodes implemented a general rule of release: the number of diamonds that De Beers put onto the market every year should roughly match the number of engagements taking place. The rocks they held back formed a "buffer stock."

After Rhodes died in 1902, leadership was briefly controlled by stakeholders and an amalgamation of competing companies. Ultimately a German man named Ernest Oppenheimer rose to the top. Oppenheimer continued to consolidate the diamond monopoly through buying up mines and seizing land. But while these brutal displays of power could keep diamonds and their wealth in white hands, it couldn't make the general public desire diamonds any more than they already did. And since the stones are not actually all that rare, it was becoming harder and harder to convince people that they needed to buy from De Beers. They needed to control demand as well as supply. Diamonds would always be useful in manufacturing, and there would always be some demand for diamond dust and its polishing abilities, but when it came to jewelry, diamonds were an option. They weren't *the* option. Diamond prices fell during the Great Depression, and demand didn't pick up when the country's economy began to recover. Young Americans were buying flamboyant, colorful stones. "Not diamonds," writes Finlay, "which were seen as colorless, like the war years."

The first big advertisement of De Beers's new campaign with firm N. W. Ayer & Son ran in the *New Yorker* in 1939. It was a wordy beast, part of a multipronged effort to reeducate the public about the importance and appeal of clear rocks. "The beautiful flame of a diamond is unquenchable," read the copy. "Once you have chosen yours, it will become a permanent symbol throughout your years and far beyond them. However modest, your wife will never relinquish it to more affluent circumstances." Clearly, this message needed to be streamlined. In 1947, copywriter Mary Frances Gerety helped to stabilize the entire diamond industry with a late-night brainstorming session that yielded four little words: "A Diamond Is Forever." It was simple, yet genius. The slogan played on the one thing that truly sets a diamond apart—its hardness, its chemical structure—while discouraging ideas of resale. You were supposed to keep diamonds, not pawn them, because diamonds were symbols of eternal love and personal worth. The size of a diamond didn't just reflect how much someone could spend—but how much they were willing to spend. And best of all? It was catchy.

With this campaign, De Beers didn't just stop people from selling their old diamonds, they also contributed to the elaborate scaffolding of fake history that had begun to obscure the stones, a false narrative that incorporated elements of mining's darkness into the light-filled rocks. It wasn't just De Beers; there were many merchants with skin in this particular game. With the help of jewelers, diamond dealers, and magazine writers, word spread that selling a diamond was "bad luck." There was some precedent here: cutting diamonds had long been rumored to be a dangerous, poisonous affair, and diamonds of unknown origin were often painted as cursed or haunted, which only further increased the stone's legendary status. Stories like this have a dark romance to them, a cinematic appeal that speaks to our desire for narrative arcs. In reality, diamond miners were treated terribly and died frequently, the stones were often taken from exploited people in colonized land, and they could ruin a person's life, particularly if someone went into debt to buy one. But these facts are rather boring compared to the magic and mystery of haunted or cursed stones. The gemstone industry allowed a little darkness to seep into their mythology to act as a smokescreen for the real, banal environmental sins of mining and the human-rights offenses of funding conflict abroad. It also further obscured the truth: that in the case of a diamond, the cost of production is entirely unrelated to the price of the final product. When De Beers began marketing their stones as the ultimate expression of love, they were trying to ensure a world in which the diamond market would never crash again. So far, their plan has worked brilliantly.

De Beers has even survived being cast as a corrupt, villainous force in a major Hollywood blockbuster. In 2006, *Blood Diamond* became an international hit and sparked a PR crisis for the company. Although De Beers was never named directly, it was obvious to canny viewers that the Van De Kaap diamond cartel was a thinly veiled stand-in for the Rhodes legacy. Starring Leonardo DiCaprio as a white Rhodesian mercenary and Djimon Hounsou as a Mende fisherman both seeking the same pink diamond against a backdrop of war-ravaged Sierra Leone, the action film brought public attention to an ongoing problem. Diamonds that had been likely mined by warlords using slave labor were allegedly making their way to the De Beers warehouse (often with the help of several middlemen). Diamonds were turned into money, which bought tanks, machine guns, and other tools of mass death. The same gemstone that helped fund a brutal conflict could then be set by a jeweler, transformed into a stunning pink ring, perhaps, or a set of brilliant-cut earrings. But De Beers was adroit as ever. As reports began to circulate about their shady buying practices, the company hired management consultants to help them reform their supply-chain issues and create more goodwill for their product They rebranded themselves as what journalist Alan Cowell called the "squeaky-clean crusaders" of the industry, the leading source of "conflict-free" stones, and introduced a new logo, the "Forevermark," to further distinguish their stones from others on the market. Despite the fact that De Beers changed their practices only when it proved absolutely necessary, the company somehow managed to turn what could have been a wholesale cultural rejection of their product into a "virtue," wrote Cowell for the *New York Times*.

The desire for lab-grown diamonds to catch on took decades, but it seems that they're finally poised to rival the "real" thing in the American jewelry market. For a time, the stigma of "synthetic" diamonds was too great, but between 2017 and 2019, sales of mined diamonds reportedly dipped while sales of grown diamonds rose 20 percent. Some have attributed this to the values of the new generation of consumers that are coming of marriageable age: Millennials and Generation Z. Unlike older generations of Americans, these groups have less material wealth overall, and less attachment to the idea of a diamond engagement ring. According to a study conducted in 2018, nearly 70 percent of Millennial-aged respondents said they would consider buying a lab-grown diamond for an engagement ring. The same report also showed that nearly half of retailers said lab-grown diamonds were "absolutely" detracting from their diamond sales. Meghan Markle has been spotted wearing lab-grown diamonds in her ears, and speaking for Millennial women in America, where Markle goes, we follow.

But this isn't a story of the new, green option overcoming the old, bloody, and pollution-tainted choice. Lab-grown diamonds are more ethical, to some extent, but they also use a lot of resources to make; their claims of being carbon-neutral are widely debated. Creating a diamond in a laboratory involves taking a "seed diamond," (that is, a tiny fragment of mined diamond) and surrounding it with pure carbon, like graphite. This small pile is then bombarded with heat and pressure. It can take weeks to grow a diamond in this way, and it takes a good amount of energy (often derived from fossil fuels) to encourage the graphite's atoms to break their bonds and re-form into that cubic, crystalline structure that makes a diamond so hard and so clear. But some lab growers don't use just plain graphite. You can pay to have the cremated ashes of a loved one turned into a diamond. Our bodies are, on average, made of around 18 percent carbon atoms, so a small portion of a corpse can be chemically rearranged, set in precious metal, and worn around town, if you should so desire.

The companies that have profited off diamonds aren't going quietly into the night, either; they're joining the lab-grown game. In May 2018, De Beers announced it would launch Lightbox Jewelry, a pastel-branded line of colorful "laboratory-grown" diamonds that "may not be forever," according to CEO Bruce Cleaver, but instead are "perfect for right now." This move "stunned" and "shocked" the diamond industry, partially because previous De Beers representatives had vowed not to "cannibalize" their own industry. But it quickly became obvious that Lightbox wasn't intended to replace the classic solitaire ring but to add more twinkle to a woman's daily life. They were disrupting themselves! You only get engaged once (or twice or perhaps thrice), but you have dozens of birthdays, which means you have dozens of opportunities to buy pink or blue stones from Lightbox! De Beers's marketing team was careful to note in their online materials that natural diamonds are "very rare," while man-made diamonds have "no limit." Even while selling their lab-grown choices, it behooves De Beers to mention their mines. And even when you're buying a lab-grown diamond, you're still helping maintain the diamond myth, as well as the corporations that benefit from their production.

My small gray diamond chips are "post-consumer" or "reclaimed" stones, but they're implicated in this system too. They're overpriced shards of carbon. I knew this, but I wanted them all the same. Desire is like that, overriding your common sense. Desire can sometimes be consciously reshaped with enough willpower and analytical thinking, but not always. Sometimes, I feel as though my passion for beautiful things splits me into multiple people. There's a person who desires recklessly, who hedonistically craves all the shine, all the glimmer, all the light in the world, who wants to hoard and steal and own. There's a person who notices the shadows and dwells on them, mulling, thinking, doubting, detracting.

There's one last version of myself that surfaces, sometimes, in the presence of great and undeniable beauty. She just wants to be, to sit in awe. To tell you that your ring is beautiful, and to mean it. To appreciate a bit of sparkle, simply and purely. To relish and then to let it go. She's the one I'm trying to be.

Turquoise has always been, in my mind, the inverse of a diamond. We love diamonds because their rigid, geometric forms sparkle and flash with fire; turquoise, matte, globular, and organic, does no such thing. Yet unlike diamonds, which need to be faceted and fixed, turquoise awes in its raw form. There's a certain magic to that; it needs so little help from us. It is a remarkable color; to say that turquoise is the color turquoise doesn't even begin to scratch the surface. The stone can be many different hues, from cold winter sky blue to glaucous bloom gray-green. It can look as brilliant and lush as a bed of moss in late spring or as fragile and sweet as a newly hatched robin's egg. It's a stone with great chromatic range that is mainly found in arid regions, which makes its blues and greens only more shocking. Unlike the tropics, with their outrageous neon blossoms and birds, our planet's dry swathes are decorated with neutral color schemes, and against this backdrop, turquoise shouts.

A mineral made of relatively common elements—copper, aluminum, phosphorus, hydrogen, and oxygen—it is one of the earliest gems discovered by humans. Like orchids, turquoise has been found on every continent, save Antarctica. Our English word for the gem most likely comes from the French "pierre turque," meaning "stone from Turkey." While deposits have been found in England and Europe, up until the 1400s, it wasn't as commonly mined, nor was it as highly valued as some of the other gems that traveled the Silk Road. Turquoise never fit as well into the aesthetic of white kings and queens. They've historically preferred the glitzier gemstones made up of orderly arranged crystals (the diamonds, the beryls, the many shades of quartz). European royalty liked to set their crowns and tiaras with translucent rocks that let light flow through them like ice. Turquoise, like jade, coral, jasper, and amber, has visual warmth; it eats the rays of the sun.

In many cultures, turquoise functioned as a symbolic echo, a stray piece of the heavens. Different Native American tribes had their own names for turquoise, but the one used most often in copy materials for turquoise traders and dealers is "fallen sky stone." Some groups believed turquoise came directly from the sky, while others felt that it was a link between the earth and the sky. My favorite myth comes from the people of the Hopi tribe, who described the stone as a waste product made by the mystical lizards that traveled between the underground world and the surface. (Turquoise, the loveliest piece of crap.) Navajo warriors are said to have worn turquoise into battle, since it was a powerful protector, and Navajo women threw the stone into the river when they wanted to pray to the rain god. Turquoise also protected you from the thunder-storm; braid a bead into your hair and you won't get struck by lightning. Many of these myths were collected by nature writer Ellen Meloy in her Pulitzer Prize–nominated book, *The Anthropology of Turquoise*, but there's plenty more to be found online. According to another legend— this one is particularly beloved by retailers—Native Americans used to dance in the rain, crying tears of gratitude for the moisture, and their salty excretions poured off their faces and into the earth, where it pooled and mingled with the rain and became turquoise.

Saying Native Americans "believed" something to be true is a bit disingenuous. It's a bit like saying Americans "worship" fame. We do, of course, but it's not as simple as all that. Indigenous Americans are a wide-ranging group with an equally wide range of beliefs, identities, allegiances, and faiths. Many of their faiths are considered "closed," meaning they are discouraged from sharing their secrets with outsiders. Sometimes, members of a closed religion will even plant false stories, putting up a smoke screen to protect their own spiritual beliefs from the prying eyes of others. What I know, as an outsider, is vague. Tribal people of the American Southwest valued turquoise and imbued it with meaning. They made art with it, they collected it, and they traded it. Some people use stones to heal themselves, while others respect them purely for their beauty. As Meloy pointed out, turquoise could have contradictory meanings: it was both "family wealth and sacred, for oneself or for sale." I don't doubt that some tribes performed rain dances and linked the ritual to the formation of turquoise. But like the objects sold off reservations to tourists—"the Indian's idea of the trader's idea of what the Anglo thought was an Indian's idea of design," wrote Meloy, paraphrasing an ethnologist—I wonder about these myths. Which ones are authentic? Which ones are real? Is it even my right to know the answer to that question? I want only the real stories, not the marketing myths, regardless of what I'm owed. It's a kind of greed that doesn't sit well on my soul.

As bad as I am at deciphering legends, I'm far worse at spotting a faux rock. I was at a flea market in Woodstock, New York, a few years ago, examining a pair of earrings, when my shopping companion nudged me and whispered, "I don't think that's real." Once she said something, it became obvious. The texture wasn't right—the round cabochons didn't have the waxiness that distinguishes turquoise. The color was too uniform, too bright. They were too good to be true, for pieces that blue usually go for a lot more money. Those stones hadn't been mined, but made.

While those dangling drops were probably plastic, there are plenty of stones sold as turquoise that are actually howlite. Howlite is a pale, opaque stone that resembles crowns of cauliflower and can be dyed almost any color, making a great canvas for dishonest jewelers. However, it's considerably easier to scratch than true turquoise, and it gives up its chromatic secrets when dropped in a vat of nail-polish remover. You can test your suspiciously affordable baubles at home, but I doubt many vendors would let you do this in the store before purchase. (Another test of gem-quality turquoise? Lick it. Geologists often use their tongues to tell stones apart. Good turquoise should stick to your tongue a little and have a substantial weight. If it's too slick or too chalky, you've got a fake.)

According to Jacob Lowry, executive director of the Turquoise Museum in Albuquerque, New Mexico, only around 5 percent of the turquoise sold in America is genuine "gem grade" turquoise. Whether a stone receives that designation depends on many factors, including color, weight, how it was cut, and where it was mined, but all gem-grade turquoise is naturally formed underground. Little of the good stuff goes into American jewelry shops, explains Lowry, because our local market for turquoise is uniquely opaque and impoverished. The highest-grade turquoise is almost always sold abroad. Here, Lowry suggests, turquoise is viewed as a token at worst, a "cultural artifact" at best. People in America are unwilling to pay the "real" value of the stone. We've become accustomed to buying inexpensive knockoffs and low-grade rocks. "In the American southwest, the history of turquoise has never been studied or written," Lowry continues. "It was assumed and marketed. The entire purpose of the turquoise industry in the American southwest is tourism." People visit New Mexico looking to spend $50 on a silver-and-turquoise ring, while customers in Japan will pay up to $1,000 a carat for high-quality turquoise. Given the difference in expectations, you can't blame gem dealers for taking their best wares elsewhere.

Lowry's blunt analysis of the local market came as a surprise to me because I've always loved turquoise and until recently I believed it was a part of some rustic, noble, distinctly American aesthetic. (A problematic assumption but a common one.) As a little girl, I remember spreading out my mother's fine turquoise jewelry on her bed and marveling at the color. Turquoise may not have the glittery, reflective qualities of diamond or quartz, or the vibrant depth of an emerald, but there's something about the gem that makes me want to touch it, feel it on my skin, or press it against my lips. There's a sensual quality to turquoise, otherworldly yet still tangible. It makes perfect sense to me that people around the world have associated this stone with deities and elements, water and air and the glorious afterlife. Heaven and earth.

Turquoise is usually found in tandem with other valuable substances. Mines that produce gold, silver, copper, and uranium will also sometimes unearth turquoise. Since mining has always been a hazardous and difficult form of labor, it shouldn't come as any surprise that the early mines of North America were frequently manned by slaves. This was true before the Spanish arrived. There was a long history of Maya, Aztec, and Iroquois people enslaving their prisoners of war. Once the Spanish arrived and began taking over the mines in the early 1500s, conditions became considerably worse for Native people. According to an essay by Andrés Reséndez on "the other slavery" (whose book on the subject won the 2017 Bancroft Prize), people living around the silver-district mines were the first to be "pulled into" the system, meaning they were rounded up by Spanish soldiers and forced to work in the mines. When there were no more able-bodied people around locally to enslave, the Spanish started buying Native slaves from other regions (New Mexico, Texas, California) and bringing them south to work in the mines. "Native slavery engulfed the entire North American continent, but the timing varied by region," writes Reséndez. While the enslavement of Black people in the eastern regions of North America stopped after the Civil War, "Native slavery continued to thrive during the nineteenth century" and proved "nearly impossible" to end.

Under colonial rule, Native craftspeople began creating the distinctive style of jewelry that the Southwest has become known for, with gracefully sweeping vines of silver, pendulous squash-blossom pendants, and inlaid floral designs. In the 1800s, waves of Egyptomania and Japanomania swept through Europe, and as a result, there was a very real obsession with all art forms considered "exotic." This included turquoise, a stone often associated with the Middle East. Women began getting married with turquoise engagement rings, often set against bright yellow gold.

Demand was further increased because turquoise was considered a suitable adornment for European men and women; it had a reputation for being a rather masculine stone, good for protecting the wearer against falls from horseback (among other disasters).

By the nineteenth century, many of America's turquoise deposits had been depleted, but the appetite for Southwestern jewelry had not. The style has come in and out of fashion many times during the twentieth and twenty-first centuries. People want a slice of the magic of New Mexico, the "Land of Enchantment," that harsh and unforgivingly beautiful place. Although there are few working turquoise mines today, and what they bring up tends to be quite low quality, I still love those flawed stones. I don't share Lowry's distaste for cheap, touristy, Southwestern-style jewelry, particularly since there is so much of it available for purchase directly from tribal members. I think it's possible to appreciate an aesthetic and enjoy the artworks of a group without appropriating their style or culture, but key to this process is sourcing. The fewer steps between me and the maker, the better I love my purchase. And it's not because I get a better deal or because I like to haggle. (I very much do not.) The things that I love most and longest are those that are draped with a web of positive associations, a memory net that links person to place to thing. I take a lot of joy in buying from an artist who is still perfecting their craft, someone who is working out the kinks in their design, using lower-grade stones, and offering flawed seconds. My favorite earrings are sterling silver hoops inlaid with a geometric pattern of turquoise, mother-of-pearl, and lapis lazuli that I bought from a Zuni artist at an outdoor fair in New Mexico. When I wear them, I remember driving into Taos in the snow with the top down on our rental convertible. I remember how warm the desert felt compared to Maine, how the light turned pink in the evening, and how the woodsmoke smelled in the air—dry and soft. I remember the face of the young artist, engaged and open.

When I visited New Mexico as an adult, I went with the secret hope that accompanies most homecomings. I wanted to awaken memories of my childhood, to find kinship in place, to return to a place where, in philosopher Glenn Albrecht's terms, my heart would be at ease. But I didn't even recognize my old house. Nothing was like my memories, not the neighborhood, not the food, not the sunsets. Yet somehow, that didn't matter; it was beautiful even if it wasn't mine. I was a stranger there, no longer a child of the Land of Enchantment. This happens often in adult life—knowledge, memories, stones can all be false. But the earrings are real. It turns out that the "traditional" Native designs I always admired are a mishmash of influences, born from Spanish colonial rule, Native artistic traditions, and the demand for "exotic" or "authentic" jewelry. Yet does this make them any less pretty? Who cares if someone wants to lie to me about their legends?

In writing about British curry, author Bee Wilson asks the related questions: "How can you explain that a cultural phenomenon people know and love is really a cartoon version? And at what point do you give up and accept that the cartoon now has its own separate life?" Curry isn't made of gemstones and metals, but the principle is the same. Curry and turquoise are both created out of brutal clashes of people, violent imperialist histories, misunderstandings, and misinformation. Yet the end results—the steaming bowl of yellow stew, the shining pair of inlaid silver earrings shaped like blue moons—still give so much pleasure. They still bring joy and enrichment to so many lives.

I have a confession to make, one that makes me a little uncomfortable because it reveals a certain desperation that drags at my words, my work. Inside a black leather pouch, next to my makeup, my emergency medication, my stash of tea-tree toothpicks and my little roll of Tums, I have a milky blue stone. I believe it's opalite, but I don't know for certain. I bought it at a New Age store in Portland, after picking up my medication for anxiety—my daily dose of off-brand Zoloft, my to-be-used-sparingly orange bottle of Ativan.

I carry this rock with me everywhere I go, not because it's pretty, though that's part of why I bought it. It's a soft color that changes with the light. It can appear pale green or gray or even teal. Up until very recently, I had assumed it was a "natural" stone, made underground. That seems unlikely, now that I know about opalite (and now that I remember how cheaply I bought it). Best-case scenario, this is a piece of "common opal," which is the name for opal that doesn't display iridescence. There aren't iridescent flecks in my stone, so this is possible. But worst-case scenario, my worry stone isn't a stone at all. It's a piece of glass, manufactured to look like opal, sold alongside pieces of cheap quartz. It could contain plastics; it might be a sham.

I carry this worry stone for the same reason I pick up my Ativan: I get panic attacks. I have since I was a very little girl. I was an anxious child. At the age of eight, my parents brought me to a therapist because I hadn't slept for more than a few hours in days. I would lie awake in bed until five a.m. running though disaster scenarios. During the waking hours, I was unafraid of the things that scared my siblings. I would swim in deep water, try the neighbor's skateboard, and eat unidentified berries. But at night, I became paralyzed with fear. I was afraid of carbon monoxide poisoning. I was afraid that I'd have to go somewhere and there wouldn't be a bathroom. I was afraid my parents would die. I was afraid I'd have to read aloud in class or speak in front of a crowd of people, all eyes on me. I was afraid of loss and humiliation, two things that still scare me now, though not as much.

The worry stone is one of many I've owned, small rocks designed to be held in the palm of the hand and stroked, petted, turned over and over in a self-soothing motion. My favorite is the stone I picked up on a beach in Iceland. It's black and leathery smooth, and I keep this one next to my bed. It does help to hold them when I feel my brain running too fast. Worry stones are just one of the many tools I use to return to my body. Over the past decade, I've learned how to meditate and control my breath. I've learned that I can lower my heart rate and thus stall the adrenaline response that pushes me into an all-out panic attack. I also use the Ativan when I need to. I dissolve it under my tongue, letting its sugary flavor flood my mouth, and signal to my overactive amygdala that help is coming, just wait.

The Ativan works because it is part of a class of highly addictive psychoactive drugs called benzodiazepines (or benzos for short) that essentially decrease brain activity. I'm tempted to call one thing "real" (Ativan) and another "fake" (worry stone), but that's not really the truth. Lab-grown diamonds are diamonds, London blue topaz, although it's been treated with irradiation, is still topaz. The worry stones and the Ativan exist together, in the same space. They both work, despite the fact that I got one at a CVS and the other at Leapin' Lizards.

Growing up in the early 2000s and the age of the hipster, I have a tendency to worry about "authenticity"—a big buzzword during the height of my social media use. And while holding dyed or manufactured stones would have once made me feel like a fraud, I've come to a gentler understanding of their appeal. While I wouldn't purchase opalite now, I don't feel the need to discard this pretty, milky thing with its orange glints and green winks. Color is something that makes people happy, and crystal stores are spaces that feel soothing, welcoming, joyful. "Crystals are bullshit in the sense that everything is bullshit," says Jaya Saxena, author of *Crystal Clear: Reflections on Extraordinary Talismans for Everyday Life*. She puts it surprisingly bluntly for someone who wrote a book about crystals, yet this doesn't mean Saxena hates gemstones or the people who use them in religious practices. She doesn't believe that green crystals vibrate at a certain frequency, nor does she believe that giving someone a rose quartz will make them love you. But she recognizes the need humans have for spiritual connection with the physical world. We need to project meaning onto the world around us. It doesn't make someone stupid, she says, for believing in their own private collection of stones. "I try to give people more credit," Saxena says. "I don't think you and I are the only people in the world who use our stones as metaphors."

I didn't understand this until recently, but metaphors are, in a very real way, magic. When I turn a gemstone into a source of solace, when I hold a rock to calm myself, and when I send out good vibes into the world, I'm practicing a form of magic that has been around for as long as humans have been alive. I'm creating links between things, pathways of meaning that get stronger the more often we travel them. In *Magic: A History*, Oxford archaeology professor Chris Gosden defines magic as a mode of activity that emphasizes "human participation" with the universe. "Rumors of the death of magic," he writes, "have been constantly exaggerated." Magic isn't about understanding coldly from a distance or worshipping like a supplicant. It's about being in the thick of it, a spinner in the net rather than a fly. "Through magic we can explore mutuality," Gosden posits, adding that "human intelligence is one element of the broader intelligence of the world." Living things communicate with one another, even though we don't always speak clearly. Magic allows for a greater understanding of the world. It is intertwined with both religion and science, and while we often think of these three frameworks as though they're in direct opposition, Gosden points out that we don't have to choose. We have space for many different beliefs inside our brains. Although we tend to denigrate magic as something for children and the childlike, we've been practicing magic for as long as we've been people. No culture is without its magical practices, its superstitions, and its folk beliefs. Holding stones and hoping for calm—it's a form of magic. If I believe it works, it will. It's *just* the placebo effect.

Yet here's the thing about the placebo effect: It's real. It works. It heals. It can be just as effective as synthesized drugs. The placebo effect happens when our brains tell our bodies to heal, and our bodies listen. It's neither purely medicine nor is it purely magic. It's not a miracle, but it is miraculous. It inspires within me a tremendous respect for our cellular structures, for the mysteries of the human brain and body. Thinking about the placebo effect, I feel an almost spiritual awe. It's scientifically backed magic. If you believe that meditating on a piece of malachite will ease your headache, that might also work. And if the pain is gone, and the anxiety is alleviated, why do we laugh at those imaginative enough to try?

4.
SPIRALING

On the ancient appeal of shells,
pearls, and mollusk-made wonders

Here is an incomplete list of things I remember purchasing in Province-town, Massachusetts: a hot-pink knife with iridescent sheen and a three-inch blade; a bag of purple glass beads; a pair of novelty heart-shaped sunglasses; a decorative mirror shaped like a seashell; my first box of tampons at age twelve; boxes of fudge; and two bags of beige, ivory, and rose seashells. Some shells were swirled and round, big moon snails, others were milky cones that blushed pink in the sun.

I've been to Provincetown more times than I can count, thanks to the benevolence of a childhood friend. My family didn't go on vacations, due to our general dysfunction and my parents' deteriorating marriage, so the weeks I spent with Lily's family at the Cape were special, a glimpse into what a peaceful home life could look like. We spent those weeks playing in the sand, reading in our twin beds, and browsing the stores in P-Town (as her parents called it). Even as a kid, Provincetown was my favorite place to go shopping. There are few places on Earth like Provincetown for shopping—for doing anything, really. A small seaside town on the tip of Cape Cod, it's where Kennedyesque blue-blood aesthetics rub up

against the funky freakadelic joy of an aging, out-and-proud generation of LGBTQ folks. It's a place where people wear boat shoes to drag
shows. It's a place where stores selling lobster buoys and nautical rope
bracelets sit next to shops advertising sleek glass dildos and equally sleek
glass bongs. The aesthetic, if you were to go by the architecture alone, is
decidedly quaint and Protestant. But if you were to go by the wares for
sale, it's anything but staid and sober. It's wild in the summer and sleepy
in the winter. It's beachy and quaint, but quite cosmopolitan in its food,
theater, art, and nightlife. It's a cultural mishmash beloved by many, including me. And above all else, Provincetown is kitschy.

Perhaps that's why, when I think of seashells, I don't imagine Florida.
I've never found so many seashells as I did when vacationing in Naples. I
came home from Florida with a nasty sunburn and a suitcase filled with
seashells wrapped in tissue paper, still stinking of their former inhabitants. (They now live in a glass cabinet, alongside a coyote face I bought
near the Canadian border and a jar of feathers I've collected over the
years—my little cabinet of curiosities). It was ridiculous, how easily you
could spot a whole sand dollar. Still, when I think about shells, I think
about Provincetown, a place with cold Northern beaches and eerily silent
winters. You won't find too many shells on the National Seashore, aside
from the translucent yellow jingle shells (aka "mermaid's toenails") or
the occasional scallop or Scotch bonnet. But you can buy a glittery pink
seashell bra to wear while eating seashell-shaped hard candies, burning
your new seashell-shaped candle, and admiring your new necklace: a
tiny gold charm shaped like a scallop. You can buy lamps covered in
shells and ribbon belts with repeating shell patterns. Mollusks, crustaceans, and other types of sea creatures are readily available for purchase,
whether you want to eat their soft bodies, wear their hard armor, or
enjoy the pulverized by-products of their secretions.

In contemporary American culture, seashells are quite obviously
kitsch. They haven't stopped being beautiful, but their beauty is obscured

by our frenzied repetition of their architecture. Their complicated bio-logical forms are rendered far less impressive when mass-produced in plastic and sugar and soap, stamped onto substances intended for quick consumption. This is how I viewed shells for most of my life—as products for purchase. I saw false shells more often than real ones, and even the real ones had been painted or dyed or broken or sloppily shot with a dose of hot glue. The shells of my childhood were trinkets, symbols, and gas-station logos. Objects of little sophistication but holding mass appeal. I associated shells with Disney mermaids and merchandise, my cousin's Malibu Barbie doll with her shell-shaped accessories, and grocery-store greeting cards with their vague platitudes and inoffensive graphics. It was easy to assume that seashells were universally beloved, part of a shared culture that included ice-cream sundaes and summer road trips and threadbare beach towels. These are soft, easy, American pleasures, as insubstantial as a McDonald's bun.

According to cultural critic Elaine Scarry, beauty "seems to incite, even to require, the act of replication." In her slim 1999 philosophical volume, *On Beauty and Being Just*, Scarry optimistically argues that beauty inspires goodness in humans because of its captivating and generative powers. Beauty, she writes, takes us outside our petty concerns and inspires in people an "unceasing" desire to replicate, reproduce, and mimic. According to Scarry, flowers make us want to draw, birds make us want to stare and marvel, and Hollywood stars make us want to have sex to produce offspring. Despite the many types of beautiful things that exist in this world, she believes that certain shared attributes exist, "one of which is this impulse toward begetting. It is impossible," she writes, "to conceive of a beautiful thing that does not have this attribute." Shells certainly fit the bill. They're replicated and remixed endlessly and at every scale. From grand houses of worship (the Great Mosque of Samarra in Iraq features a 171-foot-tall spiral minaret) to miniature speckles of bodily adornment (mermaid-themed nail art is a genre of its own), shells come second only to flowers in their omnipresence.

This is particularly true of the decorative and domestic arts. In the past decade, I've seen shell-themed trends come and go, from shell-shaped purses to shell-shaped bras to shell-shaped headboards. You can go online and buy yourself a gold cowrie-shell necklace by jeweler Pamela Love (in collaboration with model Ebonee Davis) or purchase a shell-adorned mini dress by influencer-beloved brand Reformation. This isn't new. In the sixteenth and seventeenth century, it was all the rage in the Netherlands to have a gaudy, gold-accented nautilus chalice on your table. Furniture makers in the eighteenth century seemed to spiralize every mahogany table leg and scallop every chairback. In the nineteenth century, it was common to see ladies in Paris walking around clutching seashell handbags. The twentieth century brought us synchronized swimmers in spangled shell bras, plus Walt Disney's fantastical shell castles and Elsa Schiaparelli's famous lobster dress (a collaboration with Salvador Dalí).

While one can make beautiful art featuring and inspired by seashells—one glance at the creamy gold vessel in Botticelli's *The Birth of Venus* is reminder enough of that fact—most shell art is fairly forgettable. While shell grottos are impressive and rather daring in their maximalist proportions, I think there's a reason many of them have been dismantled. When it comes to shells, there seems to be an impulse to embrace the sheer quantity rather than enjoy the singular shell as an object worthy of contemplation. It's a dragon-hoard approach to beauty, one that revels in the excess, in the glut, in the feeding frenzy of accumulation.

Truth be told, it's hard for me to think about mollusks without thinking about food, because that's where I'm most familiar with their squishy forms. Not everyone likes mollusks, though some are quite sweet and soft, like a plump scallop quickly fried in butter. Oysters are a divisive taste, though I personally love that briny, mucusy slurp. You can devour an entire ugly creature in one bite, a pure animal pleasure. Clams, too, have a certain appeal, particularly when fried and served in a po'boy with plenty of mayonnaise. In a way, I'm even more familiar with the shape and structure of a mollusk than I am that of a pig or a cow, even though these proteins make up so much more of my diet. I've considered the mollusk, seen it up close and personal, and I know their (lack of) contours and colors.

The fact that these blobby creatures make such distinctive, sculptural homes for themselves is truly marvelous and remains beyond our comprehension. Someday, we may understand all the mechanisms and motives that lead a sea snail to create a spiraling, intricately patterned shell that it will never personally see, but for now we just have theories. Scientists think snails make colorful stripes and dots on their shells as a form of memory, a way to communicate their own goings-on to their future selves, similar to how I use my online calendar. But there are many species of mollusks that live such mysterious lives, so different from our own. We're still discovering new species, some that thrive in the least hospitable places on the planet, others that we had previously thought to be extinct, and these discoveries just raise more questions, more channels of inquiry. It's no wonder I can't eat veal yet have no problem wolfing down a live oyster. My imagination can project my emotions into a brown-eyed calf; I can't even fathom how an oyster senses, much less how it feels.

Mollusks get little love from the masses. Instead, we love their shells. For almost all species of mollusk, that shell is the only home they will ever have, the only one they will ever build. It's the labor of a lifetime, and for some mollusks, that can mean decades.

Mollusks are an old, diverse, and successful form of life. A mollusk is an invertebrate that has an unsegmented, squishy body enclosed by a membrane called a mantle. They began to emerge over 540 million years ago, and during their time on Earth, they've adapted to survive in every type of natural habitat, save up in the air. They are much older than people, and much more resilient.

The word "molluscus" comes from the Latin for "soft," because they are; even the more defined mollusks like octopuses and squid have a floppy fluidity. As a phylum, Mollusca is a huge group that includes an estimated 23 percent of all marine organisms, including snails, slugs, clams, oysters, mussels, cuttlefish, octopus, squid, chitons, sea hares, and sea butterflies. Many of these creatures can make their own shells, and the majority of them can also produce pearls or pearl-like growths. Not all of these calcareous concretions are what I would call beautiful. Many of them are dull, ill-shaped and unimpressive. Plenty of squishy underwater creatures make purely utilitarian houses for themselves, lopsided and brown, knobby, and lacking grace. The shell of the invasive freshwater faucet snail is pretty ugly—a muddy-colored little coil that looks like my least favorite emoji—and oyster shells are nothing to write home about either.

While the exterior of a mollusk's shell often feels scaly, brittle, or chalky, the interior tends to be hard, smooth, and polished. My favorite shells are the ones that change colors like opals, shifting in the light. These iridescent marvels exist because some mollusks can produce a thinly layered, precisely composed mixture of calcium carbonate in an organic matrix that is protective and, incidentally, beautiful. Some mollusks, including abalone and mussels, line the interior of their shells in nacre, while others use it to coat contaminants. A small particle of food, or a little piece of silt or sand lodges inside their shell, and the mollusk slowly coats the irritant with layer after layer of nacre. Sometimes, this happens because of human intervention. This is how we create pearls—we place irritants inside the reproductive organs of mollusks and wait for the animal to respond to the violation, turning their pain into objects that can be bought and sold, worn and traded and worn again.

Shells are an example of beauty rising out of muck, much like the lotus flower. The ugly creature has a texture so like our own disgusting, contaminating secretions but somehow, these viscous things evolved to have complex lives of their own. Mollusks can grow a perfect pearl or fashion themselves a spiral palace. Few people would call shell-building mollusks pretty, but we're all familiar with the lines and forms of their architecture, the incredible allure of their shine. We know how even a fragment of an oyster shell can gleam with creamy golden color, how blue and green dance across the surface of abalone shells like the Northern Lights, how whelks can wink pink from their inner recesses. If you live near any large body of water, this is the kind of information you absorb passively as a child. You see a spot of color or a hint of reflection, and you pick it up, hold it, wonder.

"For centuries, many great minds have contemplated the elegant sculptures and patterning of shells and wondered what might govern their construction," writes naturalist Helen Scales in *Spirals in Time: The Secret Life and Curious Afterlife of Seashells*. She rightly identifies the spiral form as one that inspired great contributions to human knowledge in the field of mathematics, biology, and aesthetics. According to Scales, philosophers have long imagined that understanding a seashell's curve would not only add to our general zoological knowledge "but they might also catch a glimpse of the origins of beauty itself." For her, the shell appears to be a symbol for that abstract ideal, that place where wonder and desire and love commingle.

As a child, I was fascinated by the playful shimmer of iridescence, but years of studying art have woken me to the more subtle beauties of line and form (not to mention the role that negative space plays in a composition). Nature is an artist; she naturally knows how to create balance. One of the most famous examples of nature's tendency toward beauty can be found inside the chambered nautilus. A cross-section of this shell reveals not only a pearly sheen but also a close encounter with the Fibonacci sequence—the spiral starts out tight, growing larger and larger with each added revolution.

For thousands of years, people have been taking the proportions found in the natural world and streamlining them, making the spirals even smoother, the lines ever cleaner. We found rules for beauty in the arrangement of nature and standardized them even further, removing all the slight derivations imposed by fluctuating conditions. We've smoothed over all the rough edges, but this process hasn't always resulted in beauty. Often, in the pursuit of replicating the beauty and symmetry of the natural world, we've gone too far, removing all traces of chaotic, unruly, deviant life.

I remember the first time I walked through the Guggenheim Museum in New York, its form a shell-inspired white spiral. I passed a series of white-painted canvases, and none of them moved me. I was a rather moody teenager, and I knew very little of art history. But I did know something about my personal tastes. No one has ever, or probably will ever, call me a minimalist. In the structure of the Guggenheim, I didn't see the elevation of a form but the degradation of it—the elevator-music version of a seashell. Frank Lloyd Wright applied order too thickly, color too thinly, and texture too sparingly. A string of man-made pearls has the same pristine luster, the same blindingly white conformity. Like the porcelain teeth of a Hollywood might-be, the Guggenheim's architecture has always struck me as an empty triumph of human will. Impressive and tasteful, but not very much fun.

Over the millennia, shells have shifted around in our cultural esteem, but on some level or another, humans have always shown an appreciation for shells. They were used to make our first known jewelry. They were also one of our first known forms of currency.

There are many reasons that shells make good money, but cowrie shells in particular have played an important role in shaping the global economy. At various points in history, the cowrie has circulated among people in Asia, Africa, Oceania, and parts of Europe, serving as a stand-in for value. The preferred species was the *Monetaria moneta*, aka the money cowrie, thanks to its small size, relative durability, and the fact that it's distinctive in appearance, which makes it virtually impossible to counterfeit.

Personally, I can't look at a cowrie without being reminded of that old cliché, "sex sells." Money cowries are smooth, diminutive, oblong objects with a textured slit that runs down their middle. When held vertically, the underside of a money cowrie looks an awful lot like a pair of human labia, which helps explain why they were considered such valuable fertility charms. Tilt that same shell horizontally, and it looks more like a squinting eye, hence its use as an ancient Egyptian protector against the evil eye. But no matter what flesh folds you see in their shape, cowries seem to appeal to a narcissistic impulse in humans. We're drawn to their familiar shape, their soft colors, their light, strong walls. As objects, they're equally of interest to bank historians and contemporary fashion writers. You can find cowrie shells in the collections of almost every major museum in the world. Cowrie-shell art and jewelry has been taken from ancient Egyptian mummies, sacred burial chambers in China, and nineteenth-century Kongolese priests. These pieces are sometimes considered works of fine art on par with ancient Greek or Roman artifacts, but historically they've been relegated to other parts of the museum with the rest of the "primitive" art.

Obviously, not every culture values these mollusk-made monies equally. For some people, they're sacred. For others, they're collectors' items. This disparity was particularly stark—and significant—at the dawn of the transatlantic slave trade. For people living in fourteenth-through sixteenth-century coastal Africa, cowrie shells were a vital and highly visual part of culture. They were worn by the hundreds by both men and women, on strings around the neck, on belts around the waist, sewn into clothing, and nailed onto masks. The richest members of society showed off their good fortune by piling on the shells. Warriors wore them into battle and dancers wore them for ceremonial performances. But for the Europeans who sailed into their harbors, cowries were just another tool for amassing wealth and purchasing bodies.

The slave trade was funded in no small part by cowrie-shell money. In the 1550s European merchants discovered that shells were the best currency to bring to Ghana. Over the sixteenth and seventeenth centuries, cowries arrived in Europe by the millions as part of a complex system of global exchange that helped spread both beautiful things and exploitative economic and social systems from one corner of the map to another. Traders purchased baskets and barrels of shells for next to nothing in the Maldives and Sri Lanka and brought them home to Western Europe, only to turn around and sail south across the Atlantic to the Slave Coast on the Gulf of Guinea.

In the 1680s, it took 10,000 shells to buy one slave. By the 1770s, an adult male slave cost as much as 150,000 cowrie shells. Throughout history, people have tried to attach numbers to the human soul, value to a person's body. This sale is difficult for me to conceptualize, which in some ways makes it easier to stomach. There's a distance between my life and this event, one that is widened by each year between now and then, each uncomfortable detail that I don't want to examine. Some elements of this sale I simply can't picture. Though I am familiar with the size and shape of the money cowrie, I can't imagine what ten thousand shells would look like in a boat. My brain can't multiply the object that many times. I have a similar problem when trying to imagine the scale of suffering. I know what it is to feel some pain, but I can't multiply it accordingly. In truth, I don't need to. I know it was a global practice, I know it's ongoing; I know slavery is both commonplace and obscene. It doesn't matter whether I can relate to this experience or imagine it. All that matters is that it happened.

Billions of shells were moved across oceans and continents. Millions of people were forcibly taken from their home country and tortured, brutalized, raped, and exploited. But while money cowries are no longer used as a currency, people are still being bought and sold. It's hard to integrate these facts into the fabric of my knowledge. The numbers are too large, the suffering too great, the reality too terrible.

Part of me wants to deny these things, to close my eyes and will them away, to continue on exactly as I always did. But knowledge can change us, it can shape our desires for better or worse. I no longer want to wear cowrie jewelry, not since I've learned about the cruel backstory of these tiny, beautiful things. I recently tried to wear a pair of cowrie shell earrings that I've had for years, but when I saw my reflection, my made-up face framed by those dangling shells, I felt a queasy discomfort. Unlike turquoise, a stone that has been woven into my life from childhood and holds many positive associations for me. Once, I thought of cowrie shells as surfer-girl accessories, beachy chic. This is probably why I bought those earrings in the first place. Now I see emblems of suffering and loss.

Though it may not be mine to reclaim, others have taken the cowrie and returned it to grace. Throughout history, symbols have been stolen, repurposed, corrupted, purged, and cleansed. And as we know, cowries were never just money. They were also imbued with a spiritual power. And American history isn't just a litany of suffering; its spine is made of survival stories. People have found ways to express their individual beliefs and assert their agency, even in the worst conditions imaginable. Sometimes, the evidence we have of these acts is small, like in the case of the Newport "spirit bundle." This charm was found placed under the attic floorboards of the Wanton-Lyman-Hazard House in Newport, Rhode Island, and possibly dates to the 1760s or 1770s. Contemporary scholars have little doubt that it was hidden there by an enslaved person. Made from several layers of cloth wrapped around pins, beads, glass, and a carved cowrie shell, the spirit bundle wasn't meant to be seen or handled or placed on an altar. It was probably used to perform protective magic. In truth, aside from the shell, it doesn't look like much at all, just a few scavenged objects. But in context, this was someone's prayer, their hope. This person was owned, and this may have been the only thing they, themselves, owned.

While we don't know exactly what the person who hid this magical object was thinking, we can guess. According to the National Museum of African American History and Culture cowries were likely "brought to America as talismans to resist enslavement." There's evidence of victims of the African diaspora using charms like this to curse the people who oppressed and abused them. There's also a possibility that this piece was a protection charm, designed to keep the home free of evil spirits and the occupants free from harm. Either way, the fact remains that cowries were kept as a form of resistance against white supremacy and its bleaching effects. Hiding or hoarding shells was a way to silently, secretly fight back by practicing religious rites unknown to their captors.

In 2016, the Newport spirit bundle went on loan to the newly opened National Museum of African American History and Culture in Washington, D.C. This occasion inspired the director of the Newport Historical Society to reflect on the significance of the bundle as an "effort to both preserve and create culture" in the face of extreme suffering. The religious tool can be understood, the director's note continues, as "evidence of a rich spiritual and cultural life which we do not often discuss or interpret." Tragically, he isn't wrong. The efforts to erase America's history as a nation built on slavery are ongoing. In 2022, books are still being banned, teachers are being censored for telling their students about Black history, and misinformation wars are being waged in PTA meetings throughout the country. For many white Americans, discussion is off the table, much less interpretation. They'd rather shove this part of our history back under the floorboards—out of sight, out of mind.

I've always found forgetting easier than remembering when it comes to things read or heard; I have a far harder time forgetting what I've seen. Images of extreme suffering lodge in my brain, but so, fortunately, do spectacles of beauty and pride. These days, when I see a cowrie shell, I don't think only about stolen heritage and unquantifiable suffering. I also think of Beyoncé and her collaboration with jewelry designer "Queen of Cowries" Lafalaise Dion.

In her 2020 project, the singer released a video album for *Black Is King* to near-universal acclaim. Inspired by her role in Disney's *The Lion King*, this lavish and layered multimedia artwork prompted critic Wesley Morris to reflect: "Let's take a moment, shall we, to appreciate that beauty will make you tolerate anything, including waking up at the crack of dawn to behold it. Very little compares to the rising sun." And, he adds a beat later, "not much tops Beyoncé." The film is stuffed with splendor, jam-packed with good scenes (Morris's only real complaint is that it doesn't linger long enough on individual shots). In several blink-and-you'll-miss-it moments, Dion's intricate cowrie-shell veils play a supporting role alongside other pieces of fashion, art, and jewelry made by Black and African designers. One particularly memorable shot shows Dion's veil obscuring the singer's face, bringing all focus to Beyonce's eyes as she stares regally into the distance. We're used to seeing the singer dripping with diamonds, but in this album, she also shimmers with cowrie shells. Visually, the album is a lush, opulent, and moving experience that testifies to both the power of the singer and the glorious originality of Black culture. As Morris concludes, "Beauty is a reason this film exists."

Here's something else I can't quite comprehend: the world has warmed so much that mollusks are dying en masse, cooked to death inside their own shells. An article published in *The Guardian* from 2019 describes a California beach covered in "scores of dead mussels on the rocks, their shells gaping and scorched, their meats thoroughly cooked." A *National Geographic* piece from 2020 describes how one of their previously recommended travel locations in eastern Russia had fallen from the tourist bucket list. The coastal region of Kamchatka had been plagued with harmful algae blooms, resulting in "mounds of lifeless sea urchins and starfish" washing up on the shores. "Beachgoers picked up limp red octopuses by their tentacles," reported Alec Luhn from the Kamchatka peninsula. "A patch of fetid yellowish foam hundreds of feet wide and several miles long floated down the coast." The die-off in California is considered a "canary in the coal mine" for the disaster that will be wrought by climate change. Divers in Russia estimate that, in some places, 95 percent of the organisms that once lived on the ocean floor are now gone.

In addition to these two grisly stories, in January 2021, *The Guardian* reported that the "world's most devastating climate-driven loss of ocean life" had been documented off the coast of Israel. A group of scientists from the University of Vienna found that native mollusk populations in the eastern Mediterranean have collapsed by about 90 percent. Their habitat had become too hot.

The temperature of the ocean is changing, the water is becoming more acidic, it's filling up with "garbage islands" of floating plastic debris. The surface of the ocean keeps catching on fire, thanks to the poorly constructed oil pipelines that run beneath the surface. All these factors make it more difficult for life to thrive. Some species are migrating to colder water—including the invasive zebra mussels that are devastating freshwater ecosystems around North America—but eventually there may not be anyplace else left for mollusks to go. The heat waves aren't going to stop, the algae blooms will keep coming, and the storms are going to persist. As long as climate change keeps going at this pace, mollusks will continue to suffer. So will the animals that feed on them, the sea otters and the birds. And because we're living in a vast, connected web with everything else on the planet, we will also die. Humans are suffering now from the effects of climate change; in the words of an environmental activist friend, "the climate war is already here."

There's a word for the sadness we experience when faced with evidence of climate change in our immediate environment: "solastalgia." Coined in 2003 by environmental philosopher Glenn Albrecht, this is a combination of the words "nostalgia," "solace," and "desolation." It manifests, he writes, as "an attack on one's sense of place" that can feel like "a form of homesickness one gets when one is still at 'home.'" It's a new word for a new emotion that is bound to enter all our lives at some point. For the first time, humans are highly aware of the damage that our species has caused to the Earth. We're able to understand our role as actors in this ongoing violence, but individually, most of us are powerless to stop it. I can switch to using paper straws and stop buying items packaged with five layers of plastic, but I can't stop the ocean from becoming more acidic and I'm unable to single-handedly dismantle the Great Pacific Garbage Patch.

My grief isn't just for the mussels cooked alive in their shells on the West Coast—it's for all the fathomless depths and all the sandy beaches and all the birds that glide above the water. It's for my favorite surfing beach, where I go to catch waves, play with my toddler in the clumps of fresh green seaweed, and collect empty moon-snail shells. It's for the beach I once visited in the Arctic Circle, where glittery March ice crusted the shore but no snow fell, because the snow wasn't falling like it used to. I couldn't see it, but I knew that 50 kilometers away in the Northern Barents Sea floated a new oil rig, a monstrous thing made of red and orange metal. Named Goliat (after Goliath, of David-and-Goliath fame), it was built to extract the viscous brown liquid that forms when once-living things decompose underground. During the month I spent in Norway at an artists' residency in a ramshackle old farmhouse, I thought about that rig almost every day. Its presence haunted the tiny island—the liquid wealth funded the fishing community's lifestyle while contributing to its slow demise. Instead of writing or making art, I spent most of my days in the Arctic watching the light change and waiting for the Northern Lights. I went on long walks to collect shells and stones. I rode the ferry to the mainland just for something to do. I rented a car and drove across Finland to the Russian border. Everywhere I went, I used fossil fuels. And on every shoreline, I found pieces of plastic, washed ashore by too-warm waves. I don't know why I couldn't write well there; maybe I was just too overwhelmed by the strange, empty beauty of the far north. Maybe I just couldn't handle the idea of staying still when there was so much ground to cover, so many coastlines to see, so many islands, bridges, vistas, crags, waves, lights.

There is something about the vastness of climate change that poisons the working of my mind. It's a constant pressure, a nagging sense of doom, one I can't stop thinking about but also can't bear to look at directly. It feels noxious and diffuse, a black sun glowing darkly at the edge of my vision. Loss caused by species extinction and climate change is impossible to quantify in any easily digestible way, which is part of what makes it so slippery and seemingly unstoppable. But, like the transatlantic slave trade, the use of fossil fuels has been woven into our economy, not our natures. This is an important thing to remember—even giants like Goliath can fall. Where I live, there's been a coordinated effort by the local government and activists to protect breeding grounds for amphibians, spiders, and crustaceans. Awareness of vernal pools and their significance has ballooned, affecting building codes and outdoor recreation, proving it's possible for people to be moved to change their behavior, even by the less cuddly creatures that inhabit our planet.

Maybe, if we act soon, we won't see much more species loss, though I'm doubtful. Chances are good that many types of mollusks will be lost before we even knew that they existed. (We're still naming new ones all the time—the ocean is teeming with creatures untouched by human hands.) In the immediate future, this means that it may be easier to find shells when you're beachcombing, because the creatures who made them are dying and the shells are left behind, little gravestones littering the sand. But long-term, loss of mollusk life means seashells will become scarce. It means ecosystems will be further strained as keystone species are removed from the ocean. It means we'll have a harder time finding food in the water, and that our grandchildren may not be able to find any iridescent mother-of-pearl wonder hiding under the waves. They might not ever get to know shells through tide pools and beach strolls. They might only see shells on the yellow signs at gas stations. They might be limited to gift-shop soaps and cheap polyester dresses and pink plastic Barbie accessories.

While shopping and collecting can sometimes feel like forms of replication, it's not creation. It's a response to beauty, certainly—you admire something, and so you bring a copy of it into your life, you like something, and so you pick it up and take it home. But shells are more than objects; they're part of the ecosystem. Just because one creature is done with that shell does not mean it has become useless, that it's automatically fair game to pocket. Another creature could have come along and used that empty house. Or scientists could have used it as part of their data collection. For Dr. José Leal, science director and curator with the Bailey-Matthews National Shell Museum, these shells are invaluable tools for understanding the ocean. He explains that the Florida museum isn't just a place to store and show shells. "It's a library. Why do libraries have so many books?" he asks. "People read them. We read the shells."

Leal is a lifelong shell obsessive; he grew up collecting shells near his home in Brazil. While he is cautious about using the words "global warming," he says something has certainly happened, something is still happening. Mollusks that used to be abundant are now gone. It's all tied to the demise of coral reefs, he says, but there's also the problem of commercial collectors who go out poaching in the shallows at night. "If everyone goes out and collects something alive, pretty soon there will be nothing left to tell the story." He adds, "There's also the nutrients and pesticides going into the bay. I think we can already see a decline in life in the bay here."

Even shell collecting can be fun and ethical, says Leal. "In our county, it's okay to pick up dead shells," he says, but it's always good practice to check. Some beaches ask visitors to leave shells alone and to avoid stacking cairns, walking on dunes, and wandering over to the fragile breeding grounds of migrating birds. While beach rules are often clearly stated on signs by the entrance, people break them anyway. I don't think it's out of any great malice, just the general sense of liberation that comes with vacation.

I called Provincetown kitschy, but a less generous writer might call it tacky, vulgar, or even trashy. These are all matters of taste; I happen to prefer campy films to overly serious ones, adorned architecture to stripped-clean minimalism. There's nothing wrong with desiring what some might deem "cheap tat," like shell-shaped phone cases or satiny scalloped lingerie. However, the dollar value we assign to objects makes a difference in how we treat them. We preserve the objects, buildings, species, and landscapes that we value more highly than those we deem culturally insignificant, tacky, or ugly. Plus, much of private conservation happens because a single wealthy person decides to pony up (or shell out) for a cause of their choosing. Sometimes, these people pick based on their personal history and tastes, but just as often they choose the cause du jour, the place du jour.

Aesthetics matter because they can determine value, as does rarity. Shell collectors often quest for the rarest shells, which means the high-value pieces are the ones that are either difficult to find or endangered. As a result, there are more of some shells sitting on shelves than there are moving about under the waves. "I'm not really the right person to ask about why shells are important," says Leal. He's too close to the subject.

Shells are of the utmost importance to him, objects of great interest and admiration. And yet, he admits, "Maybe shells aren't important. Maybe people are more into the Kardashians and iPhones, and that's the way of the universe. If you look just at this moment in time, maybe people aren't paying much attention to shells."

"I've had so many conversations with people about shells," Scales told me. I had reached out to her for comment about seashells after finishing her book, and I wanted to know if she was still fascinated by them, still enchanted by their magic. She told me the story of a young woman who, like me, contacted her after reading *Spirals in Time*. The woman said that now, whenever she looked at her once-prized shell collection, "all she could see was death." Scales felt bad for her, but she recognized the righteousness of this perspective. "Traditionally, people have seen shells as connections both to life and death, and I think that's something more of us need to remember," she wrote in an email. "Instead of seeing shells as disposable nautical emblems or tamed connections to nature, I think it would be good if more people saw them as they truly are—the remains of unseen animals whose intricate lives we'll never truly see, and whose world we're radically changing."

It's not a tragedy that seashells are kitschy and replicas abound, but there's something terribly sad to me about the loss of magic and wonder for the actual, smelly, living ocean. My toddler adores going to the beach, and together we search for pink, purple, and white fragments. She likes finding different shapes and sizes, and she really loves using them to draw patterns in the sand. When I'm playing with her, I find myself examining a piece of a sand dollar from the side or a long, jagged knife of white clamshell. It's not as easy to find the beauty—these aren't museum-quality pieces. They're not even kitschy or cute. They're not trashy; they're simply worthless.

But these bits and pieces, viewed in situ, are somehow more exciting than the shells I used to buy by the bagful. I don't know where they are now, nor do I remember what happened to all my plastic toys, my once-beloved shell bathing suit, or my mermaid sandals. They're probably in a landfill somewhere. Maybe I will buy my daughter some pieces like this someday, but I don't know. I'm hoping we can make do with our summer days on the beach, our memories of making mandalas out of shell fragments, combing out tangles of seaweed, and watching snails move slowly in tide pools, ugly protrusions waving in the water. Kitsch is fun and entertaining, but I believe we need more than that to live whole and thoughtful lives. We need the knowledge of death, the acknowledgment of suffering, the awareness of harm, the awakening of sorrow and grief, even for things as voiceless as the mollusk. Pearly plastic is still plastic; the sheen is just never quite the same.

5.

LIVE FAST, DIE PRETTY
On wearing war paint, faces full of lead,
and the makeup of makeup

I was fifteen when I began using a safety pin to separate my eyelashes, a practice I came up with on my own and didn't think twice about, until it became a liability. I had been wearing extensive eye makeup for years; I favored a look with big lashes, thin black eyeliner, and glittery eyelids, halfway between underage raver and suburban mall punk. Back then, we didn't have YouTube makeup tutorials telling us how to contour correctly or achieve the perfect smoky eye. I made up my own beauty routines. I used lip gloss on my eyelids to help the glitter stick, creating a disco ball of silver shimmer. I applied coat after coat of drugstore mascara to my lashes until they were spidery and clumpy, then I used a sharp tool to separate them. Pieces of semi-dry mascara would fall onto my cheeks, and I'd wipe them off with toilet paper, batting my eyes until the lashes had lost some of their weight. Once, my hand slipped and I scratched my cornea. My eye wept ceaselessly for days. I spent my shift at the supermarket checkout with my head down, gaze averted until my supervisor asked me to leave. I was freaking people out, she said, with my steady trail of tears and emotionally inscrutable face.

Looking at pictures of myself as a teenager, I'm struck by how skinny I was and how sad I looked. My eyes were always tired, and my arms were stick-thin. Yet I was pretty, I know that now. In the pictures where I look happy, smiling with my high school boyfriend—a goofy blond kid who looked like Ryan Phillippe and died at age thirty-one of a heroin overdose—my punky makeup and pierced eyebrow actually look kind of cute. The acne I thought was so horrible and obvious isn't that bad. I didn't need all that makeup. I didn't need to do everything I did—the diets, the cigarettes, the caffeine pills, the drugs, the self-harm, the cartilage piercings done alone with a sharpened earring in my bedroom late at night. It didn't make me feel better. It didn't make me look better.

My relationship with makeup is fraught. I love it; I hate it. I never know if I'm doing it right, even now. When I step inside the grand temple of makeup (that is, when I go shopping at the Maine Mall Sephora) I still feel a girlish thrill at the sheer bounty of goods. Even though I have plenty of cosmetics at home, I can't seem to stop wanting another shade of lip tint, another type of brow gel. It's not all consumerist brainwashing either. Tending to my appearance can be healing, a minor form of caretaking, less vital than drinking another glass of water but certainly more fun. On days when I'm sunk into the gray trough of depression, I still try to cheer myself up with a coat of mascara and a slick of lip gloss, a dab of cheek stain. I feel better, having some color on my face.

This is not a modern phenomenon. Cosmetics have always healed and hurt. Often, women suffer most from trying to follow the arbitrary rules of "the beauty-game" (as Ursula K. Le Guin called it), but we're not the only victims. Men have suffered from the ill effects of poisonous makeup, damaging social standards, and extreme fashions. Nonbinary people have always faced harsh punishments for failing to physically conform. But makeup has been most closely associated, and most painfully fraught, for those of us who present as women. Traditionally, women are valued more for their physical forms than their mental capacities.

There are examples of cultures that revere and respect the intellect of all genders, but in America we tend to take after the Europeans, and the Europeans tend to take after the Romans, and the Romans believed each person had a spirit that followed them from cradle to grave. The name of this spirit for men? Genius.

While every man got a Genius, every woman was given a Juno. Juno was the name of the spirit who ruled over the hearth, the marriage bed, and the birthing process. While men were believed to have creative, generative souls, women were given over to a different realm, the world of nurturing. As a mother, I know there is some biological basis for this arrangement. I carried a child inside my body and birthed her. Her name is Juniper. While I named her after a witch in my favorite childhood novel (*Wise Child* by Monica Furlong), after she was born I began shortening her name. I didn't have any goddess in mind, but she felt like a Juno to me—it fit her nascent personality somehow.

The experiences of pregnancy, labor, and raising a daughter have been powerful and exciting. I'm proud of my work as a mother. I'm grateful that my body can create a child and that my breasts can feed her. These are worthwhile things that have forever changed how I view my physical form. Yet I still bristle at the unfairness of my assigned place in the world. Women, be they cisgender or trans, are socially encouraged to embody beauty in a way that men are not. We're expected to do more nurturing than men, more sacrificing of our time and energy, more household duties, and more emotional labor. We're less likely to be considered deep, intellectual geniuses, more likely to be praised for our shiny, pretty surfaces.

I've always wanted to embody beauty. I think most people do at some point in their lives. And like most people who want beauty for themselves, I've suffered for it. I've allowed it to hurt me, and I've been an active participant in the damage. This is a personal problem, but it's also a societal one. American consumer culture is an ugly creature, a beast that demands constant worship and thrives on the suffering of its adherents. The beauty industry is one of the many lesser gods that make up our economy. In this temple, we women come and feast on aesthetics, then feel disgusted at the glut, the excess, the sheer amount of wasted time. We strive to embody impossible ideals, working ourselves to the bone, then wonder why we're exhausted and frail, hair falling out and iron levels low. We exercise our desire until it becomes the strongest muscle in our hearts. When it comes to physical beauty, we want and want and want. What we want changes. But the fact of the wanting—that stays the same.

I'm certainly not the first person to reach for pins and needles as beautifiers. The earliest evidence we have of enhanced bodies comes from the decorated skin of ancient corpses pulled out of glaciers and bogs. There's Ötzi the Iceman who lived some 5,300 years ago in the area that straddles the Austrian–Italian border, whose skin was marked with sixty-one tattoos. There's a male mummy from Chile who lived around 5000 BCE, who was found with a cluster of dotted tattoos above his upper lip, a sort of mustache. In this same burial ground, archaeologists found evidence of cosmetic palettes, flat stones that would have been used for grinding up naturally occurring pigments to make fine, colorful powders—not too dissimilar from the eyeshadow palettes I keep in a basket next to my bathroom sink.

We don't know a lot about prehistoric makeup, but we do know that people decorated themselves, and we can guess that they did so for reasons both spiritual and aesthetic. Some people (the Iceman included) may have applied permanent color to their bodies as part of a healing ritual.

We have more documentation about ancient Egyptian beautifying practices, thanks to their famous spellbook, known commonly as *The*

Egyptian Book of the Dead. Alongside other topics, this series of writings includes information on how to properly apply kohl. This dark, thickly applied eyeliner was used by people of all genders. Not only did it look striking—especially when combined with crushed malachite to create a green glaze on the eyelids—it also helped protect their eyes from the glare of the sun. Historians believe that kohl was regarded as a magical substance, capable of protecting the wearer against curses. Some cultures still use kohl on infants for this reason. The dark spots on their skin render the cute baby faces flawed, which protects the child from the corrosive spiritual effects of jealousy. Contemporary analysis of Egyptian makeup containers has revealed that kohl may have served yet another purpose: thanks to the antibacterial properties of the lead used in the paint, it may have protected Egyptians from the scourge of pinkeye.

Across cultures, makeup has been mixed up with medicine; we have evidence that early people considered makeup a way to not only appear healthy but to become healthy. The word "cosmetic" comes from the Ancient Greek "kosmeticos," which "implied a sense of order or harmony," writes historian Susan Stewart in *Painted Faces: A Colorful History of Cosmetics*. Like teas and tinctures and bloodletting, cosmetics were a tool to help bring your body, mind, and spirit into order.

Makeup is a way to dominate one's own body, molding it into shape so that its form better coincides with the beauty standards of the time. Rae Nudson, author of *All Made Up*, says this is because cosmetics are closely tied to issues of control—both self-control and social control. In her book of essays, Nudson describes the various ways that cosmetics and makeup have elevated, degraded, empowered, and imprisoned people throughout history. While people "tend not to take it seriously," makeup can have serious benefits and terrifying consequences; it can help you land a job and it can give you cancer. In certain contexts, cosmetics are essential, a matter of life or death. While soldiers once smeared mud and dung onto their faces as camouflage, these days we have special products for that. Since the late 1990s, the United States Armed Forces have sourced their face paint from former Hollywood makeup and special effects artist Bobbie Weiner, who made her name working on the set of *Titanic,* where she transformed Leonardo DiCaprio (and his stunt double) into frigid corpses using her own formula of face paint. Word of her work spread, thanks to the magic of local morning television segments, and soon the U.S. Army was ringing her up, asking her to make them some scentless, lightweight paint that "the kids" would more willingly wear in the field.

While Weiner's line of camo compacts are perhaps the most direct example of high-stakes makeup, there are many places where gender conforming isn't optional. For a nonbinary or trans person, makeup isn't always a style choice. "Passing" to read as cisgender can be a way to avoid facing bigotry and violence. In the New York City ballroom-culture scene of the 1980s and 1990s, performers often competed in the category of "realness." As Nudson points out in her chapter on safety and makeup, "realness could act as a shield that provided some protection." Embodying femininity can be a protective measure in a world that discriminates against trans women, and makeup can often be central to this construction.

Even in less dire circumstances, people often apply makeup because they want or need the power that comes from visibility. While some kinds of face paint disguise or hide flaws, others are used for enhancement, exaggeration, and attracting attention. "It's all about surviving the world that you are in," says Nudson. "For women in the 1700s, you might fall out of favor at court if you don't use makeup. You might not get a husband." Any risk, even the risk of physical harm, tends to feel "worth it."

Because physical beauty is valued so highly, people are often willing to set aside their own discomfort in order to achieve this state. They're willing to ignore the disgust they might feel about putting something like snail mucin under their eyes, or using a mixture of crushed beetle shells to color their lips. They're willing to accept the risk that comes with injecting a known neurotoxin into the delicate skin around their eyes. In 2017, model Miranda Kerr helped to popularize leech facials, prompting at least one influencer to undergo the procedure on camera and causing known beauty obsessive Gwyneth Paltrow to remark, "Wow. I thought I was batshit crazy." But at least the snail lotion comes in a cute container and at least the cochineal-tinted lipstick goes through FDA approval. Botox gets dispensed at licensed "medical spas" under (ideally) sterile conditions, and blood-based facials aren't exactly commonplace. At least we feel somewhat liberated to discuss this normal desire for physical betterment. Beauty matters used to be much murkier; once upon a time people would smear alligator dung on their faces and brush animal fat through their hair. They ingested poison and drank urine under the cover of darkness, their fumbling toward beauty kept close to the chest, a shameful secret.

But while certain looks come in and out of vogue, there is one thing that has remained remarkably consistent throughout history. "What underlies everything is a preference for clear skin and youth," says Nudson. You'll notice she didn't say "white skin," because that's not always been the global ideal. Before the creation of a global beauty industry in the 1900s, standards for sexual attractiveness tended to vary a lot more than they do today. Not every culture in the history of humanity has valued pallor. It's hard for me to remember that sometimes; I was born into this culture and at times, I've been myopically consumed by its media and its norms. A global perspective is a difficult one to hold, particularly because aesthetics are often learned passively and through a slow process of repetition.

Most historians trace the preference for paleness back to ancient Greece, where the idea of a light-skinned, golden-haired, dark-eyed beauty was born. In order to look more like the fabled Helen, people were perfectly willing to put poison directly onto their skin. In Latin, this lead-laden face product was called cerussa nativa, which later became known as Venetian ceruse. Made by heating up a mixture of lead powder and vinegar, then combining with more vinegar and burned green fig dust, this powdery paste was used in cosmetics for centuries. While its popularity ebbed and flowed, it appears to have spiked during boom times, which is true of most luxury items. Archaeological evidence dates the use of lead in China back to at least the Han dynasty. Lead makeup seems to have been particularly popular with women in Edo Period Japan, Renaissance Italy, and Elizabethan England, though Frenchwomen used it, as did members of the German aristocracy. Basically, lead was all over the Old-World map, from Greece to England to Japan.

While some of these users may have been entirely unaware of lead's vicious side effects, it seems likely that at least a few of them entered this devil's bargain with their eyes wide open. After all, lead was a known poison. Writing in the second century BCE, the poet and physician Nicander describes the effects of drinking a liquid form of white lead in explicit detail:

> This fluid astringes and causes grave ills,
> The mouth it inflames and makes cold from within,
> The gums dry and wrinkled and parched like skin . . .
> He soon cannot swallow,
> Foam runs from his lip . . .
> He belches so much and his body does swell . . .
> Meanwhile there comes, stuporous chill,
> His feeble limps droop and all motion is still.

Indeed, consuming lead can kill you, but first it tortures you. It damages the nervous system and the digestive system, causes memory loss and cognitive impairment. Topical application isn't as harmful, but it does cause hair loss, discoloration, and pitted sores, which necessitates the use of more white lead to cover the damaged skin. This is supposedly what happened to Queen Elizabeth I, who famously stopped sitting for portraits after her last session with painter Isaac Oliver around 1592. After this, painters wanting to depict the ruler had to rely on a schema that historians have dubbed the "Mask of Youth." While the queen continued to age for the next decade until her death in 1603, her portraits did not. In these later images, she looks neither young nor old, but rather uncanny—ghost-white and as smooth as an egg. They're pictures of an idea, not a woman.

Elizabeth's devotion to ceruse and its matte effects inspired her subjects to follow suit, and this bleached look remained popular in the region until the 1800s. People tended to pile it on thickly and wear it for days. "The excessive use of this poisonous cosmetic, in turn led to the early demise of many wealthy beauties," writes cosmetics historian Gabriela Hernandez, who rather brutally asserts that "people were fully aware of the poisonous and potentially fatal nature" of ceruse. She briefly mentions the famous Gunning sisters of Ireland, one of whom died in her late twenties from possibly using too much makeup, but this appears to be the only story, albeit purported, of a young woman perishing from her own application of cosmetics. According to some sources, Maria Gunning didn't just use lead, she also used cinnabar as blush (a red form of mercury sulfide), plus a seaweed extract called "fucus" that also likely contained mercury. Toward the end of her life, Gunning's face had allegedly begun to peel off. She spent her final year on Earth sitting in a dark room, alone, mourning the loss of her looks (and possibly, given the mercury, her sanity).

There's an ongoing debate about the degree to which lead poisoning has shaped societies. Some articles assert that Queen Elizabeth was killed by her makeup, which is probably an oversimplification. Remember, this was before germ theory, before we knew the importance of washing our hands, before we had access to antibiotics, vaccines, and antiviral medications, not to mention my lifesaving SSRIs. There are many factors that contribute to failing health. Some historians believe lead exposure was a major factor in the fall of Rome, while others have argued that lead use in medieval Europe contributed to the overall bummer vibe of the fabled "Dark Ages." Analysis of bones from medieval German and Dutch graveyards revealed high levels of lead in the remains of the wealthiest members of society. But it would be folly to assume this was due solely to their face paint. The bulk of these lead poisonings were most likely caused through accidental ingestion—this was true of the Romans, too, who had used lead pipes to funnel their drinking water. Back then, lead was hard to avoid if you had any real interaction with finery. The rich ate off ceramic plates glazed with lead, traded coins made from lead, and used creams and lotions infused with lead. All manner of pretty things were made with the malleable metal, from drinking chalices to jewelry. Yet despite the pervasiveness of the material in general, lead makeup has captured the public imagination in a way that lead-glazed pitchers or lead-lined bathtubs have not.

This is partially because of the titillating nature of makeup. Traditionally, cosmetics are something privately applied for public appearances, and we're always interested in things that bridge the gap between those two spheres. It's also because poison cosmetics is such an appealing oxymoron, and Venetian ceruse is perhaps the most extensively documented example of the paradox that dwells at the heart of face-making. It's something used to beautify that often has the opposite effect, something meant to make one look smooth and youthful that results in scarred, pitted skin. It's something once marketed as a cure, now forbidden by U.S. law. (A report published in 2022 found that there is still lead present in cosmetics sold throughout Southeast Asia, typically in kohl, lipsticks, and hair dye.) Finally, I think there's a cultural tendency to blame women for their own suffering. When a woman injures herself in attempts to fit cultural beauty standards, many people respond not with concern or compassion but with mockery.

I used to consider lead makeup a historical oddity, akin to the mouse-hair eyebrow wigs that were supposedly popular in eighteenth-century England, but now I think white lead is more important than that. Look closely at Venetian ceruse and you'll see something far uglier than damaged skin. There, you'll find the twisted logic of feminine beauty standards, the insidious lies that echo throughout white culture, and the painful, simple truth about human beauty. It fades. Even if you manage to embody beauty for one glorious moment, there is no form of cosmetic, not even tattoos, that can pin it in place.

This is what happens when you drop a tincture of *Atropa belladonna* onto the surface of your cornea: First, you feel a little coldness. It actually feels like any other eye drop—cold, wet, slick. But soon, your face starts to shift subtly. The muscles that control your iris begin to move. The iris is pulled back and the empty hole of the pupil becomes larger, more prominent. Light floods into the retina. At this point, your vision might become blurred. If you use too much, you might begin to experience symptoms of deadly nightshade poisoning. You become (according to an old medical mnemonic) "hot as a hare, blind as a bat, dry as a bone, red as a beet, and mad as a hen." Meaning: your body will heat up, your eyes will go blurry, you won't be able to sweat or cry or urinate, your face will flush with blood, and you'll start feeling delirious.

Unlike many of the other substances that adorn a vanity, belladonna isn't something that stays on the surface of your body. It doesn't paint over your flaws like a powder or a cream, nor does it color in your features, like lipstick or kohl. Instead, it incites a physical reaction, one that happens often enough during daily life, yet it's one that we can't consciously control. Pupils dilate when we're aroused, either gripped by fear or lust, and when we go into a dark room. Belladonna quite literally creates bedroom eyes. These are eyes for looking at, not eyes for seeing. Your vision gets worse, but your eyes look better.

This is far more serious than a corneal scratch. Safety pins, though awfully unsuited for makeup application, aren't nearly as deadly as that famous shrub. A member of the nightshade family, *Atropa belladonna* goes by many different folk names, including "banewort," "death's herb," and "naughty man's cherries." Most poisonings occur due to accidental ingestion of the berries, which are a deep, luscious purple. Unlike many toxic plants, they're supposedly sweet and flavorful. I wouldn't know, though the more I learn about deadly nightshade's glamorous history, the more tempted I become to pick a few, try one.

Belladonna wasn't just a cosmetic, and its associations with sex run deeper than those lustful eyes. Supposedly, the ancient worshippers of Bacchus swilled it in their wine, leading to nights of debauchery where they danced with "libidinous and orgiastic abandon." The plant has hallucinogenic effects and has been known to create a feeling of dizziness, euphoria, and even provoke a flying sensation. This might explain why nightshade has always been associated closely with witches and their gardens. Belladonna was a main ingredient in the famous flying cream of medieval sorceresses, and the plant may even be to blame for the whole witches-riding-broomsticks trope. Apparently, these trippy babes liked to lubricate smooth sticks with their herbal ointments and "ride" them. The potion would absorb into the bloodstream through the walls of the vagina, allowing them to (metaphorically) soar high into the sky, climaxing in the clouds.

During the Renaissance, women were less likely to put belladonna on their sex toys and more likely to drop it into their eyes. Paintings from the time can be scanned for clues on what the average European found attractive, and according to artists like Sandro Botticelli, Leonardo da

Vinci, and Agnolo Bronzino, beautiful women had pale, unblemished skin, thin eyebrows, golden hair, and dark eyes.

Although cosmetic knowledge tended to travel in so-called books of secrets, the eyedrops weren't a particularly well-kept secret. Often written by court ladies and nobles, these texts were a cross between a magazine, a scientific text, and a spellbook. They got passed around and copied, and while there was one widely distributed "book of secrets" (compiled by Italian alchemist Isabella Cortese), most writings of this type were intended for a small, local audience. But rumors have a tendency to move faster and farther than print. People knew that these supposedly reputable women were using witches' tricks. They were aware that women at court had ways of making themselves more beautiful than the average commoner. I imagine it was quite fun to gossip about the wealthy and powerful people and their drug-addled eyes. And perhaps the story of belladonna has been overblown; this fabled usage is what inspired eighteenth-century Swedish taxonomist Carl Linnaeus to dub that shrub with such a dramatic name. For the genus, he chose *Atropa* (for the Greek goddess of death, Atropos, a nod to the poisonous nature of many nightshades) and for this species, he picked *belladonna* (that is, "beautiful woman"). I suspect the flower has remained famous purely because of that name. And what a name! Is there anything more romantic, more intriguing than a deadly, beautiful woman?

Well, perhaps for some, a dead beautiful woman is preferable. Or a dying one, anyway. She's far less of a threat, though her body will always pose some danger to men. During the Romantic period, there was a short-lived craze for looking sickly, as Carolyn A. Day documents in her book, *Consumptive Chic: A History of Beauty, Fashion, and Disease*. While plenty of women still used cosmetics to look healthier, there was a subset of makeup enthusiasts who tried to mimic the glassy-eyed pallor of a fever. Women wore long, nightgown-esque dresses, slumped their shoulders as if exhausted, painted their lips and cheeks red and their faces white, and restricted their diets to sharpen the appearance of shoulder blades and collarbones. They wanted to look as though they were fading from tuberculosis, just steps away from the grave. "How is it possible that a disease characterized by coughing, emaciation, relentless diarrhea, fever, and the expectoration of phlegm and blood became not only a sign of beauty, but also a fashionable disease?" Day asks. It seems perfectly clear to me; as tuberculosis raged through Europe, women everywhere were dying too young, their faces clear and unlined, their hair shiny and youthful. These darling dead girls were immortalized in paintings, songs, novels, and poetry. It wasn't that the illness made them beautiful, but the loss made them precious. In death, young women were elevated to new heights. The living ones just wanted to borrow a bit of this glory.

There's a long history of folktales and mythology that heaps praise upon the corpses of young, slender, soft-skinned girls. Sometimes, the girls aren't dead, they're just magically inert, as in the case of Sleeping Beauty and Snow White. But sometimes they are literally dead, saintly and supernaturally embalmed, as in the case of the canonized French nun Bernadette Soubirous, whose thrice-exhumed 134-year-old body is still on display in Nevers, France. The idea of a beauty that never ages is both uncanny and frightening (see Bram Stoker's *Dracula*) and holy, blessed (the Roman Catholic Church has a whole slew of "Incorruptible" female saints). Over the centuries, the pretty-dead-girl trope has been re-invented countless times, used by scientists, artists, poets, and entertainers. It seems that often, the dead girl was granted more reverence than any live woman, for her body was no longer just a temptation. It became a site of desire and instruction, a place for man to find knowledge and salvation.

Fortunately, our most visible examples of the historic obsession with good-looking corpses weren't made of flesh. The "slashed beauties" never breathed. In the 1780s, sculptor Clemente Susini created the epitome of the genre, known colloquially as the "Anatomical Venus" or the "Medici Venus," to teach people about the body (and perhaps excite their own bodily responses). Like others of her ilk, she is beautiful and lifelike, with flowing golden hair (made from real human hair), even features (reflective of beauty standards of that era), supple flesh (pale and pillowy), and eyes half-closed in what could be sleep (or could be satisfaction). But though they share a blissfully worshipful expression, this girl is no Saint Teresa, whose white marble form was modestly draped in heavy robes, but rather a nude corpse dressed only in a string of pearls. Below her pristine face and neck, her torso is splayed open with all her pink organs on display, guts pushing their way out of her slender form. She lies inside her original case, made of Venetian glass and rosewood, next to other Venuses-without-furs at the Museum for Physics and Natural History in Florence. Joanna Ebenstein, author of *The Anatomical Venus,* deems her "the perfect object," a wax goddess whose "luxuriously bizarre existence challenges belief." While some have found the mysteries of the universe written in shells, and others have tried to find it in a grain of sand, Ebenstein suggests that we read this gruesome-yet-lovely object as evidence that "the microcosm really does reflect the macrocosm." In her body, we can see mankind's struggle to balance our basest desires with our loftiest goals, our love for heaven and our position on Earth.

Nearly sixty years after Susini's Venus went on view in Florence, Edgar Allan Poe would write his essay "The Philosophy of Composition," in which he asserted that "the death then of a beautiful woman is unquestionably the most poetical topic in the world." He furthered his point in his poetry and fiction, where his female characters (Annabel Lee, Berenice, Ligeia, Lenore, Eleonora, and so on) were given more presence, value, and power in death than they ever had in life. Even now, there's still an entire genre of entertainment centered on the pretty corpse. Writer Alice Bolin calls this the "Dead Girl Show" and uses David Lynch's *Twin Peaks* as a case study for the genre. An example with less cultural relevance but more personal resonance can be found in my high school wardrobe: a tank top with the words LIVE FAST, DIE PRETTY written in red glitter. As a fourteen-year-old mall punk, I had thoroughly absorbed that morbid message. Even then, I knew that living women simply couldn't embody this type of frozen, innocent, pristine beauty.

Makeup can bring a person a bit closer to this obscene ideal, as can nonsurgical cosmetic procedures like Botox and fillers. While some people use Botox for gender affirmation or other medical reasons (it can help with migraines, severe sweating, and lazy eye), most customers purchase injectables for their antiaging properties. By injecting known toxins into our skin, we've found a way to stop our faces from creasing, our eyes from crinkling, our foreheads from showing strain. We've figured out how to embalm the living, and while the results are sometimes quite good, they're just as often rather uncanny. Although many people don't consider Botox a form of makeup, I think it's akin to belladonna drops. Botox is a temporary body modification made from toxins that is administered into the face. It transforms you from within. It's a way of securing or prolonging a natural state, an attempt to defy change, time, and sunlight. It's a dose of socially sanctioned magic deemed nonthreatening because of its purpose. It helps the individual to step closer to their own version of Elizabeth's schema, to better embody their uncanny, ever-living self.

Although Botox is becoming more common—particularly "preventative Botox," which is gaining in popularity among professional women in their twenties and thirties—it is still prohibitively expensive for the average American worker. (A single unit of Botox costs more than what a worker makes through federal minimum wage in an hour. The average dose is around twenty units. You do the math.) And unless you've visited the eye doctor recently, chances are good you haven't had any derivatives of belladonna dropped into your orbs. But perhaps you've snapped a selfie on your phone, added a filter, and shared it on social media. This is something I used to do fairly frequently. Like many people, I liked to add a filter to even out my skin tone. With a few quick swipes and clicks, I could remove my dark under-eye circles, smooth out that patch of discolored skin that appeared on my right cheekbone after I gave birth, and add definition to my eyes and lips. I didn't have to do any of this myself; someone had already created a program that can recognize the planes and shadows of my face and "fix" them. Or if you prefer to look on the sunny side of things, I could use a free program to "enhance" my already existent beauty. There are filters that can make my lips bigger, my eyes brighter, and my skin smoother—all at once.

Some filters give me big, cartoonish eyelashes, as fluffy and thick as an animated doe. Most of the makeup filters mess with your eyes. No matter how good your eyes are, they could always be better. Bigger. Whiter. Brighter. They could glow green or blaze with blue fire. But fundamentally, these are computer programs that work on a flat image to make it even flatter. Even with the glitter, the colors, and the cat ears, the "augmented reality" of social media is always less dynamic than the real thing. It takes a photograph (already a flattened rendering) and further obscures the truth, creating an abstraction of an ideal. These pictures become caricatures, cartoons, avatars—schemas.

In 2019, *New Yorker* writer Jia Tolentino coined the term "Instagram face" to describe the combined effect that filters, fillers, reality television, social media, and makeup have had on a generation of attractive women. She rightfully calls it "one of the oddest legacies of our rapidly expiring decade: the gradual emergence, among professionally beautiful women, of a single, cyborgian face." She describes the new ideal as youthful and heart-shaped, with plump skin, no pores, high cheekbones, catlike eyes. It "looks at you coyly but blankly." It's a white face, but it's also "ambiguously ethnic." In her attempts to understand the rise of the Face, Tolentino visits plastic surgeons, interviews makeup artists, and talks to social-media influencers. The process unsettles her. Afterward, she admits, she has to avoid looking at her own face too hard. Leaving a plastic surgeon's office, she is flooded with "a very specific feeling, a kind of bottomless need that I associated with early adolescence, and which I had not experienced in a long time," she writes. The Face has eclipsed her own.

I reached out to Tolentino several years after she published the *New Yorker* piece to ask whether she still felt haunted by this social-media specter, this pretty but uncanny image that could, with the right surgery or filter, be hers to wear. Over email, she told me that her feelings were mixed. She still bleaches her hair and wears concealer. She knows her appearance has more likely helped her than hurt her (a phenomenon often referred to as "pretty privilege"). But overall, she worries less these days about the problem of physical attractiveness. The Face, while still a phenomenon on social media, can't hurt her now. She's moved on to other topics and redirected that energy into new places. "I've been trying to feel my way to the place where I'm taking pleasurable care of my physical form the way that I would take care of (and celebrate, even periodically beautify) a backyard garden or a living room," she says. "The difference between caretaking and improvement, maintenance and optimization, is very existentially stark to me." Once a frequent visitor to social-media sites, she has been working to reject "the underlying surveillance-capitalism factors that produce Instagram Face," which we both agree continues to worsen. Tolentino concludes: "I can't feel anything through a screen, really, and I really can't feel beauty through a screen anymore. And in real life, so many faces are incredibly fucking beautiful, mainly because they are there, right in front of you, alive."

The truth of this is hard to refute. Digital beauty is removed, displaced, and (for now) two-dimensional. It lacks the texture and sensory appeal of in-person beauty or even the immediacy of a face in a mirror. A filtered and made-up face on a screen has neither voice nor scent nor grace. It's as charmless as an infinity rose. And yet, these images still have some hold over me, especially when I'm lonely. I live in a rural area and I work from home, so I often turn to the Internet for connection. In the digital world, advertisements are everywhere, which means beautiful young women are everywhere too. It's impossible to avoid them. When confronted with a deluge of filtered, photoshopped, and made-up faces, I can't help it. I get envious. (Especially if I happen to open my front-facing camera by mistake and catch a glimpse of my own bloated, unadorned, rapidly aging face.) Despite my best efforts, I still feel some compulsion to diminish my body, to shrink and diet, to work toward a version of myself that takes up less space. I still want to look good in pictures. I don't have the energy to chase the dead-girl beauty as doggedly as I once did, but I haven't purged her from my brain. I still find myself wanting.

A few months ago, Juno took a bristly brush to her face and scratched the soft skin around her eye, leaving a red welt and a single bloody scab. It was my fault. See, I haven't been able to detangle my self-worth from my appearance and you would know that with one glance at my eyes. I wear mascara every single day, almost without exception. No beauty product has ever felt as essential to me as mascara, not even the functional goos like my tinted moisturizer (with SPF 30!) or my favorite lip balm (which makes my mouth smell like sugared mint). My lashes are a source of great personal pride. I've been told they're unusually long, that they might be my best trait, despite the fact that they're rather blond at the ends. And so, every morning I take a plastic tube and twist off the top, pull out the wand, and brush the tar-dark, mud-thick product onto my face. I frequently do this in front of my daughter; I do everything in front of her. She's old enough now to mimic my motions. She play-acts being me, which means sometimes she wants a "baby cocktail" and sometimes she types on a tiny phone and sometimes she mangles her own face.

It's the normal stuff of childhood, I know. Kids mimic their parents when they're very young, and as they age, they grow out of this phase. But I do wonder sometimes what I'm teaching her. I can talk a big game about Instagram filters and Botox, but I can't quit mascara. I have probably twenty different types; I wear waterproof mascara to the beach, brown mascara for a subtle, professional look, thickening mascara for when I want to look sexy, curling mascara for when I'm feeling tired and want my eyes to pop, and even a tube of white mascara that I can use to prime my lashes for even more mascara. I have mascara in the car (in case I want to apply it while I'm driving) and mascara in my purse. There's even a tube in the diaper bag.

Like any deeply ingrained habit, it's hard to pinpoint when mascara went from occasional tool to absolute necessity. It happened years ago—sometime in junior high, I think. Like any American kid who grew up watching cartoons, I've always been aware that long eyelashes on an animal signaled femininity and desirability. Even though hyperlong lashes tend to occur more often on human men than women, in the world of cartoons, lush lashes mean you're looking at a lady. As a small child, I remember watching Disney's *Robin Hood* over and over, captivated by the magnetic voice of the rapscallion fox, who became my first real crush. His love, the lady Maid Marian, looked almost exactly like Robin, save for one detail. She had long, fluffy, dark eyelashes, as did Faline (Bambi's female counterpart) and Daisy Duck (love interest for Donald Duck) and Minnie Mouse. Notably, none of these anthropomorphic characters were given big, kissable lips—that might have felt like a bridge too far. But they all had falsies, feathery feminine lashes.

According to a timeline compiled by Maybelline, mascara has a six-thousand-year history, though that's using a broad definition of mascara that includes all eye-darkening pigments. The invention of petroleum jelly in the 1860s ushered in a number of new cosmetics, liquid mascara among them. Yet the popularity of painted lashes paled in comparison to the importance of having carmine-slicked lips. Made from the shells of crushed bugs, this vibrant red is still on the market today (look for "natural red four" or "crimson lake" in your favorite lipstick or blusher). For much of the nineteenth and twentieth centuries, lipstick was seen as the essential enhancer. It was lipstick that identified the free-spirited flapper, lipstick that American women reached for when they wanted a frugal wartime pick-me-up, and lipstick that signaled a teenager's entry into adulthood. People used mascara, eyeliner, foundation, and blush, but none of these were as profitable as lipstick.

However, mascara was a slow and steady gainer on the market, as were false eyelashes, which were patented in 1911. The use of false eyelashes went mainstream thanks to their appearance on Hollywood star Seena Owen in the 1916 film *Intolerance*, set in ancient Babylon. Most makeup historians tend to blame a combination of Egyptomania and Hollywood for the rise of darkened lashes as a signifier of femininity, though there were doubtless other social factors, including the influence of makeup mogul and socialite Helena Rubinstein (founder of an eponymous cosmetics line).

But while starlets in the 1920s and 1930s wore plenty of eye makeup, lipstick reigned supreme until the 1960s. There are several reasons for this, but chief among them is personal safety. During the first half of the twentieth century, mascara was comparatively a lot more dangerous than lipstick. The earliest lipsticks were made with fruit juice and rose petals, but even commercial lipstick made with unlikely ingredients (bugs or deer tallow) wasn't dangerous. But lengthening one's lashes tended to be a riskier proposition than coloring lips. Even though Owen's fake lashes were a hit with studio executives, the actress suffered for their wear. One day, when shooting had nearly wrapped, Owen showed up to the set of *Intolerance* with her "eyes nearly swollen shut," recalled her costar Lillian Gish in her memoir. In the 1930s, over sixteen American women lost their sight (and one ended up dying) from the use of lash dyes made

with toxic coal-tar derivatives. These injuries inspired First Lady Elea-
nor Roosevelt to push for better regulation of the cosmetics industry, and
in 1938 the FDA, for the first time, took action against the companies
that made and sold such irresponsible products.

The makeup of makeup is still a major issue for wearers. While many
of the ancient recipes for cosmetics seem laughably gross, it is probably
safer to wear a powder of dried reptile dung than it would be to slather
yourself in a layer of "forever chemicals." Per- and polyfluoroalkyl chemicals, PFAS for short, are known endocrine disrupters, which means they
can mess with the hormonal systems of many species, including humans.
Environmentalists believe that PFAS are responsible not only for the rise
of barren, hermaphroditic frogs but also many instances of human disorders, including cases of thyroid disease, infertility, and cancer. There
are thousands of different types of PFAS chemicals, and while scientists
don't fully understand their effects, we have plenty of evidence that even
very small amounts can be hazardous to human health. In addition,
these compounds don't break down easily in the environment, so they
tend to hang around in the air, water, and soil for decades, if not longer
(hence the sinister nickname). Yet American companies are still free to
use PFAS in a variety of industries, from farming to fracking to textiles
to cosmetics. A study published in a 2021 study from the University of
Notre Dame found that 82 percent of the waterproof mascaras tested
contained high levels of PFAS as well as 62 percent of long-wearing liquid lipsticks. These are products we wear on particularly vulnerable,
thin-skinned parts of our bodies, like near our mouths or tear ducts. The
chemicals, once absorbed into the body, can cause all sorts of harm, and
yet most brands don't disclose whether they contain PFAS, making it
"nearly impossible" to avoid them entirely.

Of course, you could opt not to wear any makeup. But I haven't yet
changed my habits too much, partially because I already have so much
makeup, it would be a shame not to use it. But also because I want my

eyes to look girlish and fetching. I want my reflection to have color and definition. Like so many people before me, I'm willing to accept a certain amount of risk in order to gain a better face.

This is perverse, I know. Fortunately, I have hope that my desire for beauty will fade as my proximity to the arbitrary ideal is lessened with time. "Beauty always has rules. It's a game," wrote Ursula K. Le Guin. "One rule of the game, in most times and places, is that it's the young who are beautiful. The beauty ideal is always a youthful one. This is partly simple realism. The young are beautiful." Born in 1929, Le Guin was too old to ever suffer under the tyranny of Instagram Face and, as she freely admits, she never had enough beauty to really "carry on" about it. "I resent the beauty game when I see it controlled by people who grab fortunes from it and don't care who they hurt. I hate it when I see it making people so self-dissatisfied that they starve and deform and poison themselves," she wrote. Still, physical beauty matters to her. She continues to "play the game . . . in a very small way," buying the occasional lipstick, a new silk shirt. Like Tolentino with her bleached hair or me with my mascara wand, Le Guin plays the game a little, here and there. She chose to keep some cosmetics, to admit to some vanity.

But Le Guin was in her seventies when she published *The Wave in the Mind*, and with her age, she gained perspective. Being close to death, watching her own mother grow old and die, seeing her friends die— these things helped hammer home the difference between the static "beauty-game" archetype and the shimmering "ideal beauty." Even for such a precise and generous thinker as Le Guin, "ideal beauty" proves a hard concept to define and identify, and an even harder concept to embody. This kind of beauty happens, she wrote, "where the body and spirit meet each other." It's a beauty that exists in memory and that we experience not as a single moment but as a collection of gestures, sounds, smells, motions, memories—it's a total beauty, one that radiates from a person. It isn't enhanced by makeup and it can be stripped away through screens and fillers. It can be flattened out of existence. And yet this, *this* is what I want, what I know I already have in some small amount: "beauty not skin-deep but life-deep."

With this in mind, I'm vowing not to buy any new makeup until I run out of the products I own. I threw out my waterproof mascara out of concern for PFAS and I spent the past summer with raccoon eyes on beach days. I won't go to Sephora (not even "just to look"), and I won't give in to those constant Glossier ads that appear like clockwork on my Instagram. Forgoing Botox isn't a hardship—I can't really afford it anyway. But even if my circumstances change, I plan to resist the pull of injectables and accept my creases and lines as they come. I can't promise to like them, but I can try. I don't filter my photographs, but maybe I'll stop posting selfies for a time, reserving my smile and smolder for those who see me in person. Maybe I'll even play with a bare face, let the world see me without my eyes adorned. But even more important, I'll let my daughter see me more often this way. She already knows my face and loves it, more than anyone ever has before. For this one person, I can change. I have changed.

6.
DIRTY, SWEET, FLORAL, FOUL
The rank backstory of perfumery

My nose is stuck in the 1990s. Like denim trends and shoe fads, scents cycle in and out of fashion every few years in American culture. Sometimes, you'll have a scent that defines a decade. Women in the 1960s tended to favor mature, intense white florals mixed with natural musks (the jasmine-forward classic Chanel No. 5 had gone mass-market by this point). In the 1970s, patchouli and smoke-forward scents dominated shelves (a direct response to the popularity of YSL's Opium). In the 1980s, consumers seemed to want big, brash florals and pungent spices (the epitome of which was Giorgio Beverly Hills). For the majority of the twentieth century, perfumes were highly gendered and sexualized, dictated by marketing out of Hollywood, London, Paris, and New York. Beautiful women, according to popular media, smelled.

I bought my first perfume in the late 1990s, a time when androgynous, so-called "clean" scents were all the rage (think Calvin Klein's CK One and Obsession). Public perception of perfume had begun to shift; it was no longer popular to fill a room with your scent. Instead, people wanted to appear fresh, scrubbed, washed—sanitary. As a hormonal preteen, I was no exception. From sixth grade to eighth grade, I stockpiled bottles of Heaven that I purchased at the Gap with my $20 per week allowance. I probably went through a dozen bottles before I outgrew it. Unlike many of my classmates, I wasn't a fan of Bath & Body Works or Victoria's Secret scents (both, I thought, were too fruity and too girly, too strong). I believed that *my* mall scent was different and more grown-up. My beloved perfume smelled, according to the perfume site Fragrantica, like orange blossom, jasmine, green leaves, lemon, and carnation. At the bottom, sunk below the brighter, fresh notes, lay a swamp of sandalwood, moss, and musk.

I no longer spray myself with Heaven before leaving the house, but I'm still a fan of grassy, green scents and white flowers, citrus blooms and smoky woods. I like androgynous smells and marine, salty fragrances. I've never gone for vanilla or "gourmand" scents—those perfumes that smell like pumpkins or marshmallows or cream and I have trouble appreciating certain old-fashioned florals, even the classic scents that I feel I *should* love. My nose remains somewhat limited; I blame this on my adolescence, that hormone-drunk period where my body devoured my mind. My desires felt like discoveries back then. I was an explorer plumbing the depths of myself, unearthing tastes like treasures, polishing them until shiny, presenting them to the world.

Back then, I took it for granted that I could buy my way into that confident, elegant femininity that some women seemed to naturally inhabit. I wanted very badly to have a signature scent, and so I chose certain notes that I felt were evocative and sophisticated. I didn't know that the jasmine flowers I loved so much were naturally laced with a molecule called indole, a chemical compound that is also found in corpses, feces, and on the oil that covers pubic hair. I had no idea that the smells I'd come to covet above all others had been scientifically engineered to reek like the wounded insides of a whale. Then again, few people know what's actually inside the lotions and potions they wear. Perfumery has always been a specialized realm—but that's by design. You're not supposed to understand the mechanics of your cravings. You're not supposed to see behind the curtain.

You may know that for thousands of years, perfumers created scents mainly from plant products, tinctures and oils made with billions of petals and stems. But you might not know that perfumers also have a long history of bottling and selling the by-products of animal pain and suffering. Not only are these supplementary materials terrifically expensive, but most true mammalian products often come at a cruel cost. Whales have been murdered for their oily blubber and concealed stomach bile; civets are caged and prodded for their fear-induced anal-gland secretions; and musk is harvested from the glands of slaughtered deer. Then there's the element of decay; although perfumery is described by some as a history of "purification," it's also a history of putrefaction.

It might seem counterintuitive or the stuff of moralizing fiction, that sophisticated, cultured people would want to cover themselves in something so nasty. Olfactory distaste is usually reserved for outsiders, not gatekeepers. Yet perfumery is a highly specialized art form that has always blurred the line between attraction and repulsion, pleasure and pain, good health and bad hygiene. It's highly subjective and often quite personal. You might love the smell of fresh sweat on your partner while loathing the smell of a coworker's floral lotion. Scent can also be fraught with fear. Most of us are afraid of smelling and being sniffed, but we're also endlessly fascinated by the scents of others, particularly those we deem admirable for some reason. There are even Christian legends about the smells emitted from saints. Unlike regular people, saints emit a whiff of sanctity to go with their upstanding moral code. Even when their bodies are rotting and maggots are breeding in their self-inflicted wounds, a saint smells like summer (and the maggots look like pearls).

In my quest to understand the draw of dark scents and ephemeral arts, I spoke with doctors who study the nose, perfumers who feed the organ, and even a zookeeper who spends her days breathing in the pure, undiluted scent of civet discharge. They had various theories as to why darkness seems to be an essential element of beauty, yet they all agreed on one thing: It's all about context. In the right context, even the smell of death can be appealing. In the right context, animal waste can be more desirable than gold. Disgust can be transformed into lust, then love. In the right context, with the right music playing in the background, you begin to root for the glamorous hit woman or the sardonic drug dealer.

They also agreed that sex is part of this equation, and it's the easiest explanation to trot out. But perfumery is about more than just smelling pleasant. We want to smell intoxicating, and truly intoxicating things are often a little bit nasty—they have an edge that cuts deeper than simple sensory pleasure. And as we've already seen with our black obsidian mirrors and our pale, cursed stones, encounters with the beautiful are rarely entirely enjoyable. If that were the case, Thomas Kinkade's light-dappled cottages would be considered the height of fine art, and we would all walk around misted lightly with lavender and vanilla. Instead, we adore the luscious gore of Caravaggio's canvases and dab our pulse points with concoctions containing the miasma of swamp rot, the cloying smell of feces, and the pungent, tonsil-kicking fetor of death. Beauty is sharp, it is intense, and it comes at a cost. Just as desire and repulsion walk through the same corridors of our minds, so, too, do beauty and destruction move hand in hand. Whenever you find something unbearably beautiful, look closer and you'll see the familiar shadow of decay.

One of the first known perfumers in history was a woman named Tapputi-Belatekallim. According to clay cuneiform tablets dating back to 1200 BCE, Tapputi lived in ancient Babylon and likely worked for a king. Surviving clay tablets describe her process of distilling and refining ingredients to produce a fragrant balm made of oil, flowers, water, and calamus, a reedlike plant similar to lemongrass. It's miraculous how modern her scents seem—or rather, it's surprising how little has changed. Tapputi used scent-extracting techniques like distillation (capturing a scent in water vapor) and tincture (capturing a scent in alcohol) that perfumers still use today. According to some sources, she was the first to mix grain alcohol with her scents, creating perfumes that were brighter, lighter, and had more staying power than anything else available at the time. This could be true, but she might also have been one of many perfumers working in that ancient kitchen, mixing batches of fragrance for her royal employer. There is quite a bit of mythology surrounding Tapputi, much of it modern, the product of a media hungry for stories of pioneering women. Still, Tapputi has become something of a patron saint for women in perfumery, and her contributions matter to us today. At the time, her scents may have played a religious role in ancient culture, but they may have simply been another way to prettify the body and please the senses.

In 2003, archaeologists unearthed the world's oldest-known perfume factory, in Cyprus. Archaeologists theorize that this mudbrick building and the perfumes it produced caused Greek worshippers to begin associating the island with Aphrodite, the goddess of sex and love. These ancient perfumers were using plant-based ingredients like pine, coriander, bergamot, almond, and parsley, among others.

These perfumes all sound rather pleasant, don't they? I can imagine dabbing almond oil mixed with a bit of bergamot on my wrists, catching a botanical draft of scent here and there as I move. It makes sense that people would want to smell like plants. I can even understand why curiosity might compel someone walking along a beach to pick up a chunk of marine fat and sniff it. It's a bit harder to understand the moment when perfumers made the conceptual leap from smelling the glandular sacs of dead musk deer to dabbing it on their pulse points. Yet at some point, this happened, for starting after the Crusades, Europeans became obsessed with musk.

Like many luxury items, musk came to Europe from the Far East. Derived from the Sanskrit word for testicle, "musk" refers to the glandular products of small male Asian deer. These little sacs of animal juice were harvested from the bodies of slain deer and left to dry in the sun. In its raw form, musk smells like urine, pungent and sharp. But after being left to dry, musk develops a softer scent. The reek of ammonia fades, and it becomes mellow and leathery. It stops smelling like piss and begins to smell like fresh sweat, or the downy crown of a baby's head. Musk gained a reputation as an aphrodisiac; according to some legends, Cleopatra used musk oils to seduce Mark Antony into her bed. Musk is a base note in many perfumes, even ones that don't smell overtly musky. Musk can help pin other scents in place, making those light herbal or floral scents last longer on the skin.

For medieval Christians, musk wasn't just a nice-smelling substance— it was a preventative medicine. Back then, many Europeans believed in something called the "miasmic theory." According to this branch of thought, illnesses like dysentery and the plague weren't caused by poor hygiene but rather by "bad air." Miasma, which comes from the Greek word for pollution, was also known as "night air." This term was used to describe foul-smelling vapors emitted from decaying matter, which supposedly had the power to fell even healthy citizens. Before germ theory, Europeans generally believed that gross air was responsible for the spread of disease, so it makes sense that they'd begin investing in long-lasting, powerful perfumes like musk. One luxury item available at the time was the pomander ball, a round locket-like metal accessory designed to hold nuggets of musk. Men and women wore the pomanders, sometimes on their belts, sometimes around their necks. They were often incorporated into rosaries, so you could hold a pomander and sniff its contents while you prayed.

Musk was just one of many ingredients used in this kind of aesthetics-based medicine, but it was one of the more popular scents. Musk smells good. It's a mellow scent, one you're probably intimately familiar with, since synthesized versions of the aroma have been on the market since the late 1800s. These days, real musk is rarely used in commercial perfumes, thanks to the ease with which we can replicate the animal scent. There are many different types of faux musk. Some smell sweet, some smell a little sweaty, others are rather nutty, but they're all inspired by the same basic idea. We no longer believe in night air, but we still associate musk with cleanliness and healthiness, despite the fact that synthetic musk molecules have been suggested to be endocrine disruptors (meaning they can mess with hormones) and some studies have claimed a link to a higher rate of tumor formation in mice.

"No state, federal or global authority is regulating the safety of fragrance chemicals," said Janet Nudelman, senior policy director for Breast Cancer Prevention Partners and a cofounder of the Campaign for Safe Cosmetics. Every day, almost every single American is possibly exposed to potentially toxic chemicals hiding under the big umbrella term "fragrances." These scents, once thought healthy, could be slowly seeping into tissue, breastmilk, organs, babies. Unfortunately, it can be hard to figure out which molecules are hiding in your soaps, lotions, perfumes, and colognes. While other countries have banned the use of potentially toxic fragrances, the United States doesn't regulate the use of these musk molecules. It's also not easy for the average consumer to figure out what products might be safe, since "musk" has become an umbrella term for a number of different smells, molecules, formulas, and chemicals. The safest option is to avoid purchasing scented body products altogether (including laundry detergents), but this would be too mighty a sacrifice for many of us sensualists.

We can't just switch to using the genuine article either. In 1979, musk deer were listed as an endangered species, so it's no longer legal to use natural musk in commercial perfumes. However, Tibetan musk deer are still killed for their glands, and a brisk trade in poaching has resulted in some illegal musk showing up online. Musk is also used in some traditional Chinese and Korean remedies, which helps the substance remain one of the most valuable animal products on Earth. In his book *The Fly in the Ointment*, McGill University professor Joe Schwarcz points out that musk is "more valuable than gold."

Civet is a lesser-known fragrance, though it also appears frequently as a note in perfumes. Like musk, most contemporary civet is created in a lab, made to mimic the glandular secretions of a small, furry, nocturnal creature. Civet smells even more animalic than musk, according to people who have actually sniffed it. "They have a general odor about them that is very pungent," says Jac Menish, curator of behavioral husbandry at the Nashville Zoo. Civets are uncommon zoo creatures. They are neither felines nor rodents, though they're commonly mistaken for both. Although few visit the zoo just to glimpse this offbeat attraction, the Nashville Zoo has several banded palm civets because the zoo director "just loves them." (You may have heard of civet coffee, a product made by force-feeding Asian palm civets coffee beans, then harvesting them from their poop. Society, it seems, has come up with several odd ways to make money from civet asses.) When they are startled, frightened, or excited, civets "express" their anal glands, and the greasy liquid "shoots right out." The scent hangs in the air for days. "I guess I could see if it was diluted it might not smell as offensive," Menish concedes. "But it can be really bad if it hits you."

Unlike musk, civet can be collected without killing the animal. But it's not a cruelty-free process. Civets are kept in tiny cages and poked with sticks or frightened with loud noises until they react and spray out their valuable secretions. Commercial perfumers no longer use genuine civet in their fragrances, but James Peterson, a perfumer based in Brooklyn, owns a very small vial of civet tincture. "It smells terrible when you first smell it," he says. "But I have some that is five years old, and it gets this fruity quality as it ages." The stink mellows, becoming a natural companion for floral scents. On a few occasions, Peterson has used genuine musk or civet to make "tiny amounts" of specialty perfumes, and the resulting blends have an "intensely erotic draw." Customers report that these dark and dirty smells are potent aphrodisiacs. "When it's below the level of consciousness, that's when it works best," he adds.

Ambergris is similarly subtle, often used to boost other scents. It plays a supporting role rather than a starring one, for although the smell is fascinating on its own, it doesn't project (meaning, the stank doesn't reach far). Ambergris is a naturally occurring substance that has been known to wash up on shore in waxen lumps. This valuable material is formed inside the body of a sperm whale. A common misconception is that ambergris is vomit or feces, when the reality is a bit more complicated. Like a pearl, ambergris is born of irritation. According to Christopher Kemp, author of *Floating Gold: A Natural (and Unnatural) History of Ambergris*, the formation process of ambergris begins inside a whale's digestive system when a mass of claw-shaped horns accumulate in a tangle, scratching the poor creature's organs and irritating their bowels. As the mass gets pushed through their body, it grows and slowly becomes "a tangled indigestible solid, saturated with feces, which begins to obstruct the rectum." Once the whale expels the mass into the ocean, it begins to mellow out. The black, tarlike wad is bleached by the ocean until it becomes smooth, pale, and fragrant. It ranges in color from butter to charcoal. The most valuable ambergris is white, then silver, and finally moon-gray and waxy. It's believed that only 1 percent of the world's sperm whale population produces ambergris. It's very rare, very bizarre, and very valuable.

Whales have historically been killed for their bodily products, including their oil, spermaceti, and their stomach contents, so humans may have discovered ambergris while processing whale corpses for other goods. It's also possible that humans came to discover ambergris through beachcombing (and presumably sniffing their every ugly find). Our appetite for ambergris dates back to ancient times. The Chinese believed it was dragon spit that had fallen into the ocean and hardened, and the ancient Greeks liked to add powdered ambergris to drinks for an extra kick. King Charles II of England liked to eat ambergris with eggs, which was apparently a fairly common practice among the aristocracy in England and the Netherlands. It shouldn't be surprising that people engaged in some light coprophagia—smell and taste are so deeply linked, and while I can't attest to the taste of ambergris, I can say that it smells beguiling. Given the chance, I would sprinkle some silvery whale powder on my eggs, just to see what it was like.

Ambergris has an unearthly fragrance. It smells like the sea, but also like sweet grasses and fresh rain. It's amazing that something made in the bowels of the whale could smell so pure. If you found fresh ambergris, midnight black and sticky and stinking, perhaps you wouldn't want to eat it. But with distance and dilution, ambergris is transformed from animal garbage to human ambrosia.

According to natural perfumer Charna Ethier, ambergris can smell like "golden light" or a "flannel shirt that has been dried on a clothesline on a warm summer day." Although every piece of ambergris smells slightly different, Ethier is referring to her own personal sample, which she characterizes as "soft, fresh, and ozonic." In contrast to most professional perfumers, Ethier doesn't use any synthetics in her perfume, nor does she use animal products in her commercial work, opting instead for plant-based scents. Ethier's ambergris is "quite old" and reportedly beach-found ("I hope it is," she says).

Ethier is the owner of Providence Perfume Company in Rhode Island. I went to her shop because I wanted to smell the real deal, the authentic scents, the kind of perfumes a woman might have worn in the 1700s. Inside the airy store, I found Ethier waiting in a wrap dress and heels, her smile expertly slicked with lipstick, her dark hair perfectly coiffed. Instantly, I felt a mess in my travel-rumpled denim shirt and winter boots, but once the tour began, I forgot to care about how I came across. I was too riveted. After sampling several of the artfully blended perfumes that lined the shelves, Ethier took me behind the register and opened up her cabinet of olfactory curiosities. The piece of heavy wooden furniture held dozens of vials, bottles, and jars, each one containing a different scent, among them: ambergris. Next to her hundred-year-old cade oil (a foul-smelling liquid made from juniper trees, purchased at an estate sale) and below her collection of floral absolutes and herbal essences, there's a tiny glass vial of ambergris tincture. Unlike floral absolutes or essential oils, real ambergris is simply too expensive to use in a commercial product—not to mention the fact that Ethier couldn't sell it in the United States. Here, sperm whales and their fatty lumps are considered endangered, so you can't buy or sell products derived from their bodies. This isn't true elsewhere. The going rate for ambergris is around $25 per gram, putting it on par with platinum.

There's a reason people are willing to pay so much. Ambergris is a "miracle ingredient" for perfumers, says Ethier before I take a sniff. "It makes everything better." That's why we use these strange animal fats, these oily slicks of stink and clumps of funk. They enhance our favorite floral scents, undercutting some of the frothy sweetness of nectar with a reminder of darkness, making the entire concoction feel somehow more real. Animal products are the antiheroes in this drama—even when you hate them, you still, just a little, love them. That's how siren songs work, and ambergris sings the loudest. To me, it smelled soft, warm, inviting, intimate, like the way my old husky/hound dog smelled after we washed her in oatmeal soap and let her romp in the tall summer grass to dry. Once, Ethier made a perfume using her most prized ingredients. She mixed one-hundred-year-old sandalwood essence with ambergris tincture and frangipane and boronia absolutes, two flowers native to Central America and Tasmania, respectively. It was the first time she'd used ambergris, and this one-off perfume was so lovely that "it was like gold-washing something." She remembers wistfully, "It was so beautiful."

Smell is the most underrated and mysterious sense. "In the Western tradition smell ends up associated with the dark, the dank, the primitive and bestial, with blind and subterranean bestiality that moves in ooze," wrote William Ian Miller in his philosophical examination of our basest emotion, *The Anatomy of Disgust*. He argued that smell "ranks low in the hierarchy of senses" and that the "best smell is not a good smell, but no smell at all." While we no longer think smell brings disease, nor do we imagine the devil is padding about the surface of the earth smelling of sulfur, we still associate smell with all things lower, including the lower parts of the body. It's associated with lower morality. "The language used in sin and wickedness is the language of olfaction gone bad," wrote Miller. A person can stink, but so can their actions. A government can reek of corruption. A hypocrite might wear the metaphorical stench of their deceit.

In her 1908 autobiography, *The World I Live In*, Helen Keller called scent the "fallen angel." Smell was, she knew, associated with wickedness through no fault of its own. "For some inexplicable reason, smell does not hold the high position it deserves amongst its sisters," she wrote. Keller mapped her world by smell—she could smell a coming storm hours before it arrived and knew when lumber had been harvested from her favorite copse of trees by the sharp scent of pine. In contrast to touch, which she called "permanent and definite," Keller experienced odors as "fugitive" sensations. Touch guided her; scent moved her. Without smell, Keller imagined her world would be lacking "light, color, and the Protean spark. The sensuous reality which interthreads and supports all the gropings of my imagination would be shattered."

We don't often think in terms of color and light when it comes to smell, perhaps because we have so few words for scent that we borrow from the lexicons of our other senses. Even though smell is our most ancient sense, it is also one that seems to elude language. (Our so-called lizard brain is also sometimes termed the rhinencephalon, literally the "nose brain.") "Smell is the mute sense, the one without words," wrote Diane Ackerman in *A Natural History of the Senses*. "Lacking a vocabulary, we are left tongue-tied, groping for words in a sea of inarticulate pleasures and exaltation." We've had eons to come up with words for the precise smell of fresh-turned earth or the exact scent of a blazing beach fire, and still the best we can do is "earthy" and "smoky."

Perfumers speak their own language, but their words have recently begun to trickle down into popular culture through beauty magazines and blogs. Not only do beauty gurus and their superfans speak of absolutes, oils, and tinctures, but they can also rattle off compounds like coumarin, eugenol, and ambroxide. A trained master perfumer (or "nose") can pick out precise scents within a layered perfume. They don't just call something foul—they can pick out the pungency of musk or the reek of tobacco, ingredients that are delicious in small doses but overwhelming when used out of balance.

Professor Schwarcz's book offers one reason why we're drawn to animalic scents, citing studies that suggest people with ovaries could be more sensitive to musk, particularly around ovulation. He cautiously speculates that musk might resemble chemicals produced in humans to attract potential mates.

Over the phone, he is even more wary of speculating about a possible evolutionary explanation for our fragrance preferences. "The sense of smell has been studied thoroughly, with surprisingly little results in terms of what we actually know. It's such a complicated business," he said. "We don't know why musk is more attractive to some people than others. We don't know why it smells differently when it's diluted, but we know that it does." When I asked whether we like musk because we're programmed to enjoy the smells of bodies, he was quick to turn our talk toward the "issue of pheromones," which "may not actually even exist at all" in humans, despite our desire to attribute various observed phenomena to the invisible messengers. According to Schwarcz, much of what the general population thinks they know about pheromones only applies to certain nonhuman species. For instance, boar pheromones are well understood, easy to replicate, and used by farmers to increase the farrowing rate amongst their stock. Some of the perfumes that boast "real pheromones," like Jovan Musk and Paris Hilton's eponymously named scents, may indeed contain pheromone molecules—but only ones that pigs would find very enticing. However, the marketing copy used to promote supposedly scientifically backed fragrances doesn't often reveal this inconvenient fact. Instead, we're led to believe that human pheromones can be bottled and sold, that attraction is quantifiable, that desire follows certain logical lines.

But like Diamond Doris and her learned lust for diamonds, we covet the scents that we're told to want by magazines and advertisements. When we walk into a department store, we're often drawn forward not by the smell of a perfume but by its persona. We're all familiar with this kind of imagery, the pretty pictures of celebrities with glossy lips and perfect hair, photoshopped spokeswomen for femininity and its accoutrements. They help sell us desire, but they also help sanitize and sublimate it. Behind the pseudoscientific marketing talk and the glamorous girls hides the same rutting impulse. Commercial perfumers market scents as pheromone-laden because they know that calling them "secretion-scented" would be a harder sell. They are coyly tiptoeing around the issue, which allows consumers to do the same. Most people don't want to admit even to themselves that they're looking for a product that mimics human stink—vaginas, anuses, armpits—but those are the base notes in so many scents, including my beloved "clean" fragrances. If you think that's disgusting, well, I think that's also the point. If we can unhitch it from shame, gross can be good.

For perfumer Anne Serrano-McClain, co-owner of MCMC Fragrances in Brooklyn, it is the tension between foul and sweet that elevates a fragrance from consumer product into the realm of art. This is key when it comes to repugnant ingredients, from indolic florals to musky secretions. The indecent element becomes a secret of sorts, a gruesome piece of marginalia scribbled alongside the recipe, visible to only those in the know but appreciated by all. The foulness whispers below the prettiness, and combined, these various elements create a scent that smells paradoxically clean and dirty, light and dark.

"Indole is what makes the scent of jasmine interesting," she says. "It makes you want to come back and smell it again—it has an addictive quality to it." Unlike citrus scents, which are one-note and rather simplistic, florals have an element of decay, a whiff of putridity. Serrano-McClain rightfully points out that this is part of what makes flowers themselves attractive to bees and other pollinators. Corpse flowers famously smell like dead bodies, but so do many other blossoms, just to a lesser extent.

Plus, humans are by nature "just a little bit gross," Serrano-McClain says. Like civets, musk deer, and whales, we shit, we secrete, we mate, and sometimes we vomit. But we also give birth and create beauty, and for Serrano-McClain, it's this life-giving ability that links blossoms and humans. "I think there is a depth to anything that is made of life and creates life. There's something inherently sexual in that," she says. "Even though something like civet will smell gross on its own, it adds an element of reality."

I think most people would admit that real sex has its ugly elements. Even good sex is kind of gross, especially if you're not participating in it. It's a fundamentally awkward and transgressive act—one that also happens to be life-giving and life-affirming. Even the most vanilla sex involves crossing barriers of the body and swapping fluids that would be, in any other context, considered repulsive. Sex is also contaminating, both in a literal sense and a figurative one. It's something that opens our bodies up to the possibility of infection, illness, and death.

Throughout the history of perfume, the question of contamination arises again and again. Sometimes, perfume was a way to protect bodies against disease, as it was during the Middle Ages. But perfume can also be a marker, a class signifier that tells people who to respect and who to condemn. "The lower classes smell," wrote George Orwell in his 1937 nonfiction collection, *The Road to Wigan Pier.* Orwell is clear that this is something he was told, but he still seems to believe it. Laborers smell, he argues, because they must labor. But that's not really why upper-class Britons kept repeating this myth. They were using this cruel maxim to keep the social order in place. A bad-smelling person, Orwell argues, is impossible to sympathize with. He can see having affection for a "murderer or a sodomite" but odorous breath is an "impassable barrier." For Orwell, this is a big reason why socialism never took off in the West. Too many people felt that there was something "subtly repulsive about a working class body."

Miller picks up on this thread, arguing that disgust is an emotion that allows for contempt—a key element in the building and maintaining of social hierarchies. If you assert that someone smells disgusting, you're making a claim about their place in the world. Hundreds of years ago, a disgusting smell was understood to be a human smell. People who smelled bad reeked of sweat, dirt, disease, death, decay, and excrement. That was before baths were widely available. In the late nineteenth century, more people moved to cities and urban areas and gained access to soap, water, and perfume. It became harder to make any sort of claim about the bodily scents of people employed in low-wage jobs or people born without family wealth. But rather than admit people are people and we all stink, the upper classes began making a new claim. They continued to repeat the myth that poor people smell, only now they blamed it on "cheap" perfume and "foreign" cologne. Perhaps the offending person smells like drugstore aftershave. Or maybe they emit the distinct scent of oud, a Middle Eastern and Southeast Asian fragrance made from the resin of fungus-ridden agarwood, which can range from feral to phenomenal (sometimes it's both).

During the late nineteenth and early twentieth centuries, the rich were no longer the class that smelled like expensive fragrances. Instead, the wealthiest members of society took pride in being scentless, which helped set them apart from the rest of society. The middle class had become the driving force behind fragrance trends, which made sense, given their growing purchasing power. I'm sure some wealthy people still wore perfume, but they kept it close to the body and in small doses. In contemporary culture, this is more or less the standard way to wear scent. I remember learning from women's magazines how to apply perfume—a spray on the wrists and one behind the ears. Anything more would be gross or, worse, tacky.

I didn't realize it at the time, but when I first started wearing perfume, I was buying into a form of cultural backlash that was related to the HIV/AIDS epidemic. Attitudes around casual sex had changed, which led to a shift in buying practices among consumers, which in turn caused perfumers to reconsider their formulations. Josh Meyer, owner of the Oregon-based cult perfume label Imaginary Authors, explains that the 1970s and 1980s were defined by "crazy, loud animalic scents" that projected strongly, announcing one's physical presence. But then, in the 1990s, "Everyone wanted to smell super clean, like hyper clean." Marine, citrusy, and soapy fragrances like CK One and Cool Water replaced the civet-heavy, musky florals that had dominated the market a few years prior. Looking back, many members of the fragrance community have attributed this shift to the lingering cultural fear of contamination. The link between sex and death had been made more visible than ever before, which meant it was no longer fashionable to smell so funky. "People realized," said one perfumer in an interview with the *New York*

Times, "that sex can kill." Once again, perfume became a tool for conveying one's status. People wanted to smell healthy, not sexy or sultry.

Until recently, I never realized the HIV/AIDS epidemic might have shaped my perfume preferences. Throughout my teens and twenties, I continued to seek out scents that weren't overtly sexual or coded as particularly feminine. I never wore syrupy florals or warm, dark musks. They felt too wrong on my body. I had internalized the messaging about clean bodies too well, and I was terribly afraid of being considered dirty. Indole, though beloved by many, scared me with its supposed shit stink.

To a lesser extent, I also thought that I didn't have the beauty necessary to pull off that kind of complicated, earthy scent. Remember: beautiful women smell. I was afraid people would think that I thought of myself as sultry, sexy, hot. That I wanted sex. That I wanted to be desired, even when I did want and still want all of these things. This is one of the lesser pains that shame can inflict—it can shut down avenues of self-expression.

Shame can also help reinforce hierarchies already in place. People associate different perfumes with people of different racial and economic backgrounds, as well as different supposed character traits. A study published in 2018 in the *American Sociological Review* used several different perfumes to examine how smells can be used to "define, distinguish, and rank others in various races and classes." Researcher Karen Cerulo, a professor of sociology at Rutgers, presented the participants with three perfumes and found that her subjects were pretty good at decoding the intended demographic and setting. They knew the difference between a drugstore bargain-bin scent and an expensive night-out scent, and they were able to identify which of the perfumes was meant for daytime office wear. When tasked with developing a profile of the person who might use each scent, Cerulo's participants showed a clear tendency to link the cheapest scent (the big drugstore floral) with elderly women, lower-class women, and with Latina women. The other big racial link that people made was between the fanciest perfume—the sultry, night-out scent—with Asian and Black women, possibly because of the inclusion of patchouli and other "exotic" notes. Finally, Cerulo found that the perfume marketed toward office workers was linked with whiteness. One study participant, a Black woman, told Cerulo that the "clean, fresh smell" was the kind of thing a young white girl would wear because "a Black girl, for example, [she points to herself] would view this as boring."

A boring white girl is, all things considered, not a terrible way for society to see me. Cerulo points out that her findings indicate that we don't just have ideas about who likes what (Black women like spice, white women like citrus, Latina women like florals) but also who belongs where. The expensive scent was linked to exclusive events and elite places, nights at fancy restaurants or the opera. The drugstore scent was tied to church halls, bingo nights, nursing homes, and bathrooms. The middle scent—that light, supposedly inoffensive one—was tied to leisure activities like bicycling, going to the beach, or walking outdoors. Participants were also more likely to be specific and detailed in their answers when they were describing the fragrance that they associated with their own race. "This suggests that when we define a smell as 'ours,' it conveys a richer, more multidimensional experience than that associated with 'them,' thus reinforcing social identities and reifying race and class boundaries," the study argues.

The associations we form with smells are personal, but they're also cultural. One person might smell a spicy, patchouli-based perfume and think "visiting my grandma" while another might think "nightclub." These variations exist, but right next to these personal ties, most of us also harbor some socially influenced associations. These small, seemingly harmless stereotypes add up over time. They help inform who is welcomed into various spaces and who is tacitly kept out. Not everyone is expected or allowed to wear scent. Sometimes, there's obvious reasons for this. As someone who suffers from migraines, I'm glad many health-care facilities discourage the use of fragrance. But most public situations are less clearly defined than that. A perfectly qualified job candidate could ruin their chances by wearing the wrong perfume to an interview. And how would they know? Smell is a complex cultural code; there's no definitive rule book or etiquette guide. I suspect most of us learn how to wear (and appreciate) scent from our families and close friends, many of whom harbor the same biases we do. If you grew up around people wearing oud and jasmine, you might not know that a white audience tends to associate these scents with sexual contexts, not professional ones. If you grew up around girls who doused themselves in synthetic mall-bought florals, you might not be aware that, to some people, you smell young, broke, and cheap.

It's not the worst thing in the world, to be told you've miscalculated your scent, but it doesn't feel good. That kind of shame can linger with you for years, especially if you already felt like you didn't fit in. I still remember the moment when an older colleague pulled me aside at an office job and told me to wear a longer skirt and tone down the perfume. He meant well, but I can still remember how my face burned.

In 2020, the ongoing debate about perfume in public temporarily paused as people around the world retreated into their homes. Shared spaces, including schools, offices, and stores, all closed, and Americans were advised to "shelter in place." For months, I saw no one outside my im-mediate family and the occasional grocery-store clerk. I did not dress or groom myself to appear in public. In order to stay safe, and to keep other people safe, I had to sacrifice that element of my life. It wasn't night air that caused the pandemic, but it was spread via our exhalations. Suddenly, all human breath had been rendered suspect and deadly. We became morbidly aware of our own secretions and the contaminating power they held. Most of us went to great lengths to avoid getting sick. We wore masks that hindered our ability to smell. We used globs of hand sanitizer multiple times a day until our skin began to crack and bleed. We scrubbed our hands with soap, over and over, while singing "Happy Birthday" in our heads. I remember washing my hands in a grocery-store restroom next to an elderly woman who hummed the song grimly while we both slathered ourselves in pink, scented soap.

During this time, I began wearing more perfume than I ever had before. It became part of my self-care ritual. I sprayed perfume onto my sheets before I went to bed. I spritzed my sweaters before putting them away in my drawers. At first, I leaned heavily on one scent—one compound, in fact. I became enamored with a scent called Not a Perfume by the indie fragrance house Juliette Has a Gun. It's an alcohol-based spray perfume with one note, a molecule that has been described as dry, waxy, musky, and clean. Some have touted it as the first "invented" scent, but this is hard to confirm. This strange molecule was synthesized in the 1950s by industry scientists seeking to create a dupe for ambergris. Depending on who is manufacturing it, you'll sometimes see this fragrant terpenoid called Ambroxan or Cetalox. Some perfumers just refer to it as amber, while others call it gray amber. It's difficult for me to describe what it smells like, because my nose has no real waypoint for something like this. It smells like Charna's tincture of ambergris, I suppose. On my skin, it smells like woodsmoke and maybe soap. It smells powdery yet a little wet. My husband says it makes me smell fantastic. "It's so you," he says. "It makes you smell like you're happy."

As the months of quarantine dragged on, I continued to wear Not a Perfume, but I started supplementing it with other scents. I'm no perfumer, but I finally understood what a good perfume does—it changes as you wear it, shifting, moving, marking the passage of time. The top notes fade into the drydown; the heart notes and base notes emerge.

Natural ambergris is constantly evolving. I wanted my scent to change too. I began purchasing samples from a variety of different makers, mostly independent houses that specialized in unconventional perfumes, scents that tried to evoke the smell of a thunderstorm or a desert at dawn, a raging fire or a quiet old church.

My goal was not to smell clean, nor to smell healthy, nor even to smell beautiful. I wanted to smell like an experience. I wanted to layer sensation onto my body, to give myself something to ponder. My mind was troubled and running in circles, so I tried to provoke my senses into taking the reins. I bought very soft sweaters and spent hours looking at images of famous paintings online. I listened to rain sounds captured in the Slovakian Alps on my phone. I put on perfume that smelled like the Danish coastline—cold, salty, evergreen, sharp. I was creating sensory anchors, ways to tether myself to the present moment.

We're still living under the threat of disease, and I'm still at home, wearing my perfume for no one but family. I'm vaccinated, but I'm not entirely safe. I have no illusions that smelling good will protect me from viruses, but I do think conceptual, strange perfumes have been helping me breathe. Removed from the possibility of public perception (and thus the influence of shame), I'm free to discover my preferences. Through a process of trial and error, I've learned what smells good on my body and what molecules turn rancid as soon as I apply them. Although I love the smell of roses, I dislike rose absolute and I can't stand a heavy jasmine scent. A slight fecal whiff (skatole, the organic compound is called) is tolerable but only when mixed with tobacco. I'd rather smell like ozone, tar, and gasoline than lilies, a flower that reminds me too much of corpses. My favorite perfumes all smell like trees, lumber, and firewood. I've begun to pick out the differences between different pines in my perfume, different types of resin and smoke. It's a pleasure to know these things about myself.

I use the skills of perfume sampling outside too. Over the past few years, I've taken a half dozen foraging workshops and two overnight wilderness-survival courses. Scent is a form of information when you're in the woods, seeking food and trying to avoid disaster. The black trumpet mushroom, the first fungi I confidently picked and ate, has a fruity, musky scent that distinguishes it from the similarly shaped devil's urn. I've become better at locating sweet fern, wild mustard, and garlic. Smell helps us determine choice edibles from toxic lookalikes. But even when I'm not snacking on tree tips and spring leaves, I've come to embrace the power of scent as a grounding mechanism, as a way of knowing a place, being closer to a place. It helps me figure out the landscape of Maine and feel rooted within it. It's a quiet state, that of sensing attentively. Perfume requires even more work than most plants, though the stakes are certainly lower. But even when I'm breathing in a new sample scent, looking for an elusive leather note, I feel present, focused, and attentive, in tune with my body. I'm not thinking about current events or worrying about the impending climate crisis. I'm not even thinking about sex or death, though sometimes I am thinking about those two things. For the most part, I'm simply perceiving. It's a process that feels elusive, ephemeral, abstract, and engrossing.

I have over one hundred tiny vials of perfume samples stashed in boxes under my bed. Collecting and sampling them has become my hobby or my vice, I'm not sure which. I've become more careful about where on my body I spray them. For instance, when I was breastfeeding, I never applied perfume to my torso, and I rarely apply perfume to my neck, opting instead to put it in the crook of my elbow. It feels safer than spraying it close to my face or hands, though I don't truly know if it makes much of a difference. I've recently begun buying perfumes made by smaller, newer perfume brands, like Imaginary Authors, Ded-Cool, MCMC Fragrances, Olympic Orchids, and Vilhelm Parfumerie. They seem to provide greater transparency about ingredients and better customer service than the corporate-owned designer houses, but unless

I start formulating scents myself, I'll never be entirely "safe." But ultimately, I've decided that some risk is acceptable to me, particularly since there's such a great sensory reward. Plus, I want to partake in this part of human culture; I want to support the people who create art for our senses, beauty for our noses.

I'm less sanguine when it comes to my daughter. She loves to smell, and I enjoy watching her eyes light up as we sniff cinnamon, saffron, and oregano from the spice cabinet. I like how she selects an incense stick with great care, and when I watch her blow on the flaming end, I feel such pride that she's learning these bodily joys, these grounding rituals. But I no longer let her watch me put on perfume because it makes her ask for her own. I don't spray anything on my skin where she might nestle her little cheek. What's acceptable for me feels entirely too risky for her. I don't know that these perfumes are harmful, but I also don't know they're not.

Plus, I wouldn't want to cover her smell. She's a toddler now, so that intoxicating newborn mix of milk and amniotic fluid, new skin and baked bread—that's worn off. Yet she still has something special, a human scent that tells me so much about how she's feeling. I can smell a dirty diaper, of course, but I can also smell sickness on her mouth (sour like bad milk), stress in her hair (sweaty, sharp). She smells different when she's tired. She smells best when she's happy, sleepy, worn out from running in the tall grass with our yellow dog. When I hold her close and breathe deep, I'm flooded with oxytocin and information. My mind lights up. The experience is aesthetic, analytic, and animal.

I can't bottle it or capture it, but I'll never forget it.

7.
WOMEN AND WORMS
*The prismatic sheen of silk
and its fairy-tale logic*

The prom dress I wanted was out of my budget. I wasn't going to go to prom at first—the boy I was in love with was in rehab and the guy I was dating was going with someone else—but enough of my friends decided to go as a group that I figured it was worth the price of admission. Except tickets were expensive, limos were even more so, and the dress I wanted? It was more than my mom was willing to spend.

But she did seem relieved (borderline thrilled) that I wanted to go. She was happy I was going to do something normal and relatively social for a change. I think this is why, once she saw me in the dress, she offered to pay for the entire thing. Not just the $200 she had initially allotted, but the whole expense. I didn't have to use my grocery-store wages after all.

The $400 dress was, we agreed, very special. The fabric was silk chiffon with a hint of stretch and the color was a shimmering seafoam blue. The bodice was tight and textured but the skirt was a collection of diaphanous silk strips that moved like a cloud of fog around my hips when I walked. I had never owned something like that before, something so light and delicate. It wasn't as formal as most gowns in the evening section; it wouldn't have looked good with a formal updo and manicured nails, and I had no plans to spend my money on either service. I wanted to look ethereal and effortless. Most important, I wanted to look unique. This is why I asked my mom to come with me to the "fancy mall," the one with the real bamboo trees growing in the glass atrium, the one that had a Neiman Marcus *and* a Barney's. I didn't want to buy something from the prom section at Macy's.

The request was selfish, and I think I knew that at the time. But I didn't know that my mom was heading into credit-card debt. I also didn't know the alimony battle wasn't going well with my newly re-married father. I wasn't aware that my desire for pretty things was hurting my siblings, who were jealous of the time and energy my mother spent trying to make me happy and shiny and cute. She put a lot of effort into my appearance. I looked like her; she was proud of my looks. And she always enjoyed when I looked angelic and "natural," hippie-chic, like her.

When I arrived at prom, I realized quickly that I wasn't going to have a good time. There were many reasons for this (I was already drunk, the music was bad, my friends were nervous, a homophobic ath-lete was already shooting off his mouth about my newly out gay friend, et cetera), but there was another reason I advocated for leaving early. There was another girl, a friend of mine, wearing *my dress*.

"I told her I was going to get this one," I hissed to my best friend, Sara. "She knew. She totally copied me." I felt the silk of my dress, the luminescent blue fabric that had already taken on the smell of sweat and cigarettes, and I felt a deep, nauseating sense of guilt begin to form at the back of my throat like a sob. I knew it wasn't important and I knew I should be cool, calm, and gracious about this who-wore-it-best scenario. But I was filled with ugly feelings of inadequacy and disappointment, anger and resentment.

At the afterparty, I changed into my distressed denim shorts and stashed the dress in the trunk of my car. I kept thinking about what I was going to tell my mom, how I could spin this into a tale that would make her happy. I wasn't entirely self-centered. I saw that my mother was sad and suffering with problems of her own, though many of these problems were mine too. My dad had left to marry a younger woman, her father had died just the year before, and we were all still devastated from the suicide of my teenage cousin. We were sad, nothing could fix that, but I still wanted to be happier, for her. I knew how much my decisions meant to her. I had recognized that I was her proxy, her avatar, her echo. For her, I tried to be lighter, sunnier, kinder than I really was. I tried to be grateful for all the things she bought me, and I tried to spare her some of my personal sadness. When we bought it, that dress meant the world to me. It made me feel graceful and feminine in a way that I never had before. One of the reasons I used to love shopping with my mom was because it made me feel like we were in a movie montage, a mother-daughter duo trying on clothes to upbeat jazzy music, pulling faces at each other when an outfit looked wrong. I've always loved fairy tales and rom-coms, two genres that revel in a pat story and bow down to the power of a makeover. Two genres that recognize the power of a good dress.

Here's a fairy tale of sorts: Once upon a time, there was a queen who was as clever as she was pretty. She was married to the Yellow Emperor of China, and like most ladies of status, she didn't have to work in a garden or toil over a pot. Instead, Lady Hsi-Ling-Shih was able to sit all day under the trees, drinking her cups of tea, looking at flowers. One day, she was doing this when she heard a little splash. She looked into her teacup and there, among the dregs of leaves, she saw a curious bundle. The great lady fished it out with her delicate fingers and saw that the bundle was an insect, wrapped in a soft white substance that had begun to unwind. She picked at it a little with her fingernails, revealing a long, fine thread. It was a single piece of raw silk. She looked up and saw dozens more bundles attached to the glossy green leaves of the mulberry tree. She put down her teacup and called her servants. She had an idea.

Whether or not this happened is a matter of faith, not history. Like many ancient tales, it follows the rhythm of a fable. The Yellow Emperor's reign does roughly coincide with the beginnings of China's silk production, but whether a queen pioneered the practice or someone else discovered the preternatural strength of this insect-made string, we'll never know. There's a similar story told about tea itself that involves the same basic ingredients: a boiling cup of water, an errant object, an intelligent observer who just so happened to be the emperor. Both technologies could have been sparked by this type of royal windfall, but it seems more likely that ideas bubbled up in a less sycophantic manner.

The important thing is that silk has always been closely tied to royalty. Even now, high-quality silk fabric remains a luxury good. Although I often feel broke compared to some of my peers, in the grand scheme of human life, I'm among the richest people who have ever walked the earth.

Several months ago, I donated a silk blouse that I bought at a J.Crew store in Boston before graduating from college. It was lavender, sleeveless with ruffles, purchased in anticipation of entering the white-collar workforce. The shirt didn't suit me, but I held on to it for years because it was real. It wasn't "silky," as so many garments are labeled, but actual silk—soft as belly skin, faintly iridescent, hard-to-care-for, easy-to-stain silk.

I owned this blouse for over a decade, moving it from Philadelphia to Boston to Portland to the woods of Maine. I can remember wearing it only twice, yet I kept it, because it was silk. I also kept a cobalt dress, a wine-colored skirt, and a black blouse for the very same reason. After having a child and swearing off office work, these clothes did not fit my body the way that they should. They also no longer fit my life-style. I wear denim to pick blackberries and wool to paddle the marshes for good reason—those are fabrics that perform a function. The denim protects me from prickers, while the wool keeps me warm, even when wet. During a bout of pandemic-inspired closet purging, I finally faced the fact that my life is almost entirely devoid of silk-worthy moments. I was not using these business-casual garments. I had been hoarding them in my closet, letting them go to waste for years—someone else could have been wearing them all along. Unlike my prom dress, which I hope to give to my daughter someday, these pieces meant nothing to me. I bought them just to have them, kept them because I felt I should, and gave them away only when I realized my closet was stuffed to the brim, the wooden bar sagging in the middle from the weight of all those un-worn, unloved clothes.

My jammed closet feels normal to me, but it isn't the global or historic norm. My grandmother didn't have this kind of luxury at her fingertips. The fashion industry, and its glut of waste, is a staggeringly new devel-opment. Moths have been around for at least 200 million years. Most silk comes from the *Bombyx mori*, a species of domesticated moth that began its relationship with humans some seven thousand years ago. In the long arc of the universe, it's a bit of a baby. J.Crew was founded seventy-six years ago, and I was born forty years after that. Of course, you can't really compare the history of an entire species with that of a single human life. Yet in this age of mass extinctions, it seems to make a certain kind of nar-rative sense. I'm constantly measuring my human life—the harm I may inflict—against countless animal lives, against the continuation of species, against the wellbeing of the world itself.

Fortunately, the *Bombyx mori* is in no immediate danger of dying off. We love its thread too much. Like mollusks, the creature that creates such beauty is no great looker. In the adult stage, it's a rotund, furry, white-winged bug with feathery brown antennae. It can't fully fly because its body is too large for its wings. This doesn't matter, because few *Bombyx mori* ever get the chance to try; they're boiled alive before that can happen. A few are allowed to live long enough to mate, thus guaranteeing future generations of productive victims, but since they lay hundreds of eggs at a time, you don't need that many adults to ensure offspring. Over the centuries of domestication, we've changed their bodies and artificially sped up their life cycles. Compared to their wild moth cousins, these bugs both live fast and die young. The majority are hatched from eggs, fed a steady diet of green mulberry leaves until they're chubby little caterpillars, and then killed as they attempt to undergo metamorphosis inside their cocoons. The caterpillar creates its protective shell by spitting out a mixture of enzymes through a triangular orifice. This liquid hardens upon hitting the air. The bugs spit and they spit, turning around and around until their bodies have disappeared under layers of polymers. In that cozy little bundle, they get ready to make wings. That's when we strike. Splash, into the drink they go.

The basic recipe for production hasn't changed since the days of the empress and her fatal teacup—not for any great respect for tradition but because we haven't figured out a better way to do things. When the *Bombyx mori* emerges from its cocoon, it does so by softening the threads, thus breaking what could otherwise be a continuous strand of silk. This is why we don't prize silk from wild moths. While there are other species of moth that produce silk, every one of them destroys their shelter in the process of exiting it. The only way we've discovered to stop them from releasing their digestive enzymes is by boiling (or baking) the creatures alive before they're ready to emerge. The pupa dissolves, leaving only the thread.

And what a thread it is! Thanks to its zigzag arrangement of hydrogen bonds, silk created by insects is incredibly strong and elastic. The prismatic and regular shape of the strands account for the fabric's lustrous, almost iridescent quality. After discovering how to unwind the cocoons, Neolithic Chinese weavers began spinning these pieces together, making first threads, then, using a loom, weaving cloth. In 2019, archaeologists discovered the body of a child, partially wrapped in a piece of carbonized fabric, buried in a tomb in the Neolithic Yangshao culture ruins in Central China's Henan Province. At more than five thousand years old, this burial shroud is the oldest known example of silk cloth. (Archaeologists have also found evidence of silk's existence pre-dating this fragment, but since the fabric is biodegradable, these artifacts are mainly silk-adjacent objects like tools for weaving and spinning.) The complexity of the weave suggests that it came from a time when the technology had "matured rather than just begun." I can only imagine how precious that bundle must have been, how terribly sad someone was to bury it under the soil, how much care must have gone into that final act of parenting. This is something people have been doing for as long as we've been people: when you lose a beloved person, you sacrifice something to the ground or to the air. A burned boat or a buried piece of silk.

For several thousand years, silk remained an exclusively Chinese product, one of the many objects that traveled along the Silk Road. This wasn't a single highway but a network of trade routes that Yo-Yo Ma has called "the internet of antiquity." The Silk Road, literally and figuratively, knit societies together. The four-thousand-mile network of rough roads allowed caravans of travelers, laden with valuables, to traverse deserts and scale mountains. Merchants brought bolts of raw silk in its natural pale-ivory state as well as elaborately woven and embroidered luxury fabrics. Some were decorated with swirling patterns of abstracted gold clouds, others featured painted birds, flowers, and landscapes. People in Rome loved the stuff, though it scandalized the more conservative writers of the time. Pliny the Elder wrote that silk was being used by dressmakers to "reduce women's clothing to nakedness." He goes on to suggest that the practice of wearing silk was a symptom of the degeneration of Roman culture, an attitude reflected in the Roman sumptuary laws that prohibited men from wearing the luxury fabric.

Silk wasn't the only material carted between China and Europe; people brought tea, jade, porcelain, spices, and paper from Asia. The traders returned with horses, glassware, and fur. People, too, were traded along the route. Evidence of slave markets has been found all along the route, from Dublin in the west to Shandong in the east. Like social media, which has been used to both connect people around the globe with loved ones *and* foment genocide abroad, the Silk Road brought beauty and destruction. Some research has suggested that the bubonic plague, which devastated medieval Europe, was another— albeit unintentional—export from Central Asia.

"It is hard to overstate the importance of the Silk Road on history," states the National Geographic Society's entry on the subject. Presented as a neutral source for school-age children, it provides an understated but still clearly biased overview of how these trade routes functioned, one that emphasizes the importance of violence, money, and power. "Religion and ideas" spread along the Silk Road, towns bloomed into cities, and the spread of information "gave rise to new technologies that would change the world." As often happens in history writing, we're told to look not at the embroidery or gowns or other luxury goods but rather the tools of warfare and dominion. Horses went to China and "contributed to the might of the Mongol Empire" while gunpowder flowed west, changing the "very nature of war in Europe and beyond." Weapons, disease, wealth, slaves—the Silk Road had it all.

But the history of silk isn't a simple story of soft goods in exchange for hard muscle, one animal technology for another. And it's not just about those quantifiable forms of power, like money and military might. It's also a story about people: goddesses, peasant women, concubines, wives, daughters, brides, babies, and slaves. It's a story about economics, certainly. Yet tangled within these tales of public exchange, there's also flashes of intimacy, glimmers of resistance, and a sturdy sense of hope that accompanies the radical act of mending.

The association between women and textiles is an ancient one. In the case of silk, the connection is especially strong. Silk is a fabric that was supposedly discovered by a woman, was predominantly woven by women, and offered women a rare chance for self-expression. While women in ancient China weren't given a lot of freedom, they were expected to do a great share of the household work, particularly spinning and weaving. "The production of silk was bound up, from at least the time of Confucius, with ideas about women's appropriate place in society," writes Kassia St. Clair in *The Golden Thread*. From 2000 BCE onward, women were expected to "stay at home and devote themselves to weaving." Often, there would be three generations of women under one roof, all focused on the care and rearing of thousands of little worms. While this was no doubt hard and oppressive work, the cultural significance of silk production could allow talented women a chance to make a meaningful contribution to their household (as well as providing an outlet for creative expression). During the Shang dynasty, people began worshiping a silkworm spirit or goddess, a practice that continued in some form or another into the nineteenth century. Worship of a female deity was unusual, notes St. Clair, and went against traditional Confucian values. But this goddess was special; she oversaw the creation of one of China's most beloved inventions and famed exports. For St. Clair, the belief in a goddess can be read as evidence that even the poorest women were able to take pride in their labors, perhaps even finding a level of self-respect and purpose through their work.

Since literacy wasn't common among women until the end of imperial China, historians tend to look at secondary sources for hints on how the average woman lived. A piece of surviving silk-themed art from the eighth century shows a highborn woman surrounded by the trappings of silk production, but rather than lusting for her ruler, she's subverting his laws. The 1,300-year-old piece is an aide-mémoire, used by a storyteller to illustrate his tale. *The Silk Princess* is recognized as one of our best surviving examples of the Khotanese school of painting. The image is bold and graphic, almost cartoonish to my eyes. The center of the panel shows our main character: a lovely young princess in full wedding gear. On her left stands an attendant, whose outstretched hand points dramatically at her royally adorned head. Atop her dark curls sits an elaborate headdress in which she has hidden silkworms, mulberry seeds, and cocoons. To the right, we see a seated four-armed deity, perhaps a patron spirit of weaving, and a figure working at a loom. Together, these figures represent the "just-so" story of the Silk Princess. Like all just-so legends, we'll never know if this really happened, but the story remains useful for how succinctly it explains a cultural phenomenon—in this case, the spread of sericulture knowledge over the Asiatic continent. According to the story, an ancient Chinese princess used her bridal finery to smuggle the necessary tools for silk production out of her father's kingdom (the land of silk) and into her future husband's realm (the land of jade). She betrayed one man to enrich another, and in the process, she made herself unforgettable.

It seems unlikely that this is how silk slipped beyond the borders of China, but it's not impossible. Silk technology could have been discovered by an intelligent queen and spread abroad by a disobedient princess. Women were some of the primary laborers in the production of silk, though they weren't necessarily its number-one consumers. Men were just as likely to wear and own silk, and before paper became readily available, silk was often used as a medium for artistic expression. People embroidered silk tapestries, painted ink scenes on silk, and wrote works of literature, poetry, and scholarship on bolts of silk. Around the third century, sericulture began fully kicking off in communities outside China, so we know the secret got out somehow. For a bit, silk remained geographically close to China, but over the course of several hundred years, the technology spread to India, Japan, the Middle East, and North Africa. At some point in the sixth century, envoys from the Byzantine Empire were sent into China to pilfer the secret of silk, an act of attempted knowledge-theft that pre-dated France's attempts to woo Venetian mirror-makers by over a thousand years. Legend has it that the two monks dispatched by Emperor Justinian filled a pair of hollow bamboo walking sticks with moth eggs and mulberry seeds before making the hike back to Byzantium, shaking their ill-gotten biomaterials with every step. We know this isn't how it happened—the journey would have killed the eggs—but it speaks to the power of silk that it has spawned so many fantastic fables and quest narratives.

Even though silk wasn't a Byzantine discovery, the empire wasn't interested in sharing their new knowledge with the rest of the world. They didn't even want to share it with all their own citizens. According to Trini Callava, author of *Silk Through the Ages*, silk production was "considered an art, at the same level as architecture, painting, and sculpture. The position of weaver could only be inherited." The silk industry became an imperial monopoly and the silk textiles an important tool for social control. Fine textiles were used to promote and uphold royal and ecclesiastical hierarchies. Silk was a way to make visible differences in status and wealth. Famously, Phoenician noblemen took to wearing intensely hued silk garments that had been dyed with large violet strips using the secretions of a carnivorous sea snail. The production and consumption of this purple cloth was strictly regulated by the state. Sumptuary laws were enacted to keep these symbolic garments off the bodies of the lower classes. It seems like it was never enough to simply import fine Chinese silks; rulers wanted to take this powerful symbol and remake it in their own image, adding color and texture to the blank slate.

History is, according to professor Christopher J. Berry, "the history of opulence, not of (basic) need." The stories that get passed down through generations and across cultures aren't about people simply surviving. They're about people finding ways to achieve objects of desire. Likewise, the story of silk is not just a tale of cloth, argues Callava. "It was about witnessing human industry procuring distinction according to a specific aesthetic. They were about a sense of opulence and distinction, as moving principles, and the definition of civilizations." Silk's power doesn't come solely from its beauty, nor from its practical use. It comes from its ability to mark members of the elite, its ability to inspire imitation, and its ability to make visible the rules of social order. Like any luxury, silk is about excess. It's above and beyond what we need.

One particularly striking example of this excess appeared on the global stage in 1981. It was a dress, but it was also more than a dress—it was a statement of national values. Princess Diana's wedding dress wasn't just voluminous or fancy or expensive, though it was all those things. The $115,000 gown was a sweeter-than-sweet confection, a pouf of ivory silk taffeta that had been embroidered with sequins, trimmed with frilled lace, and decorated with ten thousand pearls. I can't decide if I find the dress beautiful, though she certainly looked lovely in it. But while thousands of brides wanted to copy that dress (and many designers did copy it in the puff-shouldered years to come) Diana's dress was one of a kind. It was made from British silk, farmed and milled at Lullingstone Silk Farm, which the royal family had been using for some time. At the time, this was the only operating mulberry silk farm in Britain. (Most British silk mills imported foreign silk and wove it on-site). The *New York Times* reported that the mill staff had to "scramble" to produce enough silk. "They drove daily to neighboring counties, stopping at all houses with mulberry trees and asking to pick the leaves," wrote Terry Trucco. "No one at Lullingstone seems certain just how many cocoons went into the Princess's gown, but a woman's blouse uses 600." That's a lot of effort for an outfit that will only be worn once, yet it was worth it to the royal family. The entire event, dress included, was a performance of soft power, the kind that often gets outsourced to women.

Unsurprisingly, there have been numerous attempts to create and market silk alternatives. People have tried very hard to figure out ways to make an identical product through a different process, but to no avail. Some of the attempts to remake sericulture for a Western market have had disastrous effects. If you've ever seen the tree-killing eyesore that is a gypsy moth "egg mass," you know what hell an amateur lepidopterist can unleash. In the 1860s, artist Étienne Léopold Trouvelot began raising over a million gypsy moth larvae on his property in Medford, Massachusetts. Some adult moths escaped the laboratory and promptly began mating and eating and laying eggs. Ten years later, the trees in Trouvelot's neighborhood had been stripped bare of leaves. We still can't make silk fabric from gypsy moth tents, and we're still dealing with their ravenous descendants. In 2016, the damage wrought by gypsy moths on the Rhode Island forest was visible from space, and firefighters were concerned the too-bare branches would present a risk of fire.

Even with money from our military budget, our most recent attempts to revolutionize the sericulture industry have been largely unsuccessful. For years, I've been reading about efforts to genetically modify other living creatures so that they can produce silk enzymes. We've tried reprogramming moths, yeast, and even goats. Supposedly, scientists hope to create an alternative source of spider silk, which could be useful in making better, lighter body armor. The alternative silk could also be useful in surgery or creating prosthetics. Theoretically, we could also use this fantasy material to create nearly indestructible blouses and buy-it-for-life bras.

I suspect that even if we could make faux silk, people would still want gowns and blouses made from the real thing, woven from unbroken threads of animal proteins. When it comes to silk, people crave the strength, sheen, *and* the story. How else can you explain the continued practice of weaving sea silk? Made from the fine filaments that attach a Mediterranean clam to the seafloor, this odd and incredibly rare fabric has been speculated to be the inspiration for the fabled Golden Fleece of Greek mythology. "When you have a piece of sea silk in your hand, it's so lightweight you don't know it's there," says Joyce Matthys, one of only two living sea-silk artists (that Matthys knows of, at least). A longtime shell collector, Matthys became inspired to try her hand at spinning silk from byssus hairs after she read an article about Italian weaver Chiara Vigo, who once called the byssus threads, "the soul of the sea." When I ask Matthys what made her so interested in the fabric, she replies, "Oh golly gosh, I hardly remember. I read about the woman in Sardinia. She was claiming to be the last person who knew how to create sea silk." She remembered how, after a storm, she'd seen similar hairy shells on the beaches of Sanibel: "I thought, maybe I'll see if I can find some that still has the dead animal in them."

Matthys spent the next four years combing the beaches of Florida, searching for stringy fragments of mollusk fiber. Eventually, she was able to collect two small Ziplock baggies full of byssus. She cleaned them with Dawn dish soap and used hair conditioner to soften them slightly. Then, she taught herself to spin ("I'd never spun a thing in my life," she tells me) and eventually, after months of working with the delicate material, she managed to crochet a small square of fabric. At first, it didn't shine. It was as brown and boring as a piece of sugar kelp. She read that sea silk needed to be submerged in an acidic liquid in order to get the desired effect. "Back in antiquity, they used cow urine," she says. She dropped some lemon juice onto the square and watched fearfully as it appeared to dissolve—all that work, down the drain. Matthys began to panic. "But then I took it outside," she says, "and it shone like gold. It was so beautiful." Now, the three-inch strip of the cloth sits near cases of pearly seashells at the Bailey-Matthews Shell Museum on Sanibel Island. While this rare fabric was once reserved for "the very rich," these days sea silk doesn't have a value. "Oh, you can't sell it," she says. "Who would buy it?"

Matthys says she was drawn to complete her obscure task because of the "history and the mystery." A similar impulse led Madagascar-based artists Simon Peers and Nicholas Godley to begin harvesting golden orb spiders (named for their saffron-colored silk) back in 2004. It took years, over a million spiders, and around half a million dollars to create a hand-woven brocade cloth that is reported to be the first of its kind. In 2009, the American Museum of Natural History in New York City held a glitzy event to honor the unveiling of this cloth, which was worn around the party by socialite Tinsley Mortimer. A press release described the cloth as being "imbued with metaphor and poetry, with nightmare and phobia, with tales and myths that resonate with us all." While the publicist who wrote that was trying to drum up excitement for their events, the breathless tone (for once) feels warranted. Spiders have an unsettling place in our symbolic register—they're weavers, tricksters, goddesses, mothers. Poisonous and feminine. In Jungian psychotherapy and dream analysis, spiders are representative of the part of our personalities we suppress and keep hidden, our so-called shadow selves.

People had tried weaving with spider silk before, but it's not an easy material to harvest. It is not a fiber for the masses. That glimmering yellow garment is a piece of art—we know that because it resides in a museum, because it's beautiful, because you can't buy it or make it yourself or touch it. It has an aura to it, a sense of specialness that comes from its physical qualities and its emotional value.

These other silks, the spider and the sea, are more than just curiosities. For me, they help clarify the appeal of moth-made silk. Their rarity evokes a time when all silk was miraculous. The labor that goes into each piece reminds me of the countless cocoons and hours and hands that went into the development of all such garments. Even my ruffled lavender blouse seems more appealing in hindsight, its existence made possible by nature's chaotic brilliance and human ingenuity. Their museum-bound presence puts fabric back into a place of honor. I'm so used to viewing textiles as things to possess; it feels useful to be reminded of all the objects of beauty that exist beyond my reach. My appetite can't be sated, much less glutted, so it must be curbed. A simple lesson, yet I find myself learning it over and over.

When I first started reading about silk, I thought the darkest part of its history might come from the outrageous toll of insect death. There is something disturbing about winged creatures being bred too fat to fly, raised to glut themselves as wriggling worms, bind themselves in coffins, then die. I imagined I'd find myself in a similar position to David Foster Wallace at the Maine Lobster Festival, wondering whether it was "all right to boil a sentient creature alive" just for human pleasure. In what might be his most famous essay, Wallace grappled with crustacean anatomy, moral philosophy, culinary traditions, and personal beliefs. "Consider the Lobster" holds up as a piece of writing, but when I went to reread it, I was struck not by Wallace's many funny observations or where he ultimately landed on the question of boiling lobsters, but rather his preoccupation about whether it even makes sense to write about this stuff at all. "Is the previous question irksomely PC or sentimental?" he asks immediately after wondering if it's "all right" to cause so much animal suffering. Published in 2004, "Consider the Lobster" pre-dates our obsession with wokeness and the conversation about virtue signaling by decades. Even then, reluctant hedonists were wondering how to explain our society's choices and our personal desires.

Like Wallace, I am afraid of coming across as mawkish and preachy, but that's the risk you run when you grapple with morality in the public sphere. Unlike Wallace, I don't feel particularly confused over the issue of lobster death, grisly as it may be, and as callous as it may sound to some readers. Living in Maine, I've boiled plenty of lobsters and heard them scramble about in the pot. I've even grilled lobsters, a process that involves cutting a live lobster lengthwise with a big knife and then waiting around until the two halves stop flailing their claws about (this can take upward of ten minutes). I don't enjoy these experiences, but I did find them rather fascinating. I felt the same way when I witnessed my dog quickly and cleanly kill a baby squirrel. It was sad, on some level, but more than that it was interesting. Death is a part of life, after all. Plus, my lifestyle does harm to the planet and to people. I know enough about how various industries work to know that harm is standard, the rule not the exception, especially when it comes to the production and processing of animal products. I eat meat that I buy at a grocery store that was likely produced in a factory farm and packaged in a plant by underpaid workers. I wear leather shoes I purchased at a mall from some brand I can't name, mass produced somewhere far from my home using hides that were tanned using God-knows-what chemicals. And I still wear silk, though these days, it's mostly purchased secondhand.

I have tried, but I can't make myself care about silkworm death; I don't know if I think it's "all right" to boil creatures alive. It's probably not. But on the list of questionable things humans do, it ranks low. Especially when you consider the children.

Was my prom dress made by kids? It could have been. While America once was home to plenty of textile companies, most of the industry has been moved abroad, mainly to countries that have lax labor laws and less government oversight than ours. Similar to the floral industry and our media's annual "blood and roses" reports, every few months we get a fresh glimpse into the hell our general indifference (and our taste for cheap fashion) has wrought. Here's another: "Boiling cocoons, hauling baskets of mulberry leaves, and embroidering saris, children are working at every stage of the silk industry. Conservatively, more than

350,000 children are producing silk thread and helping to weave saris," explains a 2003 report from Human Rights Watch titled *Small Change: Bonded Child Labor in India's Silk Industry*. Many of these children work twelve or more hours a day, six or more days a week, "under conditions of physical and verbal abuse." These kids are usually "bonded" to their employers by their parents, who receive a small loan for their child's future work. According to Human Rights Watch, this money (sometimes as low as $21 at the time of the report) often goes to pay off another loan, to pay for medical services or funeral services, or simply to buy food. The bonded children are paid nothing or less than minimum wage, and those who are paid usually see none of their earnings. They're given little to no education—it's easier for employers to take advantage of illiterate workers—and many are bonded for life. Diseases pass freely around the crowded workshop. Children are subject to sexual, physical, and psychological abuse, and the dangerous nature of the work can leave sericulture workers crippled for life. According to a 1997 sericulture textbook, this is an industry that preys on vulnerable people because it "does not require great skill but only delicacy in the handling of the worms and it is ideally suitable for the unskilled family labour, particularly womenfolk, aged, handicapped, and children."

The 2003 report is a follow-up to a 1996 report that urged the government of India to put a stop to the practice of enslaving children born into poverty. While some steps were taken to address bonded labor in the textiles industry, Human Rights Watch estimated that there were between 60 to 115 million children working in India (of whom at least 15 million are bonded). When they revisited the issue in 2003, they found no reason to change this estimate. While other sectors use these practices too, the textiles industry is regulated more closely by the Indian government since silk has such a high cultural value. Researchers from Human Rights Watch believe this is a space where the authorities could enact change quickly and effectively, should they feel so inspired.

Decades later, in 2021, a twenty-two-minute documentary made by CNN's Freedom Project attempted to capture the scale of this ongoing tragedy through footage of hot-pink saris shimmering under studio lights juxtaposed with scenes of face-blurred laborers, hands submerged in troughs of hot, dirty water as they sort bobbing cocoons. Another image shows the worms, wiggling like maggots, as they eat their way across an emerald sea of leaves. Bonded workers in hijabs tell their stories from behind black cloth. It's a good piece of reporting. It relays information clearly, explaining that these girls are subject to frequent abuse and injury. But in the age of constant content creation, it feels less like a call to arms and more like a single serving of humanitarian concern fed into my media diet. The nature of television is to consume so passively, sometimes it feels like the news flows through me like my arsenic-rich well water. It's bad for me, slightly. It's mostly good for me.

But there comes a tipping point. After years of reading about the fashion industry, seeing almost daily reports about its abuses compiled by writers like Whitney Bauck, Aja Barber, Jasmin Malik Chua, and Alyssa Hardy, something changed. The documentary came into focus as part of a bigger picture, and I began to understand more deeply what I was wearing and what it meant. I stopped thinking about clothes as items I could want and buy on my phone and began thinking of them as objects that were made out of labor. I've been able to see the truth of my food for years now, thanks to friendships with small-scale farmers and first-hand knowledge of the labor that goes into growing something to eat. But for years fabric (even sheer fabric) remained impenetrable. We don't see this part of textile manufacturing in America. We don't see the dead moths, much less the trapped children. We're able to ignore so much of the darkness that we wear on our bodies because of distance, denial, and obfuscation. It takes some moral interrogation to find peace with fashion, and some moral calculus to settle on decisions that best reflect our values. It's harder work than getting dressed.

I've learned enough about the fabrics that I prefer—silk, cotton, and wool—to realize I haven't been paying properly. Not proper attention, nor the proper amount of money. "The further back you go in the supply chain, the more opaque it becomes," says *In Intimate Detail* author Cora Harrington. A lingerie expert and lifelong lover of luxury garments, Harrington has been thinking about these issues much longer than I have, and she's unwilling to offer any pat answers to my question about what is "all right" when it comes to buying clothes. "It's very difficult to make any ethical decisions as a consumer," she continues. "The average person doesn't even know the right questions to ask, and then you need to rank your own priorities." Many people, Harrington points out, think their values should be everyone's values. A vegan may think silk is a terrible material, worse than any plastic-derived fiber, while an environmentalist might like that silk can biodegrade and will not sit for centuries leaching chemicals into a landfill. No textile on Earth can be manufactured, shipped, and worn without causing some level of damage. That's the nature of consuming in the twenty-first century.

But there are still choices we can make to mitigate the damage we do. "For me, I'm more concerned with child labor than silkworm larvae," admits Harrington. "People might say that's speciesist, and some people might find that unethical." She tries to purchase objects that were made fairly and without underpaying someone, which often means she's buying more expensive items than most people. Once, she went on social media and "broke down" the cost of a $1,000 lingerie set. Even though there were machines involved in the making of the garment, the piece was still made by artisans. Lace must be hand-drawn, she explains, and even machine-made appliques have to be sewn on using tiny, invisible stitches. This type of object is necessarily a luxury good. It was not created to serve a practical function (though it can) and it was never intended to be available to everyone. Like the spider-silk cape, these pieces of high-end, under-the-clothes clothing exist primarily to serve aesthetic and social functions.

Buying a luxury item can be a way of showing one's allegiance to the elite class, it can be a way to reinforce social norms, and it can be done purely for the individual pleasure, the aesthetic experience. I don't believe it is morally repugnant to purchase a beautiful, expensive silk nightgown, hand-painted and decorated with lace cuffs, nor do I think it's gross to own a silk thong, so long as you make an effort to find out where it was produced and how. Fast fashion will never be ethical fashion. (Simply buying the cheapest item available is rarely going to be an ethical choice, though it is an understandable one.) Waste is human, and what defines luxury (according to economist Thorstein Veblen) is the element of excess. Beauty is tangled up with excess and overflow, and most beautiful things are wasteful to some degree. To remove these things from our lives would be to take away a very valid source of pleasure, but we don't have to partake in "conspicuous waste" in order to appreciate beauty. "Part of why I enjoy textile and fashion is because it's such a direct bridge to the people who lived before us," says Harrington. "When I look at a piece of Sophie Hallette lace, that's what I think about. All that craft, all that heritage, all that skill. That history is a sign of our humanity."

After speaking with Harrington, I spent hours looking up Sophie Hallette lace (made by a French fashion house that's been in continuous operation since the 1880s) and searching for secondhand silk robes. I wanted to find an object so light and beautiful that it could undress me while covering me. I wanted to feel the sensation of fabric that skims over my skin like breeze, that falls off my limbs like water, that moves with me as though we were two dancers onstage. For much of my life, I've believed that beauty resides primarily in the eyes. But I've slowly come to realize how deeply it can be experienced through other senses. It can also be accessed through the ears (a song that sends shivers racing down your spine) or the nose (a perfume that tickles a memory of spring, wet earth, and bulbs). We don't describe tastes as being beautiful very often, nor do we often talk about something feeling beautiful on our skin. But have you ever stroked your hand along a piece of wax-finished wood, the grain a faint ripple beneath your fingers? Have you ever brushed your cheek against the ear of a dog and let it twitch, velvety and warm, against your face? Have you ever slipped a silk robe around your body and felt it brush against your nipples?

Hands on plastic keys, I write this sentence, a rattling sound accompanying my thoughts, a screen emitting blue light toward my eyes. It's not an unpleasant experience but it's a far cry from those bodily pleasures. I begin to search for silk robes because the more I think about the fabric, the more I want to shed my clothes and wrap myself in the softest fibers, to bless my body with a garment that shimmers and glides. Yet I want it to be free of cruelty, free of the pain of small hands, free from the terror of poverty.

This is nearly impossible. Even if you choose not to care about boiling moths, as I do, and even if you choose to prioritize non-plastic materials, as I have, there's almost no way to live both fashionably and ethically. Perfect sartorial morality (to borrow a term from writer Quentin Bell) is impossible to reach. I could choose to believe in companies like Everlane, who promise radical transparency about their supply chain and factories, but I don't.

After looking at robes for hours, I closed my tabs and didn't buy a single one. I didn't buy the "washable silk" pajamas handsewn in California. I didn't buy the short, eggplant-colored robe from the Kew Gardens gift shop, printed with moody flowers in beautiful detail. I didn't buy the '60s silk "kimono-style" robe with hand-painted white cranes on a midnight-blue background (I couldn't have afforded that one anyway). Instead, I talked to a friend who had recently sewn her own wedding dress, and she told me about the pleasures of making one's own garments, the joy of knowing your clothing is one of a kind, born from your own participation in an art form.

I didn't dig out the sewing machine from my basement. But I did begin learning to mend. And I began listening to the works of philosophy and technology writer, L. M. Sacasas. He runs a newsletter called *The Convivial Society*, which aims to illuminate facets of contemporary life that feel wrong. In his piece, "Ill with Want," he puts it plainly:

> Endless wanting will wreck us and also the world that is our home. By contrast, our economic order and the ostensible health of our society is premised on the generation of insatiable desires, chiefly for consumer goods and services. Your contentment and mine would wreak havoc on the existing order of things. "That's enough, thanks," is arguably a radical sentiment. Only by the perpetual creation of novel needs and desires can economic growth be sustained given how things presently operate. So just about every aspect of our culture is designed to make us think that happiness, or something like it, always lies on the other side of more.

Clothing can do so much for us—textures can calm us; good clothes can ignite the libido; they can make us look professional, subversive, or even invisible. In retrospect, I'm grateful for the minor indignity of having the same prom dress as another girl. It didn't feel good at the time, but that silky, gorgeous green garment taught me something important. I didn't fully digest the lesson until later, but that was the first time I really saw how quickly a purchase can turn sour and how pointless it is to seek lasting joy through acquisitions. No dress will ever magically make someone love you, nor will a makeover ever change your life. These are fairy tales, but so is the idea that we can buy our way into personal style or moral righteousness. To buy clothing, when one already has enough, is never going to be a virtuous act.

As much as I love and cherish my ability to desire, I've found a great amount of peace in the phrase "That's enough, thanks." I'm repairing the broken strap on a dress I once wore and loved. The fabric is a mixture of silk and cotton, and it's covered in blue flowers with lawn-green leaves. Years ago, I wore it to attend a wedding, but then it broke. I found it in a crumpled ball at the back of my closet. The most remarkable thing about this object is that it's already mine. Once it's fixed, I think I'll wear it as a nightgown.

8.
DECEPTIONS AND DAMNATION
The molten glow of screens, the beauty of stained glass, and the treachery of spectacles

My first car was a beat-up blue sedan with rust along the wheel wells and a crack in the windshield. I bought it at the age of sixteen and drove it until I totaled it at an intersection in Boston, five years later. Before I said goodbye to my Dodge Neon, I grabbed a few things: a booklet of Rilo Kiley CDs, a copy of *The Secret History* by Donna Tartt, and a sterling silver necklace chain that dangled from the rearview mirror. On this chain, I'd strung two charms. The first, a red enamel Saint Christopher coin (the patron saint of travelers and surfers, I was once told), then next to that, a single scarlet figure. It was a woman's torso, complete with two pointy nipples, an ample round stomach, and soft conjoined thighs that tapered to a point. She had no feet. Like the Venus of Willendorf and countless other ancient fertility statues, she had no arms. In place of her head, she had a thick loop of glass. I called her simply my Red Lady.

I made her in a beadmaking and lampworking class as a high school student during the brief period when I thought I might be an artist of some sort. The course was taught at a nearby community college and since I refused to do any sports, small-scale glass art became my only real extracurricular. I had vague notions that I would work in glass—maybe glassblowing (which turned out to be hard, heavy, hot work that made my arms ache and my face turn tomato red) or maybe stained glass (tedious, fiddly, focused work that required too much pre-planning and not enough soldering for my tastes). I quickly figured out that I wasn't interested in "slumping," where you arrange pieces of glass on a molded sheet and then put them in the kiln to slowly fall into mushy shape. While some of these classes were offered through my public high school's art program, others required weekend trips into Boston and Worcester. The studio I visited the most was in a large industrial building outside Worcester. I couldn't always afford to attend classes, but I got to know an instructor who gave me a discount and let me use the studio sometimes for free. (Almost for free; once, I let him kiss me next to my car but when I rebuffed any further advances, the tutorials came to a halt.)

It turned out that I wasn't really interested in making beads, but I did love lampworking. It involved an open flame, which appealed to me more than the hellmouth furnace required for glassblowing, and promised instant gratification. One could learn fairly quickly how to make small vessels and sculptures. I thought I might make my own bongs, but that dream never came to fruition. Instead, I bought hand-blown pipes from other, more advanced students and made a series of small floral sculptures that my mom put into her China cabinet. Once I left for college, glassworking proved to be too expensive to continue. (There weren't many studios near my rural college campus anyway.) But I carried my Red Lady with me for years because in some small way, she reminded me that I could manipulate this brittle, harsh material. I could play with molten silica, sodium, and calcium, twirling it in the air as it glowed orange over a 900-degree flame.

I don't remember exactly when the Red Lady broke, but she did shatter. I no longer own a single glass bead, charm, or object that I made myself. They've all broken during moves or car crashes or maybe I lost them somewhere. Honestly, none of them (save the Lady) were particularly important to me. It was the glass itself I liked, not the final product. I liked to see it smolder.

There's something about the liminal, chaotic, mercurial nature of glass that appeals to me. When I was in a studio working with glass, I always wanted to touch the molten substance, to drape it across my skin, to eat it. Viewed with my adult lens, I can recognize these as intrusive thoughts about self-harm, inspired by my depressive brain. But even now, I don't believe that's the full explanation. I think glass is beautiful because it's dangerous and unpredictable. I can never quite get over my sense that something shouldn't behave how glass does, especially not something so ordinary, so useful, so common. Or rather: I shouldn't be allowed to play with it. I shouldn't be allowed to heat it up, cut it, break it, sand it, manipulate it.

Looking back, I can also see how I was using my newfound glass obsession as a way to build a sense of self, one that placed emphasis on creation rather than devotion, art rather than faith. I was an extremely religious and anxious child. My family attended Mass at St. Elizabeth of Hungary Parish in Acton, Massachusetts, every Sunday for years. I grew up staring at the stained-glass windows, waiting for them to glow and cast their reds and blues onto the floor, or even better, onto the faces of the congregation. I didn't love attending these services, but I adored the intimate quiet of the confessional, the clean feeling of divulging my sins, the alchemical process of turning ten Hail Marys into an unblemished conscience. I wanted to be loved and I was told, for a time, that God would do this, or at the very least, the Virgin Mother, who loved all children. At night, when I prayed for sleep to come easily, I didn't think of Jesus on his wooden cross, but rather Mary, glowing and angelic, backlit and sky blue. Religion brought me peace and comfort, until it didn't.

I stopped loving the Catholic Church, but I never stopped appreciating the beauty of its rituals and forms. Even now, I find myself praying sometimes. Even now, I'll catch my breath at a rose window, a cathedral spire, a flickering candle in a ruby glass, lit for someone loved and lost. While I can no longer be loyal to the Catholic Church as an institution, the aesthetics of my childhood religion have been burned into my heart, and I have no interest in healing from that particular wound.

Glass is perhaps the most frequently overlooked material in history. It is essential to our lives, more so even than plastic. A world without glass is more unimaginable to me than terraforming Mars (practically an impossibility, most scientists agree). Without this banal marvel, you wouldn't be able to use a touch-screen phone, switch on a lamp, look out a window, put on your glasses, sip from that bottle on your nightstand. You wouldn't be able to receive emails or phone calls or access the Internet. In an article for *The Atlantic*, glass is called "humankind's most important material." Douglas Main writes, "To reach you, these words were encoded into signals of light moving about 125,000 miles per second through fiber-optic cables," which climb up mountains, creep under oceans, making tracks through cities and countries, all around the globe. The glass within is thinner than a human hair and "30 times more transparent than the purest water." Glass allows us to see and be seen, hear and be heard, to illuminate our rooms and lives and thoughts.

But glass is a funny material, partially because the word itself is a general term, one that refers not to a specific chemical formula but a substance that can be manufactured according to an "endless number of recipes." Yet when we say "glass," we understand it to mean something quite specific: it's a type of material that is hard and brittle yet capable of being turned viscous and mobile with enough heat. Sometimes glass is erroneously characterized as a liquid, because even in its cooled form, it does move (albeit very slowly). Glass is not solid like rocks are solid because its molecules aren't as rigidly organized as any material with a crystalline structure. Diamonds have a crystalline structure, as does ice and hardened honey, but glass does not. While more dependable than a sheet of ice, glass is, on a molecular level, a lot less ordered.

In materials science, glass is typically considered an "amorphous solid" or as Dr. John C. Mauro puts it, glass is a "nonbinary material," neither liquid nor solid. A former researcher and inventor and current engineering and materials science professor at Penn State University, Mauro has been fascinated by glass ever since he visited the Corning Museum of Glass in New York as a six-year-old. He recalls being "captivated" by the colors and shapes. These days, he knows more than almost anyone about how glass functions, yet he retains a sense of awe for the substance. "Glass is its own thing," he says. "It breaks the mold." From a thermodynamic point of view, he explains, glass wants to become a solid. When observed on a molecular level, glass behaves more like a viscous liquid than a solid, yet we experience it like a solid because of how slowly it shifts. "Philosophically, it's interesting that we're observing glass at all," Mauro says. "We see through it, when we're looking at something else." Yet there, right under our noses, is a scientific marvel—a material that behaves in a fascinatingly unique way, a substance that resists easy categorization. It makes up our lenses, our microscopes, our telescopes, our screens, our glasses. It allows us to see the world clearly, yet so rarely do we really *see* glass.

It's this disappearing act that makes glass a strange vessel for beauty. It defies what we're taught as children about matter, that there's three states: solid, liquid, gas. Compared to other items in this book, it's practically as cheap as dirt. It's not rare by any stretch of the imagination. But glass is special despite all that.

Glass is mainly a manufactured substance. While some natural glass does exist, like obsidian and tektite, the vast majority of glass has been cooked over fires we built. As far as we can tell, glass manufacturing dates back to the Bronze Age somewhere in Mesopotamia. Some four thousand years ago, human beings began melting silica (sand or crushed quartz) and mixing it with small amounts of limestone and soda ash. According to Pliny, the invention of glass was a happy accident. The Roman historian thought it happened at a cookout on a beach with some Phoenician sailors, but since no cookfire could get hot enough to melt sand, this seems doubtful. Contemporary historians believe glass could have been discovered through experiments with ceramics or metalworking— two early crafts that called for hotter ovens and longer firing times than any loaf of bread or leg of goat.

The oldest known glass objects were used and handled like the lesser cousins of precious stones, worked cold rather than hot, chiseled rather than melted. People cut them, ground them, and set them in jewelry. At some point, our distant ancestors figured out how to cast glass in molds to produce vessels. Before anyone was blowing glass, artisans were creating glass mosaics, small mirrors, and a number of different types of vessels that could be used to store wine, perfume, drugs, and other valuable substances. Most of the glass objects that have survived from this pre-Hellenistic period are more interesting than they are beautiful. There are some graceful vases that copied the forms of Greek pottery, and there are some pretty beads that feature bright blue and yellow designs, but a lot of our early glass artifacts are rather rough. Decorations were created by slumping garish color upon garish color. Looks-wise, these objects don't hold a candle to the ceramics or the sculptures being produced at the time.

This may be because of the fragile nature of glass, but it could also be because glass was, for a very long time, considered a lesser material. When it came to art-making, glass played second fiddle to clay, stone, and metal for thousands of years (some might argue that it still does). In the ancient world, glass beads were a luxury item, but they don't appear to have had as high of a value as gold or gemstones. In an interview with *Knowable Magazine*, archaeological materials scientist Thilo Rehren said that glass "doesn't smell to me like a closely controlled royal commodity." Ancient Egyptians were perfectly happy shipping their colorful glass wares off to Greece; glass wasn't so valuable that they would have needed to hoard it. Perhaps this is because ancient people knew clay far better—they'd been working with it for thousands of years. But maybe it has something to do with the shifting nature of glass. Maybe it's always been a little unsung because we're just a little suspicious of it.

Around year zero, glass went big-time, thanks to the Romans and their regimented methods of production. Glass-blowing (a technique imported from Syria) enabled workmen (often enslaved people) to create cups and bowls much more quickly than any of the previous methods of glasswork. Glass cups could be purchased cheaply at market, and soon glass rivaled pottery in its popularity for the average Roman. Artists began experimenting more with form, creating two-faced Janus-head vases and wine bottles decorated with scenes of carnal pleasure. Builders began using glass to make windows, but since the glass was fairly murky and thick, the purpose of adding glass was probably less about illumination and more about security and insulation. We've found evidence of glass windows throughout Rome and the surrounding cities, including in the luxuriously tiled, beautifully preserved bathhouses of Pompeii.

Judging by the literature from the time period, glassmakers weren't viewed as artists but craftspeople. Generally, they made useful tools rather than luxury goods. Glass could be a marvel in the window, but when it came to the banquet hall, glass simply didn't have the same cachet as ceramics.

Nor was glass welcomed into religious rituals. The Catholic Church went so far as to forbid the use of glass chalices and plates in the sacrament of the Eucharist. In Catholicism, the bread and wine that are consumed during Mass have undergone a process called transubstantiation and thus are understood to be of Jesus's corporeal form. Eating his flesh and drinking his blood is said to preserve Catholics and make their

175

bodies ready for heaven. It's spiritual medicine. It's strangely cannibal-istic. It's too precious to be entrusted to fragile, lumpy, lowly glass, and in the ninth century, the Roman Catholic Church issued an edict that forbade the use of Eucharistic chalices made of glass (copper, bronze, wood, and brass had already been ruled out sometime in the eight cen-tury). It was far more appropriate to make a vasa sacrum (sacred vessel) out of a noble material like gold, silver, onyx, or even ivory.

Since much of the art produced in the medieval period was created in service of Christianity, this left glassmakers out in the cold. Gold and silversmiths could make chalices and platters, woodcarvers could make crosses and altarpieces, and painters were useful when it came to repre-senting the sufferings of Christ and the teachings of his father. Tapestries were necessary to warm stone walls, and clergymen could always use liturgical vestments, so there were plenty of places for fine fibers to shine. But glass? There was really only one place for it.

The oldest known stained-glass window was installed in the seventh century at St. Paul's Monastery in Jarrow, England. Archaeologist Rose-mary Cramp found the fragments of this window in 1973 and said it was "like picking up jewels." A reconstruction of this window shows a small cross made with blue, gold, green, and ivory glass. While we don't know precisely how the glass fragments were arranged, this seems like a good enough guess. In its original form, the Jarrow window wouldn't have let in too much light, but with the sun behind it, I imagine it would have glowed, a bright spot of color in the chapel walls.

The Jarrow window strikes me as something of a marvel, an act of immense creativity and devotion. Even though it's a puny, humble thing compared to the soaring panels and elaborate rose windows of the Ro-manesque and Gothic periods, the Jarrow came first. As far as we know, this could have been the seed of a movement that blooms on today. At Jarrow, there must have been some daydreaming monk who looked at a hole in the wall and thought, What if that were made of jewels? What if, instead of daylight, we let color pour down onto us? Would God approve of such fragile, bright beauty?

It must have been decided that God would approve, for the art form exploded across Europe and eventually made its way into other houses of worship, like synagogues and mosques. Stained glass, as an art form, reached its peak in Europe between 1150 and 1500. Much of what we know about the practices of glaziers and glass painters comes from the writings of Theophilus, a twelfth-century German monk who loved these objects of "inestimable beauty." Though a major reason for commissioning and building these windows had to do with religious instruction—it's traditional for stained-glass windows to show scenes from the Bible, hence the nickname, "the poor man's Bible"—there was also a real appreciation for their entertainment value and aesthetic qualities. They didn't just teach illiterate churchgoers about the lives of the saints; their "multicolored loveliness" also allowed individuals to transcend the "slime" of earth, as one abbot put it. For many people, these churches must have felt a little like heaven—at least, the heaven that was described by John in the Book of Revelation. According to his angelic-induced vision, heaven was a place with high walls and twelve gates. The walls were made of precious stones that shone blue, red, purple, green, and gold.

However, not all scenes cast in glass and lead were made purely for the glory of God. Plenty of them included portraits of the person who commissioned them, while others included images of earthly rulers. Most disturbingly, some stained-glass windows depicted demons and devils. These windows weren't created to instruct or inspire but rather to incite fear, repentance, and ideally, the giving of tithes. At the Cathedral of Our Lady of Strasbourg in France, there are several panels dedicated to the "harrowing of hell" that reveal a Hieronymus Bosch—like genius at work. The tortured human souls are carted around in wheelbarrows by their demon jailers and beaten bloody with flails and maces. Anguished, disembodied faces swim in waves of golden fire while horned, clawed, humanoid monsters frolic above. One scarlet demon even has a baby's face coming out of his belly. A similar scene at Bourges Cathedral shows Jesus prying open the jaws of a green reptilian monster to release the sinners from their prison—a far more hopeful image, though the message is still frightful. According to doctrine, hell exists and it's still full of sinners. Jesus freed some of them, the righteous, but heaven has never had an open-door policy. You could still be locked out.

The age of the lens is difficult to pinpoint, for lenses pre-date the year zero by a decent span. Optics came into its own as an area of study at the end of the first millennium in the Islamic world, where mathematicians and scientists were making great leaps in the understanding and manipulation of light. During the Renaissance, philosophers, scientists, and thinkers were all using lenses to examine the physical world—both the stars above (with the invention of the telescope in 1608) and the ground below (after the introduction of the microscope in 1625). Glass has long been seen as a material that grants literal illumination, but it's worth remembering that glass laid the groundwork for much of our metaphorical enlightenment too.

The Enlightenment was also an era that birthed the phantasmagoria, a form of theatrical entertainment that was either horrifying or hopeful, depending on how one chose to see it. Phantasmagoria were wild, eerie events during which guests paid to be terrorized by moving images of spirits, demons, and other frightening figures that were projected onto walls, smoke, or semitransparent screens. This spiritually tinged form of proto-cinema was made possible by a combination of inventions new and old, including magic lanterns, magnifying lenses, zograscopes, pepper's ghosts, and other glass-based tools that could be used to manipulate light and sight. The first phantasmagorias took place in the 1790s in a theater in post-Revolution Paris to the eerie background tunes of a glass harmonica. After waiting for a few moments in complete darkness, the audience began to see shapes emerge from the air, spectral figures that appeared to float and glide. Pale and otherworldly, these ghosts spoke, shouted, and cried. One, the Bleeding Nun, approached menacingly before retreating. Later versions of the phantasmagoria would involve the ghosts of recently deceased public figures, supposedly wrangled into submission by the powers of science. For that's how these shows were billed: as the intersection between science and religion, faith and enlightenment. They were horrible, but also a real hoot.

Phantasmagoria spread from Paris and evolved. Sometimes, these events were explanatory and showed viewers a glimpse behind the curtain, explaining how the illusions were created. Often, however, they were presented as genuine interactions with the dead, a rare piercing of the veil that separates our world from theirs that just so happened to occur in a theatrical setting. Interestingly, it didn't really matter to a lot of viewers whether what they were seeing was real. According to Tom Gunning, an art historian and film professor who studies early cinema, the appeal of the phantasmagoria was less about faith and connection and more about the sense of suspended disbelief. "One of the main things that defines the phantasmagoria is that suddenly things which were before taken very solemnly—death and ghosts and life after death—became a form of entertainment," he explains. The people who went to see these light shows were looking for titillation, spectacle, and frisson. Talking to the dead wasn't a religious experience nor was it a chance to learn from those who had passed on. Instead, he says, "It was a sensuous experience. A thrill."

These fantastical events coincided with the rise of the circus as a form of entertainment. There were suddenly many places one could go to feel awed, confused, and overcome—you didn't need to rely on your local preacher anymore. This marks the development of a "modern state of mind" defined by its fascination with uncertainty, says Gunning. "It became P. T. Barnum's stock-in-trade. This idea of 'did you see that?' It didn't matter if it was real. It mattered if you talked about it." Over the phone, Gunning draws a direct line between these early modernist events and the twenty-first-century explosion of reality television. He asks, "Is it real or not? Does it matter?" Judging by our continued embrace of the genre, I think we can safely say no.

Although we've come a long way from the freak shows and funhouse mirrors of the nineteenth century, we're still begging to be both fooled and enlightened. Humans love a spectacle. Out of all the players in the material world, I think glass is the ultimate trickster. Although glass can illuminate rooms and lives, it can also distort reality and obscure the truth. Much like how photography can appear as a record of true events while cropping out essential context, glass sharpens our vision but not necessarily our understanding. Contemporary life relies on glass more than most of us realize; it's not just in our windshields and windows, it's also in the fiber-optic cables that run under our feet, pulsing with meaning. "Right now we're looking at each other via glass screens," Dr. Mauro said during our interview, making me intensely aware of the tenuous nature of our connection. We were speaking over Zoom, a service that allows people to video chat over the Internet, using our respective laptops in our rooms hundreds of miles apart. He continued, "We wouldn't have information screens without glass. All of this is being transmitted via light signal through really thin pieces of glass we call fiber optics." Without glass, he said, we wouldn't have modern architecture, artificial lighting, natural lighting, cars, and most crucially, so much information.

Mauro stresses the benefits of glass. It enables us to store vaccines, examine cells, and gaze at the stars. But he argues that glass is, like all technology, "neutral" at its core. "When I think about fiber optics, I think about all the good things it's done to enable communication, but it's also done a lot of harm," he said. People use social media to "spread lies and hate." We use glass to tell our individual truths, but we can also use it to create false narratives. I wouldn't have been able to get the coronavirus vaccine without glass vials, but we also wouldn't have seen such rapid-fire spread of anti-vaccine propaganda if we didn't have glass screens in our pockets. We wouldn't be able to talk about the end of the world on social media without fiber-optic communication. We wouldn't be able to see scenes of war in Ukraine or Afghanistan or Syria. We wouldn't have the same sort of knowledge about atrocities happening in faraway places, and that would severely limit our ability to send aid. Without glass tubes, German glassblower Heinrich Geissler wouldn't have been able to observe cathode rays, Ernest Rutherford wouldn't have been able to discover the power contained in an atom's nucleus, we wouldn't have nuclear reactors or bombs. We wouldn't know that, when an atomic bomb goes off, it has the power to turn sand into glass, raining asteroid-like shards on the ground for people to find decades later. Maybe we wouldn't be so uncertain, so unstable in our convictions. Maybe I would still have faith.

I would not want to live in a world without windows, goblets, beads, and glasses. I'd be unable to see so much of the beauty of the world without my lightweight tortoiseshell frames. Yet there are many times when I realize I don't want to live in this world either. Here, young men can become radicalized online within a few short months and then live-stream their mass murders on social-media platforms like Twitch. Here, my little girl isn't safe at daycare, not from coronavirus and not from gun violence. In this world, we've devised miraculous tools to observe galaxies billions of light-years away, but we somehow can't manage to see ourselves clearly, our lonely and sad elderly, our violent and alienated young people, our neighbors who are hurting, and our unhoused people who live at a constant risk. While I agree with much of what Mauro says, I don't know if glass is truly neutral or if any technology can be said to be neutral. I think calling it neutral is a shorthand, like calling glass a solid. It's far more ambiguous than that. Guns are not neutral technology, nor are nuclear weapons, nor is glass. They are not bad, but they do need to be examined and considered carefully. Technology isn't inert. It's not a stone; it's a language. And like a language, we must accept its many uses. We can say prayers; we can tell lies. Sometimes, we do it in the same breath.

But that's human history. It's a chain of events, one leading to another, sometimes ending in disaster, sometimes ending in beauty. When you look at it from one angle, it can appear full of beauty, prisms of color dancing across eons. From another, it's so much hellfire.

9.

BONE WHITE, PAPER THIN

*On porcelain dishes, pale faces, and
the complicated act of setting a table*

When Tasha Graff was a little girl, her grandmother never talked about her family. But every Thanksgiving, without fail, Ingeborg (her 101-year-old grandmother) would open the glass-fronted cabinet, take down the good dishes, and set the table with pieces of porcelain that "escaped" from Nazi Germany. "Her family didn't make it out, but the dishes did," Graff says.

Graff is close to her grandmother, so she knows a bit about her life, and she's traveled to Germany to see her distant relatives who now live there, including the descendants of cousin Emma, the woman who turned in Ingeborg's parents to Nazi officers. Ingeborg's father, Sigmund, was a middle-class Jewish man, respected in his community. He was able to afford fine things like nice dishes and cabinets. He had the first car in Heidelberg, according to Ingeborg. He was law-abiding, hesitant about leaving Germany illegally. "My grandmother said to me many times that he couldn't believe his country would turn on him," Graff says. But soon enough, Sigmund realized what was looming. Hitler had already seized power and begun rearmament. In 1937, Ingeborg's father decided to send his nice things to America, and some of his children. First, his son went. Then, his daughter. Ingeborg arrived in New York City in late December 1938. "Her brother was waiting for her," Graff says. "He told her she had a bad haircut." The crates of dishes and furniture began to arrive soon after. Then, nothing. No one else could leave. "The only record we have is that Sigmund was registered as a Jew on October 22, 1940," says Graff.

The dishes are delicate things, pale and light with pretty little pink flowers and gold trim. Ingeborg has never been much of a homemaker and doesn't care at all for a well-set table, but still, these things matter. They're relics of another time and place. Using them is a way to honor the dead without speaking of them, though Ingeborg doesn't put it that way. For her, the choice to use the dishes is simple, obvious. "They're the family dishes," she told Graff. "It's the nicest thing we have."

After Tasha told me this story, I told her mine in exchange—not that I had very much to tell. My mother's family was from Germany. They left before World War II, years before the Nazis rose to power. But I still have relatives living in Austria. I've been to visit their tidy little home on the outskirts of Linz. When I was in college, I asked my grandmother as directly as I dared about our ancestry. I wanted to know about our blood ties and their involvement with bloodshed. She wouldn't tell me anything. I remember how her face closed off before issuing a vehement denial. Of course there were no Nazis in our family. How could I think such a thing?

My family is very large and very spread out. I have only one clear memory of my grandmother's silver-rimmed porcelain plates—a Christmas dinner, decades ago, ham and pineapple and ambrosia salad. I've been told the dishes are now in Alabama, with my cousin and her husband, but I can't imagine I'll ever see them again. Although my mother has inherited a china cabinet with claw feet and a little brass lock, it houses no ancestral set of dishes, just an eclectic collection of objects she likes. There's a dish from Tokyo, six painted eggs from Poland, and a green porcelain teapot my dad bought her when he was stationed in Scotland. My cabinets are similar though far less cleanly displayed. They're filled with dishes that don't match but still please me, mostly bone white and river blue. It's a color palette many people associate with folksy Scandinavian decor or fussy formal Americana, despite its deep roots in the Islamic world.

Porcelain dishes and silver cutlery, lace-edged tablecloths and claw-foot tables, silk rugs and crystal goblets—these are some of the beautiful things that were traditionally passed down from generation to generation. For most of the modern era, porcelain has been a common heirloom, a traditional wedding gift to a new couple, and a material that generally signified sophistication, upward class mobility, and maturity. During the nineteenth and twentieth centuries, owning a special set of porcelain dishes meant something, a form of consumerist propaganda for the middle-class self.

In America, this is no longer true. Fussy dishes have fallen out of favor, and family meals are becoming less common as fewer people are willing (or able) to take the time to cook, sit, and eat. Now, we're more likely to see porcelain in the bathroom than on the table. We're more likely to see it on television, winking brightly at us from the mouths of our most chaotic reality stars and magnetic actors, their smiles fixed and brightened with layers of glue and clay. We still use porcelain, and we still consume it, but it's no longer revered in the same way. The porcelain object I interact with most often is probably my toilet.

The meaning of this material has changed; porcelain no longer evokes the nuclear family sitting down to an uncomplicated-yet-wholesome mother-cooked dinner of two vegetables, a grain, and a serving of meat. I used to think this was a good thing. Mothers, I thought, had been liberated from all that.

But for Graff, the family dishes mean more now, in this post-pandemic world, than they ever did before. They went from being a source of slight curiosity to something she hopes to inherit. She used to consider them objects that would weigh her down. Now she sees the importance of having a set table and survivors gathered around it.

I'm beginning to come around to this way of thinking too. In the past five years, I've begun to crave a traditionalism I never wanted before, complete with communal dinners and nicely set tables. I've begun to understand the value of rituals that I previously dismissed as unnecessary or outdated. I can see the deeper logic now behind a big wedding with perfectly coordinated tablescapes and fresh bouquets of flowers, and I've gained a new respect for ceremonial gift-giving. Whether this is due to the pandemic or motherhood, I've yet to parse out.

Not all fine china is porcelain, and not all porcelain is "true." There are several different definitions for the material. In China, porcelain is distinguished by its bell-like sound. "Resonant when struck," explains the *Encyclopedia Britannica*. European countries tend to define porcelain by its transparency—a fine china cup allows light to flow through its fine-grained, non-porous edge. According to some, the only true porcelain is that which includes kaolin, a type of clay mineral that we use in toothpaste, paint, cosmetics, organic farming, and ceramics. However, many people consider "bone china"—a British invention that uses cattle-bone ash mixed into the clay—to be of equal quality. There are chemical differences between these various porcelains, but for the average consumer they matter little. If presented with a new set of dishes, I doubt most of us would ask whether it was true porcelain made solely with materials dug from the earth or a similar substance baked with burnt cow bones. We'd just marvel at their thin edges and slick glaze.

The first pieces of porcelain were fired over two thousand years ago in the mountains of China. What made porcelain a distinct form of pottery was the introduction of kaolin into the mineral mixture. It took hundreds of years of experimenting to create the distinctive style of Chinese ceramics that would come to obsess Europeans, with its starkly white background and delicate cobalt-blue brush painting. While English speakers have often used the shorthand "china" to refer to our nice dishes, it was more commonly known as "porcelain," a name that originated from a comment made by the famous Italian trader Marco Polo. He noted that the dishware was as smooth, light, and pale as a cowrie shell, and so he called it by the shell's Italian name—porcellana. This is also similar to a slang term for female genitalia, and according to some sources, it derived from the word for a sow's belly—or maybe a young pig. While the etymology is murky, it does strike me as funny that we humans find so many ways to insert our obsession with genitals into every sphere of life, from the garden to the dinner table.

But long before porcelain made its way to Italy, it arrived in the Middle East. In 851, one merchant wrote of "a fine clay" from China that was used to make drinking vessels so fine that "one can see the liquid contained in them." While people in this region weren't using porcelain to make their pots—they didn't have the fuel to fire such hot kilns, for one, and they didn't have access to kaolin, for another—they were still able to make finely decorated earthenware in traditionally revered colors, including cobalt blue. Some historians have speculated that the blue-and-white color scheme that would come to define porcelain in the European imagination originated in the Islamic world and was a result of many years of trading back and forth between cultures. Artistic practices don't often stay within the borders of a nation-state, no matter how hard the powerful try. Inspiration moves across cultures, countries, and times, muddying the waters in a most beautiful way and obliterating the myths told about superiority and tribalism.

While there are similarities in the westward spread of porcelain and the movement of silk, it wasn't quite as easy for other cultures to seize the secrets of clay as it was for them to plant mulberry groves. During the Yuan dynasty, merchants carried porcelain vessels, plates, and figurines along the Silk Road to trading cities in southern Spain and Italy. Medieval Europeans were immediately obsessed with these light, smooth, intricately painted pieces. They knew how to make pottery, but they couldn't make anything like *that*. Chinese-imported ceramics took on magical qualities in the European imagination. It was said that porcelain cups could neutralize poison, which made them very appealing to any rulers fearing assassination. In order to preserve an ordinary teacup, metalworkers would sometimes craft elaborate silver and gold cages and stems, turning what would have been a cheap little cup into a precious (albeit gaudy) wineglass. Known as "white gold," porcelain objects remained prohibitively expensive for most households until the eighteenth century. They were a highly desirable but not particularly accessible object of fascination for the upper class.

Meanwhile, in England, potters were using the remains of boiled, stripped, and burned cattle bones to create their own translucent plates. Bone china production began in 1748 and continues to this day. It turns out that bone ash was a genius ingredient that made for even stronger, thinner products. While some found it grisly (and some still do—vegans won't buy bone china) this innovation spread quickly around the globe and now you can find bone china factories in India, Russia, China, Japan, and elsewhere. A few artists have even experimented with making bone china from the remains of human bodies, which could be either an innovative way to memorialize a loved one or the stuff of horror novels, depending how you look at it.

As more workshops began to pop up across the European continent, a number of different styles began to compete for marketplace supremacy. The most fashionable pieces came from France, where Madame de Pompadour, mistress to King Louis XV, used her considerable wealth and whimsical tastes to influence the artistic development at Vincennes and later Sèvres. The lady favored rose hues, and Pompadour pink became a favorite color for nobles shopping for gilded tureens or fanciful vases. Porcelain was so popular that dinner itself transformed during this time period. There were suddenly all these marvelous products that could be used to transform the dinner table into a miniature landscape, complete with elephant-shaped pitchers, boat-shaped tureens, and asparagus-shaped plates made specifically for serving buttered spring vegetables. The idea that a dining table could be representative of the hosts' personalities and values began to spread beyond European nobility and into the houses of American merchants. A new era of eating had begun, one that was prettier and more public than ever before.

During the nineteenth century, the shift toward more stylized living spaces became widespread throughout the Western world as the middle class began to gain economic power and women were, for the first time, encouraged to stay inside instead of working in the fields or factories. This created an entire class of person—the housewife—whose raison d'être was caretaking, nourishing, and beautifying. During the Victorian era, there was a massive boom of consumer goods, and it became the job of the matriarch to buy them. While women were still unable to participate in many areas of society, they were encouraged to shop, attend dinners, and host parties. Fashion, previously only of great importance to the very richest members of society, came to play a larger role in the everyday lives of women in America and abroad. This is also when the lifestyle publication took off. For the first time, there were multiple magazines dedicated to women's interests, including *Godey's Lady's Book*, which held up Queen Victoria as the very model of femininity and elegance. The British monarch had everything—diamond tiaras, silk lace gowns, a storybook romance, a line of porcelain named after her, and a drug habit.

During the day, Victoria purportedly chewed gum containing cocaine to give her a bit of bounce, and she often sipped laudanum—a beverage containing a tincture of opium. Maybe this is why she didn't think it was a terribly big deal to begin introducing new users to the drug. She drank it, so how bad could it be? Or maybe she just didn't care what happened to people in other parts of the world. Either way, it was under Victoria's leadership that the British East India Company started a drug epidemic in China, smuggling in tens of thousands of chests per year.

They did it to correct the long-standing trade imbalance between the two empires. China had many desirable products that appealed to Victorian-era consumers. Thanks in part to a growing temperance movement, the British were totally obsessed with tea. It had even replaced gin as the breakfast beverage of choice. Tea drinking had become a ritualized event, one that came with an incredible number of accessories, from decorative teapots to mahogany tea caddies to silver tea urns. Many high-class ladies even had their own personalized tea blends. Tea came from China, as did the most beautiful porcelain (and the softest silk, the nicest paper, and such refined lacquer boxes). Unfortunately for the British, their own products weren't nearly so popular in China. When it came to luxury exports, Chinese merchants were able to set the price, and the British were forced to pay up. Perhaps if the populace just happened to get addicted to a substance produced in British-controlled India, well, maybe that could all change. Maybe they could get cheaper tea for their tea parties, cheaper porcelain for their tables, cheaper silk for their dresses.

Opium, porcelain, tea, silk, silver. "It's all interconnected," says Karina Corrigan of the Peabody Essex Museum in Salem, Massachusetts. The museum has one of the richest collections of Chinese export art in the world, including large porcelain urns, small porcelain crabs, and silver-caged porcelain goblets. These pieces attest to the continued popularity of Chinese ceramics on the American dinner table, as well as the tangled, damaged relationship between empires. While other museums have struggled with the question of whether they should return looted treasures to their home countries, the Peabody Essex has a slightly different problem. When I'm gazing past the glass case and at the shelves full of decorative porcelain plates, figurines, and candelabras, I'm missing a huge part of the story behind these pieces. They weren't just made for foreign tastes, thus turning them into fascinating hybrids of aesthetics and projected desires, they were also part of a larger system of exploitation. "Opium had always lurked in the background of the story we told about global trade, but we had never fully addressed the truly central role it played," explained Jeanne Goswami, formerly of the Peabody Essex Museum. "We felt that the resonance with our present-day opioid crisis made that silence untenable."

To address this darker side of art history, several years ago, the Peabody Essex unveiled an installation, *Every Eleven Minutes*, which seeks to explain how opium deaths are linked to the institution's exquisite collection of pottery. Millions of people in China and India, explains the film, had their lives ruined after British and American merchants smuggled illegal drugs into the country. In the American imagination, opium would go on to become a problem of immigrants, laborers, and sex workers, despite the fact that some of the heaviest users of opiates were rich, tea-drinking ladies. The typical American opiate addict during the eighteenth and nineteenth centuries was middle- or upper-class, white, and female. They obtained their drugs in the same place that many of us still get our fix—at the doctor's office. Often, they were prescribed opium for their "women's issues," including menstrual cramps, morning sickness, and something termed "general anxiety" or, as it was often called, hysteria.

The paradigm of the overmedicated housewife continued well into the twentieth and twenty-first centuries. While women made steady gains in their quest for equal rights, misogyny has not been entirely eradicated from American life. Many women are forced out of the workplace upon becoming pregnant, or otherwise penalized for their decision to have a family. Women in America are still asked to shoulder most of the housework, even while working equal hours at the office. "Having it all" has always been a rather dubious goal. Then, as now, housewives had both too much (stuff, duties, chores, children) and not enough (agency, money, freedom). Drugs can ease pain while providing a false sense of balance, giving the harried homemaker a whitewashed contentment.

Drugs also funded American and British prosperity—they still do, loath as most of us are to admit it. The myth of America is that our country was built by free, hardworking immigrants who pulled themselves up by their bootstraps. In reality, America was molded and shaped by decisions of the wealthiest members of society, people who inherited their money or exploited their way to the top.

Germans loved their porcelain. Augustus the Strong, eighteenth-century ruler of Saxony in Germany, was so smitten with the stuff that he diagnosed himself with Porzellankrankheit or "porcelain madness." Augustus built palaces to house his collection, which included more than 29,000 works from China and Japan. He owned thousands of blue-and-white bowls, cups, saucers, urns, and vases. He also collected figurines (both animal and human) and dozens of other art objects, some brightened with paint and gold, some glazed plain and white, many of which are still on display in Dresden at the Porzellansammlung (porcelain gallery). His varied collection of imports served as inspiration for the factory at Meissen, founded by Augustus around 1710. More than two hundred years later, Meissen would become a major source of inspiration for mass murderer and Nazi occultist Heinrich Himmler.

Himmler was a true believer in Nazi ideology. He crafted much of it himself. He was born into Catholicism, but in the 1920s he lost all interest in the Church and began building his own religion that was based on a mixture of mythology, paganism, and white supremacy. He was obsessed with returning Germany to some imagined, impossible past where "Aryan" people lived in harmony with nature, celebrating the solstices, worshiping the land, and respecting their ancestors. He was deeply attracted to the idea that German people were connected to the soil itself and that part of their status as uber-folk came out of this relationship. Porcelain, a smooth, white surface made from the landscape, must have felt like an easy symbol for him to corrupt.

In 1940, Himmler set about moving a small Nazi-founded porcelain factory named Porzellan Manufaktur Allach from its original location in Allach to the concentration camp at Dachau. It had been overseen by Karl Diebitsch (a painter who also designed some Nazi uniforms and insignia) and Theodor Kärner (a porcelain artist who had previously worked at Meissen). At first, the Allach factory made mainly art objects like medallions, animals (stags, dogs, foxes), and historical figurines (Frederick the Great on horseback), but eventually they manufactured pieces of white dinnerware for the middle and upper classes of German society. While not every worker at the factory was enslaved (some of the Christian German craftspeople were displaced to the region and given wages for their work), many of them were victims of the concentration camps. One of the most famous designs to come out of this factory was the Julleuchter. These candleholders were made specifically for Himmler to give as gifts to high-ranking members of the SS during the waning days of December. They were used on the darkest nights of the year as part of a neo-pagan feast.

Most of the pieces that the Nazis produced were fairly plain and unimpressive, according to Suzanne Marchand, author of *Porcelain: A History from the Heart of Europe*. "Part of this is because it's cheaper to produce a plain pattern, but it's also an aesthetic," she says. "It's what I call 'stripped classicism.' You strip it down to its bare bones." Hitler liked this look very much, but Marchand points out that some of Hitler's "head honchos" including Himmler had "just awful taste, even worse than Hitler's." Of course, they believed the Allach factory was making beautiful, elegant, and tasteful objects. They thought their strutting stags were chic as could be. One of the most popular porcelain models was known as Die Fechter (The Fencer), and it depicted a muscled youth, shirtless, leaning on his épée. He was, of course, white. "White porcelain is the embodiment of the German soul," stated the first Allach catalogue. The aesthetic was an attempt to remind their citizens of the neoclassical works of the late eighteenth and early nineteenth centuries, which were created using materials like porcelain, marble, and lead-white paint. Theirs was a manufactured artistic movement, done in a "very grandiose fashion," says Marchand, thus destroying the delicacy and subtlety that made German art of the Romantic period more technically successful, not to mention more aesthetically pleasing.

Not everyone feels this way. There is a serious market for porcelain made by slave labor in the Dachau concentration camp. While there are several dealers selling porcelain from Dachau online, Marchand believes that much of it is likely fake, modern replicas of concentration-camp memorabilia and dinnerware. There's even an artist, Charles Krafft, who was celebrated for years as an iconoclastic figure in the Seattle art scene for his subversive ceramics, many of which incorporated Nazi imagery (think: a blue-and-white teapot in the shape of Hitler's head). Jen Graves, writing for *The Stranger* in 2013, said Krafft's series *Disasterware* was seen as "injecting the homey crafts of European ceramic painting with violence and catastrophic events . . . poking holes in the fascist and totalitarian ideologies of the 20th century." Yet as Graves goes on to show, Krafft wasn't kidding. He was active on social media, posting about his Holocaust beliefs, and participated in discussions on neo-Nazi podcasts. He was a Holocaust denier and an open fascist who reportedly "laughed in private" at the "liberal-leaning establishment [he's] fooled with his art."

Yet even after his unmasking, Krafft continued to find a market—

albeit niche—for his work up until his death in 2020. Some still consider him an important artist, despite his plainly stated position as a Holocaust denier—or perhaps because of it. It is still possible to buy his work online and Krafft is still popular at white supremacist rallies, leading one reporter to conclude that "what cred" Krafft lost after being outed as a neo-Nazi "he has more than recovered among white nationalists."

This shouldn't be surprising to anyone. There are plenty of neo-Nazis operating in plain sight in America. There are quite a few people who would happily serve their pork chops on swastika plates. Several years ago, I attended a gun show in Bangor, Maine, as part of a travel assignment for a local publication. After spending a few minutes in the shooting gallery with a BB gun, I found myself browsing a tray of antique daggers—silver, pretty things with mother-of-pearl handles—when I stopped short. Next to that section of decorative vintage weaponry was a tray of equally polished Nazi memorabilia. There were lethal-looking knives and gold badges, as well as several patches. Behind the plastic folding table laden with these collectables sat a white man with a long black beard and a camouflage jacket. He caught my eye and smiled, big and friendly. I don't think I smiled back, but I know I didn't say anything to him. I felt queasy and complicit, guilty of looking too hard at something too dark. I went home soon after.

Whether made with kaolin or a more modern substitute, the story of porcelain is a story of whiteness. Although there are several qualities that have made this material so desirable, potter and historian Edmund de Waal argues that the beauty of porcelain can't be separated from its lack of color. Certainly, porcelain is loved by some for its sonorous qualities, and yes, it does have a tactile beauty (de Waal: "It feels clean. Your hands feel cleaner after you have used it.") And of course, porcelain is sterile and difficult to stain, which is why we can use it for teeth and toilets. But above all, porcelain is pale. Not just pale: "It is white, returning to white," writes de Waal. "It feels white . . . it is full of anticipation, of possibility. It is a material that records every movement of thinking, every change of thought." Porcelain is, in this telling, a form of magic that can turn the insubstantial (thoughts, light, cleanliness, sound, the ideal of beauty itself) into the tangible. For those who worship whiteness and brightness, for those who dream of landscapes erased by snow, walls clean of blemishes, tablecloths and silver flatware and clinking of crystal glasses, porcelain is a miracle substance. It is refinement itself.

I understand the appeal of bright-white dishware, translucent and ringing. People around the globe have coveted the resonant, translucent, seashell-thin beauty of fine porcelain. Chinese emperors valued their light, bright dishes too. But in the hands of Europeans and Americans, porcelain's whiteness became oppressive, particularly once they made the link between this material and the favorite of so many classical sculptors: Italian marble. Since it was generally accepted at this point that the ancient Greeks and Romans used white stone to depict supposedly "pure" and objective images of beauty, it was easy for white supremacists to use porcelain, a cheaper material to work with that was more plentiful, as a tool of propaganda. In addition to the white plates, white figurines, and white home goods, Marchand also points toward the eighteenth-century craze for porcelain doll heads (with "certain white complexion" and "ruby cheeks") as having had a certain sinister effect on Western beauty standards. "You can't prove this, of course," she hedges. "But I think it contributes to a certain expectation of female beauty." Though the idea of a fair-skinned maiden with a modest blush wasn't new, Marchand believes the availability of doll heads helped to disperse and solidify this standard among Victorian parents and children. At the very least, it worked to shore up white supremacy rather than dismantle it.

Although I've written dozens of articles about colors, pigments, and the emotional associations we form with certain hues, I've never felt particularly comfortable writing about white. I'm torn about the meaning of the color. On one hand, I find doll heads eerie and Nazi-owned ceramics revolting. I believe Herman Melville when he writes that whiteness has nihilistic qualities, a "dumb blankness, full of meaning . . . a colorless, all-color of atheism from which we shrink." I think white can be horrifying—it's the color of bleached bones, suffocating cold, and the "heartless voids and immensities of the universe" that "stabs us from behind with the thought of annihilation" (so writes Melville). And yet, I find myself wanting to differentiate between white and Caucasian, white and whiteness. There is nothing sordid about skin color, nothing horrible about a person who is pale. There's nothing inherently terrible about sensory information, not even a descending white fog is terrible in itself. It's what happens with it, what is channeled through it. White people are just people, a white cup is just a cup, white snow is just snow. It's what happens next that matters.

In my research on porcelain, I eventually came across images of a soup bowl that supposedly belonged to Hitler's partner, Eva Braun. It has her monogram at the top in red, and the rim of the bowl is decorated with a delicate pattern of Edelweiss and other blooms. This rim of green, blue, and pink looks like a crown of flowers set atop a white background. It is pretty, I think. It's hard to tell. It wouldn't look amiss on a contemporary "cottagecore" mood board, an image of aspirational, twee femininity. The object itself isn't evil, yet the idea of eating off Braun's plate makes me feel sick. It doesn't need to look as menacing as the swastika-emblazoned Jul plates or Krafft's violent *Disasterware* series with its blue-and-white hand grenades and floral machine guns. Its aura is just as tainted. Maybe a dish like this is never just a dish; once you know its background, it becomes capable of holding more than food. It presents a series of cultural associations that have been built up slowly over time. A plain white plate setting on a restaurant table tells a vastly different tale from that of a chipped piece of Fiestaware pulled from a dorm cabinet. Studies have found that the color of a dish can even influence how full you feel after a meal.

As an American of German, Irish, and Czech descent, whiteness (Caucasian-ness) is a huge part of my identity. Baked into that white identity is a knowledge of violence. The conditions that have allowed me to prosper during my lifetime were created purposefully by people who were, like me, white. I don't feel personally guilty about this, nor am I particularly ashamed of my ancestors. I suspect if I had access to the specifics of every single family member, I would feel repulsed at many of their actions. Lacking that, I'm left with a sense of ambivalence about the people who birthed my grandparents and their grandparents and their grandparents. I don't loathe my ancestors, but I'm not proud of them either. I don't feel particularly connected to them. I think that's what happens when you close off discussion of family history, good and bad. You create people who feel estranged. To some, being unattached can feel like freedom. If you aren't part of any particular lineage of violence, you're not responsible for undoing any harms. You don't owe anything to anyone.

I want to owe people though. I want to be more entangled in community and history. I want to break bread with people and feel the glow of hospitality, the warmth that comes with giving and receiving. I want to set a table for friends and welcome people in. And truthfully, I want this table to look a certain way. I want there to be flowers and blue-and-white vintage dishes and a rustic tablecloth—things that might signal to some a certain type of Caucasian-ness, a certain set of values and beliefs that I do not hold. I don't believe in the superiority of any group of people over another, and I don't want anyone to be forced into inhabiting a gendered role. I want people to be responsible to one another and to treat others with kindness; I want a community without hierarchy.

I'm uncomfortable with elements of my aesthetic preferences because they betray my secret conservatism. I see now the importance of family dinners, the significance of ritualized events, and the emotional and physical benefits of homemaking. I've become slightly fanatical about vintage dinnerware—I collect Villeroy & Boch porcelain from Germany, pressed-glass goblets and tumblers, and Finnish-made Moomin mugs. I have a blue-and-white Delft dish that I use for earrings, and I treasure my pair of Herend porcelain rabbit figurines that a friend bought me as a surprise. I have a Chinese porcelain vase (cobalt blue and brilliant white) and I've inherited several pieces of flower-painted porcelain from a now-defunct Czech factory. These things are important to me for a variety of different reasons, but it doesn't escape my notice that they're mainly European in origin and many of them feature the same kind of delicate flowers as Braun's disgusting dish.

It's possible to train yourself to appreciate new forms of beauty and it's possible to fall out of love with an object. It's even possible to disavow an aesthetic. I could buy a new set of dishes made ethically in America, fired at a local kiln. I could visit estate sales until I found a bone-china dining set that had been owned by some now-deceased family, an unwanted and anonymous group of plates onto which I could project whatever fantasy I can devise. But I don't want to do any of these things. It would feel false and futile—wasteful too.

After I became a mother, I began to look for other parents who were approaching the project of raising children and homemaking with critical eyes and generous hearts. It's a hard thing to navigate, this desire to create a beautiful, calm domestic space that feels linked to one's heritage without reproducing the more damaging aspects of history. Meg Conley, author of the popular newsletter *homeculture*, wrestles with these issues frequently and publicly in her writing. Conley grew up in the Mormon church in Southern California with Midwestern parents who loved to set a fine table, complete with German-made porcelain. Like me, she's grown away from her previous religious beliefs yet retains a deep reverence for tradition, ritual, and caretaking. From this position, she's written extensively about the fascist impulses behind modern kitchen design and the ways in which home can be a prison for women. She's also become aware of how women help uphold certain ideals behind the scenes, safe in the comforts of their home. "America started as a heaven-building project," she points out. "We've been trying to engineer heaven since the colonists got here. We've been justifying things like genocide and slavery saying if we are going to build heaven, we might have to do a little hell." According to Conley, even recent American wars call upon the figure of the American housewife as justification for aggression. This fabled woman is a figure of purity. Her house is clean, her children are quiet, her table is set, her food is wholesome.

"When you are raised Mormon in America, you're raised to believe that the home is apart from the economy," Conley explains to me over the phone. But she's come to realize that "nothing is ever innocent." This particular version of womanhood also excludes men from caretaking and the emotional joys of raising and feeding children. When it's always up to the woman to feather the nest, men don't get the satisfaction that comes from nurturing. This paradigm also omits people with differently composed families, people who aren't heterosexual, and of course people who aren't white and moneyed. It cuts out all kinds of people who need to be included, people who would benefit from giving and taking care, sharing, and receiving the grace of community.

But Conley has found a way to accept these dueling narratives. Simply put, she believes in the importance of feeding people. "As I've been interrogating home culture, there have been times when I've felt like burning everything down." But, she adds, beauty matters to her, and she sees great beauty in the act of breaking bread. "People who want to exploit will always use things that are beautiful for ugly means," she says. "I still have to remind myself that the propaganda I find on my countertop or sitting in my cupboard, that came second to the original use."

First came the food, the bread, the cup. First, even before we began speaking of Eve or Eva, we knew about mothers and their beauty. While that figure can be polluted and manipulated, there's always going to be value in the act of caring. You don't need to be a woman to do it. You certainly don't need fine plates to do it, but they can help create a sense of reverence for the beautiful and mundane ritual of eating together. They can signal that this space, woven into the fabric of the world and its terrible history, is an important one. It doesn't need to be bleached pure to be wholesome and nourishing. Nothing ever does.

10.

THE EXHALATIONS OF THE EARTH
*On marble statues, engineered stones,
white lungs, and small lambs*

I went to visit the dead boy because I was sick with dread. In a room with big windows, a beautiful boy lay on a piece of rough white stone. His figure was slender and delicate, his head thrown back and his eyes blank and half-closed. As I moved around the sculpture, the boy's hard skin glimmered, the marble surface catching the light and sending it back into my retinas. He was luminous and lovely. His body pale as milk, each hair a tender curl. Though he'd been carved out of marble, he looked as though he'd be soft to the touch, his skin would wear the imprint of my fingers were I to reach out and grasp his cold limbs. I didn't do it, but I wanted to. Instead, I left the museum, but I knew, from the moment I first laid eyes on him, that I would be back to visit *The Dead Pearl Diver*.

I moved to Maine from Cambridge, Massachusetts, when I was in my mid-twenties. I had taken a terrible job as a managing editor of an alt-weekly-style magazine called *Transmit*. This position was the worst I have ever held. Alongside the other young members of the staff, I was routinely subjected to verbal harassment and bullying both sexual and non from the owner/founder, a man who went by the name of Freaky

Rick. This job was hell, and at first, I thought the city might be hell for me too. It didn't have the culture of Cambridge or Boston, let alone New York or London or any of the other cities I had considered for my future home. Portland was colder than I had expected, and lonely. Maine is notoriously unfriendly to new transplants, particularly ones from Massachusetts. This decision, which had seemed like such a good idea, such a big adventure, was quickly turning sour. I wasn't sure I wanted to live in Maine. When I was working at *Transmit*, I didn't want to *live* anywhere. I had entered one of the worst depressive phases of my life, and while I didn't attempt suicide, I acted with a passive sort of recklessness that invited injury.

When I am miserable, I often feel estranged from the experience of beauty yet deeply hungry for it. I lack the momentum to seek out beautiful sights, sounds, smells, or tastes, though I know I need them to return to myself. The pearl diver came to me; that's how it felt. The Portland Museum of Art was a few blocks away from my office, and while I never had an occasion to visit for work—Freaky Rick was uninterested in art museums and instead preferred "cool" and "underground" art forms, like tattoos—I found the quiet, chilled halls of the small city museum incredibly soothing. My office was usually flooded with loud music from an act that Freaky Rick was looking to sign (he also ran an agency for local musicians) and I found it hard to think while he was there and the music was blaring.

I returned to the museum, Wednesday after Wednesday (it was free on Wednesdays) because my world felt so ugly, small, and disappointing. Mushrooms grew from the grout in my bathroom, and black mold appeared around the windows, but our landlord was always busy and rent was, at least, cheap. At work, I spent my hours editing edgy pieces of music writing and writing joke-bloated columns on food, bands, and alcohol that ran with no byline. I didn't want anyone to know how much of the magazine I wrote every month, because a lot of it was terrible, produced last-minute when one of the underpaid writers inevitably failed to submit their work. I knew it was a matter of time before I got fired. Freaky Rick had threatened to fire me more than once, and I'd watched as other employees were ruthlessly dismissed for seemingly minor reasons. But I needed the job, so I held on and tried to cope the best I could.

Seeing a sculpture, the same one, over and over, felt like a more worthwhile activity than how I usually spent my lunch hour. When I wasn't hunched over the computer, I'd usually go out and get drunk with my coworkers before returning shakily to the office. Sometimes, we'd wake ourselves up by snorting lines of crushed orange Adderall off a CD case in the supply closet. We didn't have enough money for cocaine. Maybe if we did, I would have preferred white powder to fluorescent, but I doubt it. Even then, I was aware of the cocaine trade's body count and its bloody history. It never held much glamour for me.

Visiting the art museum was a healthier habit, though it was lonelier too. Over time, I came to appreciate the finer details of the piece, like how Benjamin Paul Akers created such delicate netting to hide the boy's groin from sight, or how he sanded smooth the flesh on his arms. I came to love how the boy's long, wavy hair fanned out like a halo behind his head. I noticed his hairless face and his long fingers and toes. I saw how the light made his limbs, sprawled long, look like they had been rubbed with oil, and how the rock he lay upon was so rough in comparison to his skin. He was a gorgeous boy, dead at work, drowned in pursuit of marine beauty. He must have stayed too long underwater, seeking mollusks and their elusive treasures. I didn't consciously compare his world of physical labor to my own abusive workplace, but I suppose I did find some comfort in his morbid form. He looked so peaceful and clean, so free.

It was only later that I came to understand the full context for the piece. The sculptor, Akers, a Maine native who trained throughout Italy, showed the tragedy that happens when young people are sent out to seek their fortunes and are rewarded for physical risks. A member of the Romantic movement, Akers was sculpting an ideal, a "beautiful death" of the sort that I, too, had internalized during my depression. He created an image laden with poetry and, unfortunately, several levels of irony.

This beautiful marble masterpiece shows a sudden tragedy, not the mundane reality of bodies failing under capitalist pressure. Rarely is it one sudden disaster that befalls the worker, one dive too deep, one strike from a machine, one dose of toxin. It's usually scarring that builds up, year after year. Work ages and breaks so many of us over time. Akers himself was scarred like this. He died young, at the age of thirty-five, from tuberculosis, a condition that is typically worsened if one has prolonged exposure to silica particles—like those found in marble dust.

I no longer work in an office. These days, I write from home. I leave to do interviews, studio visits, and site tours. One of my most reliable sources of income is a design magazine that publishes home features, where my words run alongside pages and pages of gorgeous glossy photography. I like writing these stories, but I don't always enjoy going to the homes. Often, the homeowners are friendly and welcoming. Usually, the houses are tasteful and spacious, filled with well-crafted pieces of furniture and works by local artists. Frequently, they have water views, which means I get to spend my morning sipping coffee, looking at the ocean, and taking notes about the design-build process. It's not a bad job, I know.

Occasionally though, I'll meet a health-insurance executive who laughs at my questions and rolls his eyes at my muddy boots, or I'll sit down with a newly minted CEO who just cannot believe I have never been to London. These are the minor humiliations of dealing with the rich. The greater humiliation comes when I return home and walk into my kitchen with its poorly applied linoleum tiles and faded gray Formica countertops. Made of paper and plastic, they don't have the grain of wood or the depth of stone, just the matte, room-temperature feel of man-made things. But it's not the countertops that shame me; it's the wanting, the envy, the shallowness of my own emotions. "I hate my kitchen," I tell my husband, and he looks sad. He painted my old cabinets cornflower blue for me. I should be more grateful.

Whenever I spend too much time rubbing shoulders with the very wealthy, I tend to forget my own good fortune. We bought a house years ago and we have a manageable mortgage. Our house has five acres of woodland, two bedrooms, two bathrooms, and a screened-in porch. My bedroom has skylights through which I can see the moon and, on a clear night, the constellations as they move across the sky. We've planted hundreds of bulbs, and every spring I can enjoy the snake's head fritillaries, the narcissus, the crocuses, the snowdrops, and the spring beauty. So what if my countertops are Formica?

Yet I want porcelain tile and tubs for the bathrooms, and I want a slab of old marble for my kitchen. I want my shelter to look more beautiful. Instead, I have so much plastic, so much more plastic than I ever imagined, than I ever wanted.

Long before plastic began to snake through our walls and coat our floors, we lived with stone, timber, and mud. Early humans built cities out of mud bricks and temples out of stone. At first, they used whatever type of stone was easiest to find, stack, and cut, but as humanity progressed, we began to branch out and use a wider range of geological materials. The earth gives us a rich palette of rocks to work with, and people often gravitated toward the sister stones of limestone and marble.

In order to understand marble, you have to know about limestone. Limestone is the basis of most marble. Limestone is made of several types of minerals, the most important being calcite and aragonite. Some limestone is made almost entirely of fragments of seashells (this chunky amalgamation is called coquina), and some limestone is made of finer crystal particles. Limestone is often found near the surface of the Earth's crust, but as it gets buried farther beneath the ocean or the soil, lime-stone can be forced to undergo a massive change of state. Pressure (from the material sitting on top of it) and heat (from the magma that makes up the Earth's core) transforms the stone from a soft sedimentary rock into a harder, more rigid and orderly metamorphic rock. Like graphite squeezed into diamond, limestone is birthed slowly into marble.

Marble was, from the beginning of building history, a prized stone. Marble is glittery and bright, thanks to the large calcite crystals that form during the metamorphic process. It's also full of character. The color of marble depends on what "impurities" or "accessory minerals" have snuck into the mixture. Clay, feldspar, and iron oxide all add color to the stone. The distinctive veining that gives marble that cartographic look comes from water flowing through cracks in the stone, depositing minerals as it goes. Marble can be delicate and rosy pink, honey yellow, or mossy green. There's bright cobalt-blue marble, black marble, and heavily lined cream-colored marble.

Yet when we think about marble architecture and sculpture, we tend to associate it with a specific aesthetic, one that is pale, rigid, and cold. Mark Abbe, professor of classics at the University of Georgia and spe-cialist in the study of color in antiquity, says it's a common misconception that Greek statues, temples, and living spaces were bleached of color. "Though we live in a white world, this wasn't the experience histori-cally," he explains. Abbe is at the forefront of a current reconceptualiza-tion of Hellenistic art, one that argues for a polychromatic understanding of history. The statues, buildings, and artworks we have from the an-cient world were once thought to be reflective of a preference for naked stone. Now, thanks to new analysis of old images and statues, historians have come to believe that the Greek and Roman worlds were a lot more colorful than we thought. Talking to Abbe, I become newly aware that we're living in a time of unprecedented whiteness. Rarely have human cultural spaces appeared as stark and sterile as they do right now. "You go into a consumer space, a high-end or medium-level gallery or store, and there's this white minimalism that looks like a hospital. Someone could walk in and perform surgery," Abbe says. Anyone who has visited an Apple Genius Bar in the past decade or seen images of Kim Kardashian's ultra-minimalist home can probably picture this "disturbingly sanitized" aesthetic. You can find this monochromatic, vaguely futuristic look in high-end hotels, spas, and restaurants in every major American city. While minimalism has been losing steam within design communities since the late 2010s, I doubt white walls will disappear. White has become the ultimate neutral, a paradoxical sign of good taste and no taste. "Do we really even think this is beautiful?" Abbe wonders. He points out that the Greeks certainly didn't. To them marble's value came not from its whiteness but from the interplay between surface and depth. It wasn't like porcelain, a material that has always been prized for its purity. Marble was more fluid and strange, more lively and lived-in.

Instead of seeing white marble as one option among many, Western culture has elevated certain types of stone to the top of a hierarchy, turning this neutral material into a potent symbol of assumed superiority. The ugliness in marble, Abbe believes, comes more from our contemporary interpretation and implementation of the ancient Greeks' aesthetics than anything they themselves put into practice. Our current tendency to see Hellenistic works as the unrivaled pinnacle of aesthetic achievement arose from centuries of Western theory. From the Renaissance onward, the "classical" school of art has been obsessed with copying, remixing, and updating the styles and stories of the ancient Greeks and Romans. I'm not suggesting that every Renaissance artist thought this way, nor did every sculptor during the Romantic period (two eras uniquely beholden to Greco-Roman inspiration), but as time wore on, the association between neoclassical styles and supposed superiority became even more entrenched. Marble busts and ionic columns were claimed by xenophobes across the European continent as relics of some shared "ancient and glorious past." This, according to Abbe, made marble an effective "uniting symbol" for right-wing groups. It allowed them to create a fiction in which they were the sole descendants of some elevated, refined culture, one that outstripped other ancient communities and reinforced ideas of racial superiority. Both Hitler and Mussolini loved marble and embraced neoclassical art and architecture.

Although Americans are geographically removed from the site of this "ancient and glorious past," European immigrants to the New World imported their biases and their preferences, including their love for white marble. Over the past two hundred years, neoclassical marble buildings have come to define the architectural aesthetic of the U.S. federal government. Starting in the early 1800s, Corinthian columns and grandiose marble plinths began popping up all over Washington, D.C. Using marble quarried in nearly a dozen states (and some imported from Italy), Americans erected monuments that bore the names of famous white men who died for freedom—the Washington Monument, the Lincoln Memorial, the Columbus Fountain, to name a few. According to the Architect of the Capitol, a preservation organization located in Washington, the founding fathers were known appreciators of ancient Greek and Roman civilizations, and had they more marble on hand, they would have used only marble right from the start. Sadly, they could only find sandstone nearby, so some of the oldest buildings were made from that material. But with the opening of several American marble quarries in the 1800s, even these old walls could shine anew. Marble was tacked onto sandstone, marble sculptures were added to many facades, and solid marble was used to construct new, even grander buildings. Over the next century, marble became increasingly visible in American cities, and slowly those white stone colonnades were imbued with a new level of meaning. Marble now gleamed cleanly for the power of a supposedly secular, almost entirely white-ruled nation-state.

As America grew as a global power, we continued to construct a national identity based on a sense of superiority. As a child in elementary school, I was taught that America was the richest, greatest, most free, most independent, and most brilliant country on Earth. I'm embarrassed how long it took for me to understand how many of my opinions were parroted propaganda. I love the place where I live, but I'm no longer under any illusions about the greatness of my country. America has always had a dark and violent side, though I wasn't always able to see it.

It would be ridiculous to say something like "only fascists build with marble." That's clearly not true. But marble has become the go-to material for strongmen trying to display their wealth in a suitably masculine way. Donald Trump's famous New York City apartment is tiled with a variety of colorful, veined marbles and he's publicly lamented the "cheap" green marble tiles that decorate the general assembly dais of the United Nations building in New York. ("I will replace with beautiful large marble slabs if they ask me," he tweeted in 2012.) Romanian dictator Nicolae Ceauşescu had similarly grandiose taste and in 1984, he laid the cornerstone for the construction of a massive marble palace that would be used for government business and cultural purposes. Hundreds of architects and thousands of workers were conscripted to build this ornate, pharaonic structure. It still ranks as the heaviest government building in the world (and possibly the most expensive). While the Romanian parliament does meet there, and while some of it is used to house a national art museum, the building stood 70 percent empty as of 2014, according to CNN Travel. It is generally regarded as a reminder of corrupt communist excess. But at least the people of Bucharest continue their daily lives in the neighborhoods that surround the big marble palace, the city as lively and loud as any.

Compared to most of the capital cities in the world, Ashgabat is eerily empty. Few people can afford to live in the city, and many of the original inhabitants have been forced to leave due to inflation and draconian government restrictions. When reporter Stanislav Volkov was a little boy in Ashgabat, his hometown was known as the "garden city," a place full of lush plants and historic, beloved homes. Footage of the city from the 1980s shows men in turbans and long beards sitting on plush floor cushions and drinking tea, street vendors cooking skewers of meat, swans floating gracefully over the surface of public ponds, and pink, blooming roses swaying in the wind. The city streets were busy with foot traffic and old, beat-up cars. Everything changed in 1990 with the fall of the Soviet Union and the rise of dictator Saparmurat Niyazov. On his orders, multigenerational family houses were razed to the ground, centuries-old trees uprooted, and the flows of Ashgabat's many irrigation canals diverted. In their place, he put highways, palaces, airports, and skyscrapers. Niyazov disliked anything he personally found ugly or unpleasant, and so he banned dogs from the city, outlawed opera and ballet, forced men to shave their beards, and banned news anchors from wearing makeup onscreen. Instead of perennial trees with their big, shady boughs, Niyazov ordered his new city be filled with upright evergreens. Every year, more people left. Without their homes, beards, dogs, or music, they weren't very happy. Without the trees and canals, the streets were too hot. "The city's special microclimate was almost completely destroyed," writes Volkov. "In place of the old tea spots are car parks or outright wastelands." It is a silent place, "the city of the dead."

A decade ago, Ashgabat was recognized by *The Guinness Book of World Records* as having the most marble-clad buildings in the world. While Turkmenistan is currently listed as a "level three" country by the U.S. State Department (meaning "reconsider travel") English-speaking photojournalists, YouTubers, and reporters have managed to visit and relay their findings. If you have access to the Internet, you can vicariously experience the desert heat, the intimidating architecture. "It felt like entering a forbidden place," said travel photographer Amos Chapple after his 2013 trip. His images of life in the glittering white city showcase the riches bought with oil money as well as the poverty experienced by the average citizen. They show a place that is lavishly appointed and forcefully controlled. "When we drove into Ashgabat I assumed there was some kind of holiday taking place—the streets and all these beautiful parks stood deserted," he wrote. "In the area I first walked there were more soldiers than civilians."

Turkmenistan isn't a poor country. They have oil and important trade ports. But that's like saying the economy in America is booming just because the stock market is on the upswing. There's money in Ashgabat like there's money in New York. But people still die from starvation and lack of healthcare—or in the desert, from heat and lack of water. I point this out because Ashgabat isn't the only city on the globe controlled by a tiny group of unfathomably wealthy citizens. There's a lot of places like that. But not every urban landscape wears this fact so baldly. Not every place bakes its citizens.

Ashgabat is an extreme example of urban wealth disparity, which makes it both fascinating and repellant. From what I can see, it's not a beautiful place. It looks uncannily clean, too pristine. Even the cars in Ashgabat are white, as per government order. Still, I wonder what it would be like to live there, amongst all that brightness and shine. Maybe, if I lived there long enough, I'd come to love it. There must be people who do, who lead happy, relatively normal lives within that marble city.

Repetition, conformity, and familiarity are three of the most effective tools in the propagandist's arsenal. A message repeated enough times could worm its way deep into your memory, like a song. I think of it sometimes as a mental pollutant. Even if you know what you're seeing is state-sponsored propaganda, it can be hard to see how it could damage you. We're surrounded by systems of power that work in such insidious ways. It can be so hard to even identify the boot that's resting on your neck, much less learn how to resist it.

Throughout the history of marble, people have been contending with its dust. When marble is broken, the dust releases particles of silica crystals into the air. Silica dust is toxic to the human respiratory system. Repeated contact is the main cause of many different occupational lung diseases, including pneumoconiosis (that is, "black lung"), chronic obstructive pulmonary disease, silicosis, and asthma. People who work in stone, granite, construction, mining, ceramic production, and glass industries are all at high risk. Studies from around the globe, including Pakistan, China, South Africa, Australia, and the United States, have all found that people who work with marble tend to be at a greater risk for developing silicosis and autoimmune disorders than the general population. One reason marble workers are at higher risk has to do with their general lot in life; the group shows higher rates of illiteracy, lowered socioeconomic status, lack of safety rules and enforcement, and "exploitation by employers." Unlike coal miners, who get plenty of press attention, we don't often talk about the people who mix our composite quartz counters or grind our marble to make our toothpaste (yes, it is used as an abrasive in many brands of toothpaste, though it should be safe in that context). These people are less representative of some great American past than the brawny, grimy coal worker. They work in warehouses and factories—big, boring facilities that you might pass on the highway but not see, their industrial parks hidden behind "beauty screens" of purposefully planted pines. This type of dust is used in so many different products, from mortar to cement to latex wall paint, that its production surpasses that of American-quarried solid marble by quite a lot.

Silica dust doesn't kill you quickly, though I'm sure it would if you snorted enough lines of it. For most people who work with dust, the story goes like this: he inhales just a little at his job, every day, for years. His condition develops slowly enough that it doesn't even seem related to that job he hates. He doesn't perceive the damage until it's too late. First, the dust begins to settle into his upper lungs, where it causes tiny inflammations, so small they don't even hurt. He might be coughing, but that could be anything, probably just a cold. His body heals, but the damaged area is now scarred. This new, damaged tissue has a different, thicker texture. It doesn't move as well as his original lung tissue, and it doesn't take up oxygen as well. He keeps working. Over time, these patches of damage spread and thicken. Very slowly, his breathing changes. There's pain when he inhales, and he coughs when he exhales. He might also feel weak all over. He could get fevers and night sweats. His lips start to turn blue.

There is no way to reverse this damage, so even if he finds a new job working somewhere with fresher air, his lungs are ruined. Once diagnosed, life expectancy can be as short as six years. Silicosis can lead to tuberculosis, lung cancer, and kidney disease. Sometimes, a lung transplant might be an option, which could buy more time on Earth. But these aren't common procedures, and bodies often reject the new organs. There's no easy way to test for this type of condition, which can make it hard to get a diagnosis. It can be even harder for Americans to pay for treatment, since our healthcare system is so deeply broken and corrupt. And good luck getting your company to pay for your time off, much less the cost of rehabilitation.

But this fate isn't inevitable. There are measures that companies can take to make their workplaces safer. They can provide masks and proper ventilation. Spraying an area down with water can keep the particles from ascending into the air. With regular cleaning and proper protective gear, stonecutting can be a safe occupation. Inhaling a little bit of silica won't kill you. It's not like drowning or burning to death in a factory fire. This is a slow hazard, one that most people who deal with building materials in America will not face. Through my work writing home-design features, I've met many builders and landscapers who have worked in their fields for decades. Though they are exposed to stone dust, sawdust, toxic fumes, and other pollutants, thanks to precautionary measures, they can live long, healthy lives. They can get old and crotchety, living long enough to give me excellent off-the-record quotes about their fancy, clueless clients.

Not Jose Martinez, though. The thirty-seven-year-old stonecutter was diagnosed with silicosis. Martinez says he wasn't the only one from his company to have this problem; two other workers died in 2018 from the same disease. "If you go to the bathroom, it's dust. When we go to take lunch, on the tables, it's dust," he told NPR reporter Nell Greenfieldboyce a year later. "Your nose, your ears, your hair, all your body, your clothes—everything." According to the CDC's MMWR report that same year, the agency found nearly twenty cases of silicosis, in part caused by workplace exposure, mostly among Hispanic men.

While it often takes decades for stonecutters or miners to develop silicosis, this process occurs much more quickly for people working with engineered stone. Engineered stone does contain some natural marble, but it's not solid. Rather, the marble is mixed with crushed stone, like quartz, and bound together by polymer resins. While natural marble contains around 10 percent silica, these faux-marble, engineered stone slabs can have as much as 90 percent silica in them, making it a far more dangerous material to work with than regular rocks. It's not just stonecutters who are at risk. The people who mix the stone slurry and add the binding agents also encounter a good deal of silica dust. Since this is a relatively new product, it's hard to know how many people are being sickened by man-made stone and its ingredients. But even one death is too many when it's so easily avoidable. This problem is on the rise because countertop fashion has changed. More people are buying supposedly eco-friendly and low-maintenance (that is, resistant to staining) "engineered stone" or "cultured marble" than ever before. Sometimes, companies even market this product as "quartz," a name even more misleading than the others, though none of them come clean about what's in their mixture. It's stone dust and plastic. How cultured is that?

Over the last ten years, I've seen hundreds of different types of stone countertops and tiles, both engineered and natural. The faux stone never looks quite like the real stuff, though it can be appealingly glittery and colorful. It's a convenient product; cheaper and less prone to staining. It's designed to be believably stonelike and is marketed as though it is natural stone. But it's not, just as a chair made of compressed paper isn't really made of wood.

It's not unexpected for consumers to choose the less expensive option, the middle-of-the-road choice, the engineered stone rather than the quarried slabs. I understand the appeal of these fake rocks. But they're not necessary. I believe everyone deserves to live in a space that is healthy, safe, and beautiful. I think we all want houses that can hold us, that feel personal and warm. No matter how many hours I work, or how many books I write, I'm unlikely to ever secure the money for a house like the ones I visit for work. In this world, home desire feels like a particularly horrible kind of desire because it's entirely reasonable yet terribly, painfully out of reach. There's little point in lusting after a big diamond because, even if I were given one, I'd want to convert it immediately into money. I'd sell the stone and use the money to pay for my life, buying groceries, paying for daycare, purchasing a little leisure time. But a dream home? A dream home is for living within. It's not for possessing or hoarding. Ideally, it's not for showing off. It's for going to sleep, waking up, feeding your kids, loving your spouse. It's the place you take care of, that takes care of you. It's where you grieve, heal, and grow.

This is one of the many paradoxes that come with loving beauty under capitalism. I want our beauties to be shared, readily available to everyone. But I also want to have private beauties of my own. Some Marxists would say this is reasonable; we have enough houses for everyone, enough money for everyone, enough food for everyone, enough beauty for everyone. We should all live with some luxuries because they are abundant and should be shared. This is obviously not how it works.

If you are rich enough, you can live with marble in private. For the rest of us, marble is something we tend to see in public spaces or in our places of work. My brother's office is in a massive brick building in Boston that boasts a cavernous marble lobby, a cacophony of pricey greens, pinks, and browns. I've never had an office so glamorous (he's in finance) nor have I ever lived with marble. My homes have been temporary lodgings for the most part, rental apartments with laminate or cheap ceramic tile. Fortunately, you don't have to buy marble to appreciate it. And not every piece of American marble has been pressed into the service of providing image protection for bankers or politicians. It's still possible to see such stones for free, whenever you like. Provided you're willing to walk among the dead.

I spend a lot of time in cemeteries, and I have since I was a moody teenager. When I was young, I visited them because they were private and quiet—a good place to go and get high in the suburbs and make out with my boyfriend. As I got older, I developed an appreciation for New England's somber, stark beauty and Puritan past, which made historic cemeteries all the more appealing. They are not, to borrow from Freud, unheimlich or unhomely. In fact, they can be downright welcoming. Thanks to the Rural Cemetery movement in the nineteenth century, many of America's eastern cities are peppered with green spaces that were purposefully designed and built to house the dead and please the living. They have trails and ponds, weeping willows and miniature marble temples. They are spaces made for the urban-dwelling public to use for exercise and recreation, an early model for America's city parks systems. You might imagine that people went to cemeteries for long, meditative walks, but they also used the grounds for more raucous pursuits, like hunting and shooting practice, picnic parties, and carriage racing.

Mount Auburn Cemetery, near Cambridge, Massachusetts, is one of the oldest and most beautiful garden burial grounds in the country. I used to live within walking distance, and visiting Mount Auburn was one of my favorite ways to spend an afternoon. Early in our relationship, I brought my now-husband there for a date. I wasn't trying to be edgy or morose. In June, when the rhododendrons are blooming and the air is still cool, it is a beautiful place to walk—an outdoor museum filled with sculptures, flowers, ponds, and bluebirds. It's tranquil and familiar. It's also filled with the moldering dead. The sculptures aren't there for my enjoyment. They're placed in this radically sculpted plot of land to honor people, some of whom died far too young.

The graves of the children break my heart, make my low voice fall silent. You don't have to skim the dates and perform mental arithmetic to spot them. Once you're a little familiar with the language of funerary arts, you'll can easily pick out the slumped marble figure of a lamb, degraded by time and acid rain, curled hair pocked and covered in lichen, its ears and tail barely visible.

They are easier to take in than the newer lambs, small figures that hold sadness so recent that I'm afraid it might be catching. Families still commission marble lambs from stone carvers, though the practice is less common than it once was. During quarantine, I spoke with Sigrid Coffin, a second-generation Maine stone carver, one of only a dozen or so working in the United States. I was trying to figure out where marble belongs in our modern lives. Coffin prefers to work with slate (a fine-grained stone that resists weathering) but does "a fair amount" of marble headstones. "Historically, that's what you would choose if you were a sea captain in New England or if you had the means," she says. This tradition, of using marble to mark the wealthy dead, dates back to the Romans. It's still a status symbol, says Coffin, as well as a "symbol for purity and light." Recently, Coffin was visiting Swans Island when she came across a striking graveyard, filled with all marble headstones— row upon row of gray stones glittering with white. Given the difficulty of moving marble before the advent of long-haul trucking, that marble was probably quarried locally but there's quite a bit of marble available on the market from Danby, Vermont, and many of our New England monuments have been made from that stone. Danby is a large deposit that yields a "very pretty" stone, says Coffin. It's a more ethical alternative to Carrara, though many high-end homeowners still choose the imported. Danby marble, says Coffin, "has a light-gray vein to it. I haven't been to the quarry, but I've seen the Carrara quarry from afar. I thought it was snow—a huge, white gash on the mountaintop."

Listening to Coffin talk about her work, I feel pangs of envy. She is entrusted with a sacred task. Her work has such clear meaning and purpose. When she carves a headstone or a memorial, she knows precisely why she's doing it. It may not always help mourners right away, but the goal is to give them a physical place to put their grief. Sometimes, this means sculpting an object of beauty, but often it's about inscribing an already-beautiful thing, laying down a small human mark upon the Earth's vast surface. Like me, Coffin "never tires of cemeteries." She says, "There's an energy there that I don't necessarily get anywhere else."

Perhaps this is why, when a couple came to Coffin asking for a stone to mark the passing of their child, she found a block of marble and gifted it to them. She carved them a small lamb. Usually, when she makes a carving for someone, Coffin adds in elements of the person's life and personality—the boat for the sailor, the ivy for the gardener, the musical notes dancing across the headstone of a singer. But with a child so young, there's no knowing who they could have become. "What does a child have but innocence, frailty, purity, and the dimpled softness of a tiny lamb?" she asks. "What better encapsulates their short time here, with the nuances of spring, birth, and newness than this little image? And since the only medium we have to display any resounding love is stone: hard, cold, permanent stone, what is the softest, warmest, downiest representation we can epitomize?" Marble, with its sugary texture and reflective qualities, feels right for such a monumental grief.

We put so much of ourselves into stones; it makes sense that we want to believe they can shine this energy back at us. Ancient Greeks believed that marble was somehow alive, part of the Earth's grand body, sighs and exhalations from some slumbering giant. Even now that we know better, I still think we always want our treasured objects to communicate with us in some mystical way. We want them to speak, glow, exude, shine. We crave intimacy with our world, some reciprocity, some magic. In *The Book of Unconformities*, Hugh Raffles writes of Manhattan's marble and granite, these glittering minerals that form the body and bedrock of his beloved and maligned island. Underneath the city lies a piece of land that has been stolen and sold, reclaimed and partitioned off, broken down and built up, yet below the surface there remains such strength. He recounts a bit of local lore he picked up before even moving to Manhattan that posited the reason the city was so sleepless was because of the glinting bedrock, "which concentrated the city's energies like sun on a lens, forcing its residents to live life with a burning intensity." Scientifically, this is nonsense, but Raffles discovers a grain of truth in the magical tale. Places affect people deeply. It matters where we walk, on what we step. We use stones to hold our memories and honor our dead, because they can. On a primal level, we believe that stones will outlast us, that Earth will outlast us.

It will probably outlast me, personally, but whether Earth will survive humanity remains to be seen. It turns out that we don't just have the ability to carve our names into its surface but also the power to bomb the bedrock to fragments, smash the globe to pieces. Manhattan marble, with its sugared surface and soft body, gives Raffles a surface on which he can rest this thesis: "Gradualism and catastrophism are no longer contradictory; time is both immeasurably deep and inexplicably shallow, both perpetual deferral and instantaneous turmoil."

Up in Maine, my bedrock is a vast mixture of types. This is a region famous for rough granite shorelines but there's also soft rocks like shale and mudstone, igneous rocks like basalt and rhyolite, and even sparkly metamorphic rocks like marble and quartzite. I've written this book during a pandemic, mainly from my home on a wooded plot of clay-rich soil. Under my feet, I think there's granite, but I'm not certain.

During the long periods of caution and quarantine, I was unable to visit the museums, galleries, studios, and shops that used to comfort me. I couldn't go see the dead pearl boy and his glinting skin. I also didn't go out to see other people's homes; I didn't return to mine poisoned with envy. Instead, I became acquainted with the kind of time that Raffles writes about so elegantly: deep and shallow, still and churning. I lived quietly, no marble in sight save for gravestones.

It's possible I will someday be able to afford my dream home (by the ocean, with Danby marble countertops, slate tiles, porcelain in the cabinets, silk rugs on the floor, big windows, south-facing, beauty everywhere) but I know it's unlikely. The ugliness of my adult desires is more complicated than those that came before. These objects carry more weight, literally and physically. There are so many ways to enjoy the beauty of a flower without falling into its traps, without turning ugly in the process; this is less true for something like a dream home. I will likely never live in a house as nice as the one I grew up in. My economic position has shifted, and dealing with that isn't always easy. Unlike my father, I chose a career that will make me very little money, and unlike my mother, I married a man who teaches high school (and thus makes very little money). We can't buy an old oak China cabinet and stock it with porcelain, we can't install a stained-glass window above our door, we can't just get marble tiles for our house. We live with plastic floors and plastic countertops—

like most Americans, our consumption is limited by necessity as well as moral considerations.

For now, I try to find wonder and glamour in other places. In the past year, I've spent more time in graveyards than ever before, for purposes of mourning and escape. What I like best is to go to the shore and stand on the granite boulders that buttress the Atlantic, watching snow fall onto white waves. When I can't get to the ocean, there's always the river, the cemeteries, the woods, even the patch of lumber land at the end of my road. Everywhere I go, I find flecks of quartz, silica, and mica, tiny mirrors winking light. Ocean-weathered or hand-carved, half-buried or set on a plinth, these stones tell me the same thing: my days are numbered, each beauty I find will fade, degrade, break, and tarnish, and there's no point in asking for what I can't have. This is true of both objects and the more intangible things, like permanence, stability, and guaranteed good health. Time rests on the surface, in the glinting play of a moment. It's impossibly long, unfathomably deep. Against this strange dark backdrop, beauty persists.

I don't always live my life with burning intensity, but in these moments, when I remember my death and, more important, my incredible fortune at being alive, then, when I'm staring at the sea and thinking of the water crashing, then, when I'm with myself in my body, not wanting anything more than this salt air and this hard world, then, when I'm wanting for nothing, lacking nothing, loving the world as it is, on its own terms, then, I do.

CONCLUSION

From infancy to death, we're surrounded by beautiful things. Babies cooing into mirrors grow into children eating flowers. Teens covering their bodily scents who become adults, parents, homemakers. If we're lucky, we get to be elders, faces lined with age, voices thick with the wisdom of years, heads stuffed with memories of art we've seen, places we've been, people we've loved. Best-case scenario, we get old and die and our bodies turn back into matter—soil, maybe, or ashes. I do not want to become a diamond, but perhaps you do. It doesn't really matter what I want anyway; ultimately, we have no control over where our atoms end up.

But as long as I'm alive, I plan to exercise my agency, even when the problems seem too big to understand, let alone fix. I believe I can do this while appreciating the beauty of the world, for while I don't believe beauty has a moral component, I do believe it can inspire goodness, if we let it.

I want our culture to change, to accommodate more forms of beauty, to skew away from the empty materialism of the past and toward a more sustainable way of living. I want to inspire you to go out and enjoy the loveliness of the world in ways that aren't beholden to buying or selling. To walk around your neighborhood and marvel at the birds, to learn the names of the clouds, to visit a public sculpture and admire its form, to sit on a park bench and consider the tulips. So many of my best memories took place in shared spaces—libraries, cemeteries, museums, beaches, temples, cathedrals, and gardens. There are still many things I'd like to do but haven't been able to afford (visiting London is on the list) but for the most part, I'm able to find beauty close to home. I think everyone can.

There are times when, during the researching and writing of this book, I felt overwhelmed by stories of pain and suffering. There are times when I felt jealous, hurt, judged, and belittled—there are times when my desire has turned sour. There was a point where I felt desperate and despaired, ill with want.

But focusing so narrowly on beauty has had a positive effect on me that I didn't expect. Rather than drowning in beauty, I've learned how to swim in it. I've found access to forms of inner appreciation that were previously undiscovered. I've come to see that having beautiful things is only one, rather limited, way to access the experience of beholding beauty. It's a valid way, and I am not going to give up my jewelry, my clothes, my art, or my cut-flower habit anytime soon. But I've also become more attuned to beauty, more capable of creating the experience of wonder within myself. I've gotten much better at ferreting out small, exquisite details and savoring complicated, muddy colors. I've taught myself how to identify birds and spot the ones with iridescent feathers, how to enjoy the scent of a carnation wrapped in cellophane, and how to take delight in drinking from a chipped porcelain cup. It's part attention, part appreciation, and part imagination.

Mostly, this shift has been subtle. I recognize patterns in nature, see symmetry in simple compositions of objects, appreciate aromas as they waft off rotting fruit, and the like. But sometimes, it's less about tweaking my aesthetic palate and more about doing a complete 180. I first began writing about pearls in 2017. At the time, I didn't like pearls. I didn't own them, didn't want them, didn't see the point. They were too fussy for my sensibilities. But then I learned how nacre is formed inside a mollusk, how light interacts with the calcium carbonate surface, and how people once believed that pearls were the tears of the sea, the secretions of goddesses. Suddenly, every shiny seashell on the rocky beach of Maine seemed like a fragment of sunrise. In the summer of 2020, I went to the beach often, and while my husband surfed, I sat with the baby, looking at shells. I became obsessed with the sea-washed mauve, the indigo streaks, the baby-pink insides of whirled shells, the simple creamy yellow of mother-of-pearl. I wanted to keep them all, but away from the water they lost a bit of their charm. The beautiful moment had passed.

Still, once you realize how many things are iridescent, you can't unsee it. I started to collect moments in my head, shimmers of rainbow spotted on greasy water, prismatic surfaces on a deli sandwich (roast beef has the right fiber structures to create such a colorful effect), the dark-green sheen on a duck's neck. From pearls, I moved outward, casting my net wider and each time coming back with a new shiny thing to admire. I had stared long enough into a seashell, and I found myself seeing its ghosts everywhere.

Beauty can arrive when we least expect it, and often it takes a form we don't anticipate. It's not easy to pin down or predict, and it doesn't always make us purely happy. I once spent an afternoon swimming across a muddy brown pond, trying to reach the water lilies on the far shore, only to arrive and be greeted by the leathery leaves of spatterdock. This native aquatic plant has flowers that are bulbous and strange, reeking of alcohol—nothing like the delicate spears of a lotus. Yet they were egg-yolk yellow, a brilliant spot of color on a dull day. I wasn't disappointed by their presence. Somehow, when paired with the overcast sky and the pines that circled the water, they had become exquisite, piercingly beautiful. These weird flowers threw me back into my body, limbs covered in goosebumps, legs aching from the swim. They anchored me in the melancholy moment.

To use a term from psychoanalysis, many beautiful items are imbued with at least a little jouissance. This is a term coined by philosopher Jacques Lacan to describe pleasure so intense it becomes painful, joy so big it becomes suffering. I'm not trying to argue that flowers inspire sexual or religious ecstasy. No violet, however tasty, has ever turned me into Saint Teresa, eyes rolled back in marble-white ecstasy. But I do believe the experience of contemplating something and judging it to be beautiful does provide a little moment of mental elation, a petit mort for your brain. Desire feels good even though we experience it as a lack of something, a longing for something. In the evaluation and creation of desire, we experience both pleasure (enjoyment derived from sensing, perceiving, and judging beauty) and a little bit of pain.

The sense of lack can come from many places—when the beautiful thing is a person, we might feel a sense of loss that we aren't with them. If the beautiful object is a work of art, we might feel a sense of sadness knowing we don't already possess it, or that we didn't make it. In the case of flowers, I think it comes from their impermanence. Flowers are destined to die, each and every one, and they wilt and fade so much more quickly than people do. They can be handy reminders of our own mortality, which explains all those delicious oil paintings of browning petals and rotting fruit that hang in the world's most heavily trafficked museums and galleries. These vanitous still lifes are intended to turn the viewer away from the decadence of the physical realm and inspire spiritual contemplation, but they have had precisely the opposite effect on me. They've turned me into a lover of dying bouquets, wilting tulips, sad peonies, and nodding roses. They've only increased my desire to hold on to this world, even as I watch it wither and die.

Part of me wishes I could end here, to tell you that I've gotten better and you can too. But I haven't fully reformed. I still buy things I don't need, I still wear makeup, and I still write about houses that are too big for their occupants. Through my work, I promote consumerism. I make money and I spend it though I believe that many of our biggest social problems are caused by this churning. There are ways in which I resist the impulse to accumulate—I visit museums, I shop secondhand, I recycle, I reuse. And there are ways that I try to address the harm my car-dependent life causes. I pick up trash on the beach, I volunteer with kids, I donate money to charitable causes. I'm trying to be better all the time. I'm also constantly failing.

To live an ethical life is, perhaps, an impossible goal. At the very least, it's an unknowable one. There's no authority who will tell me that I've been good enough, that I've done enough for others, that I am officially forgiven for my sins. None, at least, that I recognize at this point in my lapsed-Catholic life. Instead, I have to face myself and acknowledge my choices and the harm that I cause. There is ugliness in me, still.

Yet I plan to keep trying, in my own small ways, to make the world more beautiful. I can't undo global warming, nor can I live outside the systems of capitalism and country. But I can choose not to buy from companies I know to be exploitative, and I can pick up trash when I see it. I can plant flowers and I can raise a child who appreciates plants, shells, and glittery stones as much as I do.

Even now, there are times when I consider death and long, just a little, for the end of my own life. It doesn't happen very often anymore, thankfully. Though I expect I'll always harbor some destructive desires, I'm working to live in acceptance. Like the spatterdock, my life isn't what I expected. It seems clumsy and ill-formed. I fear that it's small and unremarkable. Yet it continues, and I keep going. Because there's always a fragment of iridescence to be glimpsed in the sand, a gleam of quartz to pick from a riverbed, a swamp rose in bloom to perfume the air, a new painting, a new song, a face to admire. There's always stars more beautiful than diamonds, clouds softer than silk, and there's always the play of light on water, shimmering, calling my attention outward and upward.

ACKNOWLEDGMENTS

First, thank you to Tzipora Baitch. Not only did she edit and shape this book with clarity and precision, she also rescued this project from languishing somewhere in digital archives. She guided me gently through the publishing process from day one, and I'm extremely grateful for her patience and understanding. I could never have written this book without her; I wouldn't have wanted to.

Thank you to Kent Wolf, my agent, and the staff at Neon Literary for being cool people with great taste. Silvia Killingsworth was the first editor to show any interest in this idea; working with her at *The Awl* was deeply influential to my work as an essayist. Michelle Weber, my former editor at *Longreads*, deserves heaps of praise for her challenging queries and empathetic excisions. Thank you to Matt Giles for his thorough fact-checking and sharp eyes. Thank you to the entire team at Simon & Schuster for believing in this idea, and a special thanks to Jonathan Karp for championing it.

For their expertise and time, I'd like to thank Ian Hodder, Suzanne Marchand, Rae Nudson, Hillary Belzer, Jacob Lowry, Jaya Saxena, Helen Scales, José H. Leal, Joe Schwarcz, Jac Menish, Charna Ethier, Anne Serrano-McClain, James Peterson, Joshua Meyer, Joyce Matthys, Cora Harrington, John C. Mauro, Thomas Gunning, Karina Corrigan, Meg

ACKNOWLEDGMENTS

Conley, Mark Abbe, and Sigrid Coffin. I enjoyed speaking with you about your work.

There were many people who let me use bits of their stories, including Tasha Graff, Susan Kelleher, Meg Conley, and Jia Tolentino. Thank you for your honesty and generosity. Thank you to everyone who read sections of this book and supported it, including Angelica Frey, Haley E. D. Houseman, Safy-Hallan Farah, David Scott Kastan, Daisy Alioto, Rachel Syme, and Jaime Green. Your feedback and encouragement helped shape this text.

There are many writers, scholars, scientists, artists, philosophers, and sociologists whose work I mined for detail. Thank you to every single one of them, living and dead.

I need to thank the staff at Kerebear Child Care for being fantastic resources and consummate professionals. I feel lucky to have my kid in your hands.

Lastly, thank you to my spouse, Garrett Temkiewicz, for his support, and my mother, Susan Kelleher, for always believing in my work. I love you both so much.

NOTES

INTRODUCTION

8   **"the ecstasy within things"**: Umberto Eco, *History of Beauty* (New York: Rizzoli, 2004), 329–354.

9   **"unselfing"**: Chloé Cooper Jones, *Easy Beauty* (New York: Avid Reader Press, 2022), 224.

9   **"We do not only want to be satisfied"**: Crispin Sartwell, *Six Names of Beauty* (New York: Routledge, 2004), 25.

1. THE MERCURIAL CHARMS OF THE MIRROR

12   **French psychoanalyst Jacques Lacan:** Jacques Lacan, *Écris* (New York: W. W. Norton & Company, 2006), 93–81.

13   **we like gemstones that sparkle:** Eric Jaffe, "An Evolutionary Theory for Why You Love Glossy Things," *Fast Company*, January 21, 2014.

13   **In his 2003 book:** Mark Pendergrast, *Mirror Mirror: A History of the Human Love Affair with Reflection* (New York: Basic Books, 2003), 1–4.

14   **According to animal psychologist Diana Reiss:** Liz Langley, "What Do Animals See in the Mirror?" *National Geographic*, February 14, 2015.

14   **contributes to our quality of life:** Alison Beard, "Hot or Not," *Harvard Business Review*, October 2011, https://hbr.org/2011/10/hot-or-not.

15   **"utopia":** Jennifer Hattam, "What Happened to Turkey's Ancient Utopia?" *Discover Magazine*, July 27, 2016.

15   **"origin of home":** Annalee Newitz, "An Ancient Proto-City Reveals the Origin of Home," *Scientific American*, March 1, 2021.

15   **"catoptromancy":** Gerina Dunwich, *The Wiccan's Dictionary of Prophecy and Omens* (New York: Citadel, 2000), 95.

16   **The Roman "blindfolded boys":** Dunwich, *Wiccan's Dictionary*, 30.

16 **Nostradamus:** Dunwich, *Wiccan's Dictionary*, 74.

16 **Elon Musk:** John James and Laura Sharman, "Nostradamus Hints at Terrifying 'Great War' in Chilling 2023 Predictions," *Mirror*, March 29, 2022.

16 **use them in feng shui:** Zhu Ying, "Reflections on Life in Ancient Times," *Shanghai Daily*, July 28, 2018, https://www.shine.cn/feature/art -culture/1807289481/.

16 **The first great glass mirrors:** Sabine Melchior-Bonnet, Jean Delumeau, and Katharine H. Jewett, *The Mirror: A History* (New York: Routledge, 2014), 18–35.

16 **"The Venetian Republic nurtured them":** Melchoir-Bonnet, Delumeau, and Jewett, *The Mirror*, 19.

17 **Workers who inhaled mercury fumes:** Vasco Branco, Michael Aschner, and Cristina Carvalho, "Neurotoxicity of Mercury: An Old Issue with Contemporary Significance," *Advances in Neurotoxicology* 5 (2021): 239–262, https://www.ncbi.nlm.nih.gov/pmc/articles/PMC8276940/.

17 **"Those who make the mirrors":** Barry S. Levy, David H. Wegman, Sherry L. Baron, Rosemary K. Sokas, *Seventh Edition of Occupational and Environmental Health* (New York: Oxford University Press, 2018), 222.

18 **Following the example of Catherine de' Medici:** Wendy Moonan, "Decorative Arts Galleries Offer Worthy Complements to the Armory Show," *New York Times*, January 19, 2007.

18 **Two Venetian workers had been assassinated:** Melchior-Bonet, Delumeau, and Jewett, *The Mirror*, 37.

20 **"You painted a naked woman":** John Berger, *Ways of Seeing* (London: Penguin Books, 1972), 51.

2. MOUTH FULL OF PETALS, VEINS FULL OF WAX

27 **"Of all the flowers":** Jennifer Potter, *Seven Flowers: And How They Shaped Our World* (London: Atlantic Books, 2013), 13.

28 **pink-tinged "sacred lotus":** Potter, *Seven Flowers*, 23–27.

29 **"symbol of purity":** Sally Coulthard, *Flioriography* (London: Quadrille Publishing, 2021), 64.

30 **"non-species emotional support":** Jeannette Haviland-Jones, "An Environmental Approach to Positive Emotion: Flowers," *Evolutionary Psychology* 3 (2005): 104–132.

31 **eerie ghost orchid:** Susan Orlean, *The Orchid Thief* (New York: Random House, 1998).

31 **"every trifling detail":** Charles Darwin, *The Various Contrivances by*

Which Orchids Are Fertilised by Insects (London: John Murray, 1887), 2, accessed online, http://darwin-online.org.uk/converted/published/1877_Orchids_F801/1877_Orchids_F801.html/.

32 **Darwin may have had a personal stake:** Jim Endersby, *Orchid: A Cultural History* (Chicago: University of Chicago Press, 2016), 87.

32 **"inflatable love dolls":** Michael Pollan, "Love and Lies," *National Geographic*, September 1, 2009.

32 **"growing tropical orchids in backyard greenhouses":** Endersby, *Orchid*, 69.

33 **"Within a month":** Orlean, *Orchid Thief*, 56.

33 **One tells of an English Traveler:** Orlean, *Orchid Thief*, 63.

34 **This last find:** Endersby, *Orchid*, 114.

34 *The Flowering of the Strange Orchid*: H. G. Wells, *Thirty Strange Tales* (New York and London: Harper and Brothers Publishers, 1898), accessed online, https://www.gutenberg.org/files/59774/59774-h/59774-h.htm.

35 **Greek word for testicle:** Endersby, *Orchid*, 8.

36 **"marvelously docile":** Endersby, *Orchid*, 135.

36 **"ripe with sickness":** Endersby, *Orchid*, 169.

37 **And it wasn't until the 1960s:** John McQuaid, "The Secrets Behind Your Flowers," *Smithsonian*, February 2011.

38 **"American Spirit":** Kase Wickman, "Why Your Valentine's Day Roses Don't Look as Good as Ben Higgins'," *New York Post*, February 11, 2016.

39 **The majority come from abroad:** Ana Swanson, "The Completely Unromantic—But Real—Reason We Give Roses on Valentine's Day," *Washington Post*, February 12, 2016.

39 **discovery of nuclear radiation:** James Wong, "Gardens: Expose Yourself to Atomic Gardening," *The Guardian*, March 13, 2016.

39 **atomic gardens or gamma gardens:** Paige Johnson, *Atomic Gardening*, https://www.atomicgardening.com/.

41 **the Forever Rose:** Forever Rose, LLC, "Luxury Floral Company Forever Rose, LLC Announces New Lifetime Warranty on all Forever Rose Brand and Beauty and the Beast Rose Products," PR Newswire, September 10, 2019, accessed online, https://www.prnewswire.com/news-releases/luxury-floral-company-forever-rose-llc-announces-new-lifetime-warranty-on-all-forever-rose-brand-and-beauty-and-the-beast-rose-products-300915284.html.

42 **6 Real, Live Flowers:** Danielle Tullo, "6 Real, Live Flowers That Will Last All Year And Don't Require Watering," *House Beautiful*, October 14, 2018.

43   a "smutty" love: Amy Stewart, *Flower Confidential: The Good, the Bad, and the Beautiful* (Chapel Hill, NC: Algonquin Books, 2008), 7–9.

43   "On one hand": Stewart, *Flower Confidential*, 151.

3. BRIGHT BLUES, CURSED CUTS

51   *The Crystal Bible*: Judy Hall, *The Crystal Bible* (Iola, WI: Krause Publications, 2003).

52   cursed gems from around the globe: Levi Higgs, "Is Your Diamond Cursed? A History of Wicked Stones," *The Daily Beast*, May 27, 2018, https://www.thedailybeast.com/is-your-diamond-cursed-a-history-of-wicked-stones.

52   Yet the details were terrible: Chloe Melas, "Kim Kardashian Thought She Would Be Raped, Killed During Paris Robbery," CNN, March 20, 2017.

53   In her memoir: Doris Payne with Zelda Lockhart, *Diamond Doris: The True Story of the World's Most Notorious Jewel Thief* (New York: HarperCollins, 2019).

53   *Town & Country* and *Harper's Bazaar*: Payne, *Diamond Doris*, 12.

53   "I didn't feel any less": Payne, *Diamond Doris*, 34.

54   "taking": Payne, *Diamond Doris*, 79–81.

54   diamond-water paradox: Daniel P. Ahn, *Principles of Commodity Economics and Finance* (Cambridge, MA: MIT Press, 2019), 12.

56   "They are often bought by men": Victoria Finlay, *Jewels: A Secret History* (New York: Random House, 2006), 320.

57   comes from the Greek "adamas": Courtney A. Stewart, "Twelve Jewels: Indian Diamonds in History and Myth," The Met (online), October 26, 2018, https://www.metmuseum.org/blogs/now-at-the-met/2018/indian-diamonds-benjamin-zucker-family-collection.

57   ancient China from as early as 2500 BCE: Peter J. Lu et al., "Earliest Use of Corundum and Diamond in Prehistoric China," *Archaeometry* 47 (2005): 1–12.

57   Bead-making workshops: Leonard Gorelick and A. John Gwinnett, "Diamonds from India to Rome and Beyond," *American Journal of Archaeology* 92, no. 4 (1988): 547–552, https://doi.org/10.2307/505249.

58   capable of faceting diamonds: Dr. Gerald Wycoff, "The History of Lapidary," International Gem Society, https://www.gemsociety.org/article/the-history-of-lapidary/.

58   Began mining diamonds in Brazil: Darcy P. Svisero, James E. Shigley, and Robert Weldon, "Brazilian Diamonds: A Historical and Recent Perspective," *Gems & Gemology* 53, no. 1 (Spring 2017): 2–29.

59   A report from 2021: Maurício Angelo, "333 People Rescued from

Slavery in Brazil Mines Since 2008, Exclusive Report Shows," *Mongabay*, August 3, 2021, accessed online August 29, 2022, https://news.mongabay.com/2021/08/333-people-rescued-from-slavery-in-brazil-mines-since-2008-exclusive-report-shows/.

59 **The first South African diamond:** "The History of Diamonds," Cape Town Diamond Museum, https://www.capetowndiamondmuseum.org/about-diamonds/south-african-diamond-history/.

59 **a "ruthless" edge:** Finlay, *Jewels*, 340.

60 **the De Beers convict camps:** Farai Chideya, "Diamonds and the Making of South Africa," NPR, https://www.npr.org/transcripts/15775777?ft=nprml&f=15775777.

60 **"The Kimberley mines":** Finlay, *Jewels*, 340.

60 **Since the late 1800s:** Donna J. Bergenstock and James M. Maskulka, "The De Beers Diamond Story: Are Diamonds Forever?" *Business Horizons* 44, no. 3 (2001): 37–44.

61 **They need to control demand as well as supply:** Edward Jay Epstein, "Have You Ever Tried to Sell a Diamond?" *The Atlantic*, February 1982.

61 **"Not diamonds":** Finlay, *Jewels*, 347.

61 **The first big advertisement:** Rachelle Bergstein, *Brilliance and Fire: A Biography of Diamonds* (New York: HarperCollins, 2017), 104.

63 **De Beers was adroit as ever:** Alan Cowell, "Controversy over Diamonds Made into Virtue by De Beers," *New York Times*, August 22, 2000.

64 **sales of mined diamonds:** Pamela N. Danziger, "While Mined Diamond Sales Decline, the Future of Lab Grown Diamonds Is Much More Than Jewelry," *Forbes*, December 15, 2019.

64 **buying a lab-grown diamond:** Harriet Constable, "The Sparkling Rise of the Lab Grown Diamond," BBC, February 9, 2020, https://www.bbc.com/future/article/20200207-the-sparkling-rise-of-the-lab-grown-diamond.

64 **cremated ashes of a loved one:** Joan Meiners, "After You Die, Your Body Could Be Turned into a Diamond," *Discover Magazine*, March 24, 2021.

65 **"perfect for right now":** Abha Bhattarai, "A Diamond Is Forever and Forever Now Costs $200 from De Beers," *Mercury News*, https://www.mercurynews.com/2018/06/02/a-diamond-is-forever-and-forever-now-costs-200-from-de-beers/.

65 **"stunned" and "shocked" the diamond industry:** Benjamin C. Esty, "The De Beers Group: Launching Lightbox Jewelry for Lab-Grown Diamonds," Harvard Business School Case 719-408, August 2018. (Revised August 2018.)

67   **nature writer Ellen Meloy:** Ellen Meloy, *The Anthropology of Turquoise: Reflections on Desert, Sea, Stone, and Sky* (New York: Pantheon, 2002).

68   **"family wealth and sacred":** Meloy, *The Anthropology of Turquoise*, 109.

70   **According to an essay:** Andrés Reséndez, "The Other Slavery: Histories of Indian Bondage from New Spain to the Southwestern United States," *Smithsonian*, 2021, accessed online, https://americanindian.si.edu /sites/1/files/pdf/seminars-symposia/the-other-slavery-perspective.pdf.

71   **protecting the wearer against falls:** Fara Braid, "Turquoise Symbolism," International Gem Society, accessed online, https://www.gemsociety .org/article/history-legend-turquoise-gems-yore/.

72   **"How can you explain":** Bee Wilson, "Too Specific and Too Vague," *London Review of Books*, March 24, 2022.

75   **"Rumors of the death of magic":** Chris Gosden, *Magic: A History: From Alchemy to Witchcraft, from the Ice Age to the Present* (New York: Farrar, Straus and Giroux, 2020), 1–15.

4. SPIRALING

79   **"seems to incite":** Elaine Scarry, "On Beauty and Being Wrong," in *On Beauty and Being Just* (Princeton, NJ: Princeton University Press, 1999), 1–54.

81   **shells as a form of memory:** Elyse Graham, "How the Seashell Got Its Stripes," *The American Scholar* (Autumn 2010).

83   **"For centuries, many great minds":** Helen Scales, *Spirals in Time: The Secret Life and Curious Afterlife of Seashells* (London: Bloomsbury, 2015), 49.

85   **serving as a stand-in for value:** Maria Kielmas, "What Were Seashells Used for in Ancient Times?" Sciencing, April 25, 2017, last modified August 23, 2022, https://sciencing.com/were-seashells-used-ancient -times-7797.html.

86   **cowries arrived in Europe by the millions:** Jan Hogendorn and Marion Johnson, *The Shell Money of the Slave Trade* (Cambridge: Cambridge University Press, 2009).

86   **it took 10,000 shells to buy one slave:** Jane I. Guyer and Karin Pallaver, "Money and Currency in African History," *Oxford Research Encyclopedia of African History*, May 24, 2018, accessed August 26, 2022, https://oxfordre .com/africanhistory/view/10.1093/acrefore/9780190277734.001.0001 /acrefore-9780190277734-e-144.

87   **Newport "spirit bundle":** *Historiansplaining* (podcast), episode #114: "The Newport Spirit Bundle," https://historiansplaining.com/individual -episodes/the-newport-spirit-bundle/.

88 **"brought to America as talismans":** National Museum of African American History and Culture, "Cowrie Shells and Trade Power," *Smithsonian*, accessed online, https://nmaahc.si.edu/cowrie-shells-and -trade-power.

88 **In 2016, the Newport Spirit bundle:** "Director's Note Fall 2016," Newport Historical Society, https://newporthistory.org/directors-note -fall-2016/.

89 **"Queen of Cowries":** Audrey Lang, "Lafalaise Dion, 'Queen of Cow- ries,' Takes *Essence* on a Personal Journey," *Essence*, November 4, 2020.

89 **prompted critic Wesley Morris to reflect:** Jason Farago, Vanessa Fried- man, Gia Kourlas, Wesley Morris, Jon Pareles, and Salamishah Tillet, "Beyoncé's 'Black Is King': Let's Discuss," *New York Times*, July 31, 2020.

90 **"scores of dead mussels":** Susie Cagle, "Heatwave Cooks Mussels in Their Shells on California Shore," *The Guardian*, June 29, 2019.

90 **"mounds of lifeless sea urchins":** Alec Luhn, "Massive Marine Die-Off in Russia Could Threaten Endangered Sea Otters, Other Vulnerable Species," *National Geographic*, October 16, 2020.

90 **"world's most devastating climate-driven loss":** Jonathan Watts, "Severe Climate-Driven Loss of Native Molluscs Reported Off Israel's Coast," *The Guardian*, January 5, 2021, https://www.theguardian.com/envi ronment/2021/jan/06/severe-climate-driven-loss-of-native-molluscs -reported-off-israels-coast.

91 **Coined in 2003:** Glenn Albrecht et al., "Solastalgia: The Distress Caused by Environmental Change," *Australasian Psychiatry: Bulletin of Royal Australian and New Zealand College of Psychiatrists* 15, suppl 1. S95-8 (2007) 10.1080/10398560701701288.

5. LIVE FAST, DIE PRETTY

98 **arbitrary rules of "the beauty-game":** Ursula K. Le Guin, "Dogs, Cats, and Dancers," from *The Wave in the Mind* (Boulder, CO: Shambhala, 2004), 163–170.

99 **every woman was given a Juno:** Thomas Bulfinch, *Bulfinch's Mythology*, accessed via Project Gutenburg, https://www.gutenberg.org/ebooks /4928.

100 **There's Ötzi the Iceman:** Carl Engelking, "Scientists Have Mapped All of Ötzi the Iceman's 61 Tattoos," *Discover Magazine*, January 30, 2015.

100 **ancient Egyptian beautifying practices:** Luisa Hagele, "Ancient Egypt's Most Indulgent Beauty Secrets," *The Collector*, January 16, 2022, https:// www.thecollector.com/ancient-egypt-beauty-secrets/.

NOTES

101 **This dark, thickly applied eyeliner:** Julia Wolkoff, "How Ancient Egyptian Cosmetics Influenced Our Beauty Rituals," CNN Style, March 3, 2020 (Originally published on Artsy.com), https://www.cnn.com/style/article/ancient-egypt-beauty-ritual-artsy/index.html.

101 **"implied a sense of order":** Susan Stewart, *Painted Faces: A Colourful History of Cosmetics* (Gloucestershire: Amberley Publishing, 2017), 2–3.

102 **"the kids":** Rae Nudson, "The Business of Blending In," *Topic Magazine*, Issue No. 14, August 2018.

102 **"realness could act as a shield":** Rae Nudson, *All Made Up: The Power and Pitfalls of Beauty Culture, from Cleopatra to Kim Kardashian* (Boston: Beacon Press, 2021), 80.

103 **Miranda Kerr:** Megan C. Hills, "Miranda Kerr's New Beauty Secret Is Absolutely Terrifying," *Marie Claire*, June 14, 2017, https://www.marieclaire.co.uk/news/celebrity-news/miranda-kerr-leech-facial-514676.

104 **Venetian ceruse:** Becky Little, "Arsenic Pills and Lead Foundation: The History of Toxic Makeup," *National Geographic*, September 22, 2016.

104 **Han dynasty:** Edward H. Schafer, "The Early History of Lead Pigments and Cosmetics in China." *T'oung Pao* 44, no. 4/5 (1956): 413–438.

105 **famously stopped sitting:** Roy Strong, *Gloriana: The Portraits of Queen Elizabeth* (New York: Thames & Hudson, 1987).

105 **cosmetics historian Gabriela Hernandez:** Gabriela Hernandez, *Classic Beauty: The History of Makeup* (Altgen, PA: Schiffer, 2017).

105 **According to some sources:** Robert Hume, "Reflecting on Beauty: Maria Gunning's Sad Story," *Irish Examiner*, July 25, 2018, https://www.irishexaminer.com/lifestyle/arid-30857470.html.

106 **Analysis of bones:** "Being Rich in the Middle Ages Led to an Unhealthy Life," EurekaAlert!, October 20, 2015, https://www.eurekalert.org/news-releases/736049.

106 **wealthiest members of society:** Danny Lewis, "Lead Poisoning Rampant for Wealthy Medieval Europeans," *Smithsonian*, October 22, 2015.

106 **there is still lead present:** J. Lewis, "True Colors: Unmasking Hidden Lead in Cosmetics from Low- and Middle-Income Countries," *Environmental Health Perspectives* 130, no. 4 (2022): 42001, doi:10.1289/EHP9220.

107 **"hot as a hare":** Erin Broderick, Heidi Metheny, and Brianna Crosby, *Anticholinergic Toxicity* (Treasure Island, FL: StatPearls Publishing, 2022), https://www.ncbi.nlm.nih.gov/books/NBK534798/.

108 **"naughty man's cherries":** Micheal Largo, "Big, Bad Botany: Deadly Nightshade (Atropa Belladonna), the Poisonous A-Lister,"

240

Slate, August 18, 2014, https://slate.com/technology/2014/08
/poisonous-plants-belladonna-nightshade-is-the-celebrity-of-deadly
-flora.html.

108 **"libidinous and orgiastic abandon":** David O. Kennedy, *Plants and the
Human Brain* (New York: Oxford University Press, 2014), 132.

108 **witches-riding-broomsticks trope:** Megan Garber, "Why Do Witches
Ride Brooms? (NSFW)," *The Atlantic*, October 31, 2013.

109 **"books of secrets":** Meghan Racklin, "Before Beauty Vlogging, There
Were Renaissance 'Books of Secrets,'" Literary Hub, January 15, 2020,
https://lithub.com/before-beauty-vlogging-there-were-renaissance
-books-of-secrets/.

109 **During the Romantic period:** Carolyn A. Day, *Consumptive Chic: A
History of Beauty, Fashion, and Disease* (London: Bloomsbury Academic,
2020), 1.

110 **"fashionable disease":** Day, *Consumptive Chic*, 81.

111 **"the perfect object":** Joanna Ebenstein, "The Brief, Mystical Reign of
the Wax Cadaver," *Nautilus*, August 25, 2016.

111 **"the microcosm really does reflect the macrocosm":** Joanna Ebenstein,
The Anatomical Venus (London: Thames & Hudson, 2016), 213.

111 the **"Dead Girl Show":** Alice Bolin, *Dead Girls: Essays on Surviving
an American Obsession* (New York: William Morrow, 2018), 13.

113 **"Instagram face":** Jia Tolentino, "The Age of Instagram Face," *New
Yorker*, December 12, 2019.

117 **"natural red four":** Helen Soteriou and Will Smale, "Why You May
Have Been Eating Insects Your Whole Life," *BBC News*, April 28, 2018,
https://www.bbc.com/news/business-43786055.

117 **which were patented in 1911:** Pagan Kennedy, "Who Made Those False
Eyelashes?" *New York Times*, January 18, 2013.

117 **Owen showed up:** Kennedy, "Who Made Those False Eyelashes?"

117 **In the 1930s:** Stewart, *Painted Faces*, 261.

118 **There are thousands of different:** Abrahm Lustgarten, Lisa Song, and
Talia Buford, "Suppressed Study: The EPA Underestimated Dangers of
Widespread Chemicals," *ProPublica*, June 20, 2018, https://www
.propublica.org/article/suppressed-study-the-epa-underestimated
-dangers-of-widespread-chemicals.

118 **"nearly impossible":** Sandee LaMotte, "Doctors Should Test Levels of
PFAS in People at High Risk, Report Says," CNN, July 28, 2022, https://
www.cnn.com/2022/07/28/health/pfas-testing-guidelines-wellness/index
.html.

119 **"One rule of the game":** Le Guin, *Wave in the Mind*, 166.

6. DIRTY, SWEET, FLORAL, FOUL

122   **the oil that covers pubic hair:** Hannah Betts, "Let Us Spray," *The Guardian*, December 5, 2008, https://www.theguardian.com/lifeandstyle/2008/dec/06/perfume-ingredients.

123   **There are even Christian legends:** Jude Stewart, *Revelations in Air: A Guidebook to Smell* (New York: Penguin, 2021), 242–245.

124   **One of the first known perfumers:** Zing Tsjeng, "Don't Forget Tapputi-Belatekallim," *Cosmos Magazine*, March 15, 2018, https://cosmosmagazine.com/history/forgotten-women-in-science-tapputi-belatekallim/.

125   **This could be true:** Nuri McBride, "Tappūtī-Bēlet-ekallim: The First Perfumer?" *Death Scent Project*, https://deathscent.com/2022/07/12/tapputi-belatekallim/.

125   **the world's oldest-known perfume factory:** "Italy Discovers Scents of Venus," *Italy Magazine*, https://www.italymagazine.com/italy/italy-discovers-scents-venus.

126   **"miasmic theory":** Joseph P. Byrne, *Encyclopedia of the Black Death* (Santa Barbara, CA: ABC-CLIO, 2012), 120.

127   **"No state, federal or global authority":** Lauren Zanolli, "Why Smelling Good Could Come with a Cost to Health," *The Guardian*, May 23, 2019.

128   **"more valuable than gold":** Dr. Joe Schwarcz, *The Fly in the Ointment: 70 Fascinating Commentaries on the Science of Everyday Life* (Toronto: ECW Press, 2004), 141–142.

129   **According to Christopher Kemp:** Christopher Kemp, *Floating Gold: A Natural (and Unnatural) History of Ambergris* (Chicago: University of Chicago Press, 2012), 11–14.

130   **it was dragon spit:** Mark Wilding, "A Brief, Fascinating History of Ambergris," *Smithsonian*, September 2, 2021.

131   **The going rate for ambergris:** Kemp, *Floating Gold*, 78.

132   **the "fallen angel":** Helen Keller, *The World I Live In* (London: Hodder and Stoughton, 1904), 77, accessed online via Project Gutenberg, https://www.gutenberg.org/files/27683/27683-h/27683-h.htm#Page_77.

137   **which can range from:** "Fragrance with Fecal Smells as an Additive" from Basenotes community discussion, https://basenotes.com/threads/fragrance-with-a-fecal-smell-an-addictive-do-you-like-fecal-scent-fragrance.274384/.

138   **A study published in 2018:** Karen A. Cerulo, "Scents and Sensibility: Olfaction, Sense-Making, and Meaning Attribution." *American Sociological Review* 83, no. 2 (April 2018): 361–389, https://doi.org/10.1177/0003122418759679.

139   **"This suggests that":** Cerulo, "Scents and Sensibility," 382.

7. WOMEN AND WORMS

151 **"matured rather than just begun":** "World's Oldest Silk Fabrics Discovered in Central China," *Archaeology News Network*, December 5, 2019, https://archaeologynewsnetwork.blogspot.com/2019/12/worlds-oldest-silk-fabrics-discovered.html.

151 **"the internet of antiquity":** Janet Tassel, "Yo-Yo Ma's Journeys," *Harvard Magazine*, March 1, 2003, https://www.harvardmagazine.com/2000/03/yo-yo-mas-journeys-html.

151 **"reduce women's clothing to nakedness":** Pliny the Elder, *Natural History*, Loeb Classical Library, accessed online, https://www.loebclassics.com/view/pliny_elder-natural_history/1938/pb_LCL353.479.xml?mainRsKey=V7FKrS&readMode=reader.

152 **"It is hard to overstate":** "The Silk Road," National Geographic Society (Resource Library), last modified on May 20, 2022, https://education.nationalgeographic.org/resource/silk-road/.

153 **"The production of silk was bound up":** Kassia St. Clair, *The Golden Thread: How Fabric Changed History* (New York: W. W. Norton & Company, 2019), 65.

154 *The Silk Princess*: Neil MacGregor, *A History of the World in 100 Objects* (London: Penguin Books, 2012), 271–275.

154 **like all just-so legends:** Elizabeth Ten Grotenhuis, "Stories of Silk and Paper," *World Literature Today* 80, no. 4 (Jul/Aug 2006): 10–12.

155 **Legend has it:** Peter Ross Range, "Spin Cycle," *Smithsonian*, July 2008.

155 **"considered an art":** Trini Callava, *Silk Through the Ages* (New York: LID Publishing Inc., 2018), 83.

155 **"the history of opulence":** Christopher J. Berry, *The Idea of Luxury: A Conceptual and Historical Investigation* (Cambridge: Cambridge University Press, 1994), 183.

156 **"It was about witnessing":** Callava, *Silk Through the Ages*, 177.

156 **Princess Diana's wedding dress:** Chanel Vargas, "Every Detail About Princess Diana's Iconic Wedding Dress," *Town & Country*, August 30, 2022.

156 **ivory silk taffeta:** Susan Heller Anderson, "The Dress: Silk Taffeta with Sequins and Pearls," *New York Times*, July 30, 1981.

156 **had to "scramble":** Terry Trucco, "Home-Grown Silk for a Royal Wedding," *New York Times*, May 30, 1986.

157 **the damage wrought:** Molly Sequin, "Gypsy Moth Caterpillars Have Decimated Large Portions of New England Forests This Summer," *Business Insider*, July 19, 2016.

157 **For years, I've been reading about:** Donna Lindner, "Air Force Scientists

Study Artificial Silk for Body Armor, Parachutes," U.S. Department of
Defense, August 6, 2018, https://www.defense.gov/News/News-Stories
/Article/Article/1594185/air-force-scientists-study-artificial-silk-for
-body-armor-parachutes/.

158 **"the soul of the sea":** Max Paradiso, "Chiara Vigo: The Last Woman
Who Makes Sea Silk," BBC, September 2, 2015, https://www.bbc.com
/news/magazine-33691781.

159 **harvesting golden orb spiders:** Randy Kennedy, "Gossamer Silk, from
Spiders Spun," *New York Times*, September 22, 2009.

159 **"imbued with metaphor":** Eliza Shapiro, "Golden Girls Heather Graham and Tinsley Mortimer Lend Natural-History Museum Spider-Silk
Opening Some Glitz," *Observer*, September 24, 2009.

160 **"all right to boil a sentient creature":** David Foster Wallace, "Consider
the Lobster," *Gourmet*, August 2004, 60.

161 **"Boiling cocoons":** "Small Change: Bonded Child Labor in India's Silk
Industry," Human Rights Watch, January 22, 2003, http://www.hrw.org
/reports/2003/india/.

162 **"does not require great skill":** "Small Change."

163 **Decades later, a 2021:** *Silk Slaves: A CNN Freedom Project*, CNN, https://
www.cnn.com/videos/tv/2021/03/11/cfp-silk-slaves-doc-spc-intl.cnn.

165 **what defines luxury:** Thorstein Veblen, *The Theory of the Leisure Class*,
accessed online at http://moglen.law.columbia.edu/LCS/theoryleisure
class.pdf/.

166 **to borrow a term:** Maria Popova, "Conspicuous Outrage: Quentin Bell,
Virginia Woolf's Nephew, on Sartorial Morality, the Art of Fashion, and
the Futility of War," *The Marginalian*, September 6, 2013, https://www
.themarginalian.org/2013/09/06/quentin-bell-on-human-finery/.

167 **"Endless wanting":** L. M. Sacasas, "Ill With Want," *The Convivial
Society* 2, no. 13, July 17, 2021, https://theconvivialsociety.substack
.com/p/ill-with-want.

8. DECEPTIONS AND DAMNATION

172 **"humankind's most important material":** Douglas Main, "Glass Is
Humankind's Most Important Material," *The Atlantic*, April 13, 2018.

172 **"endless number of recipes":** Dan Klein and Ward Lloyd, *The History of
Glass* (New York: Orbis Publishing Limited, 1984), 9.

174 **According to Pliny:** "The Origins of Glassmaking," Corning Museum
of Glass, October 1, 2011, https://www.cmog.org/article/origins
-glassmaking.

174 **Most of the glass objects:** Klein and Ward, *The History of Glass*, 10–19.

175 **"doesn't smell to me like":** Carolyn Wilke, "A Brief Scientific History of Glass," *Smithsonian*, November 24, 2021.

175 **Around year zero:** Rosemarie Trentinella, "Roman Glass," in *Heilbrunn Timeline of Art History* (New York: Metropolitan Museum of Art, 2000).

175 **experimenting more with form:** R. A. Grossman, *Ancient Glass: A Guide to the Yale Collection* (New Haven, CT: Yale University Art Gallery, 2002).

176 **Archaeologist Rosemary Cramp:** Rosemary Cramp, "Window Glass from the Monastic Site of Jarrow: Problems of Interpretation," *Journal of Glass Studies* 17 (1975): 88–96.

176 **"like picking up jewels":** Audio guide of St. Paul's Monestary, featuring Rosemary Cramp, accessed online, https://www.english-heritage.org.uk /visit/places/st-pauls-monastery-jarrow/audio.

176 **A reconstruction:** Kelly Richman-Abdou, "Stained Glass: The Splendid History of an Ancient Art Form that Still Dazzles Today," My Modern Met, April 28, 2019, https://mymodernmet.com/stained-glass-history/.

177 **It must have been decided:** Virginia Chieffo Raguin, *Stained Glass: From Its Origin to the Present* (New York: Harry N. Abrams, 2003), 6–14.

177 **reached its peak in Europe:** Department of Medieval Art and The Cloisters, "Stained Glass in Medieval Europe," in *Heilbrunn Timeline of Art History* (New York: Metropolitan Museum of Art, 2000).

177 **"inestimable beauty":** "Stained Glass in Medieval Europe."

177 **"slime" of earth:** Alexandra Kelly, "Medieval Artwork: Jewels of the Middle Ages," *The Collector*, May 29, 2022.

177 **"harrowing of hell":** "Stained-Glass Demons, Strasbourg Cathedral, Strasbourg, France," *Atlas Obscura*, February 15, 2019, https://www .atlasobscura.com/places/stained-glass-demons-strasbourg-cathedral.

178 **an era that birthed the phantasmagoria:** Allison C. Meier, "The Magic Lantern Shows that Influenced Modern Horror," *JSTOR Daily*, May 12, 2018, https://daily.jstor.org/the-magic-lantern-shows-that-influenced -modern-horror/.

178 **took place in the 1790s:** Tom Gunning, "Illusions Past and Future: The Phantasmagoria and Its Specters," University of Chicago, https://www .mediaarthistory.org/refresh/Programmatic%20key%20texts/pdfs /Gunning.pdf.

9. BONE WHITE, PAPER THIN

186 **"Resonant when struck":** Editors, "Porcelain," *Encyclopedia Britannica*, January 10, 2020, https://www.britannica.com/art/porcelain.

189 **The lady favored rose hues:** Sarah Archer, "A Western Cultural History of Pink, from Madame de Pompadour to Pussy Hats," *Hyperallergic*,

February 20, 2017, https://hyperallergic.com/359159/a-western-cultural-history-of-pink-from-madame-de-pompadour-to-pussy-hats/.

190   **under Victoria's leadership:** "The Opium Trade in China," *Story of China*, PBS, https://www.thirteen.org/programs/story-of-china/opium-trade-china-bcwi05/.

190   **smuggling in tens of thousands:** Editors, "Opium Trade, British and Chinese History," Encyclopedia Britannica, https://www.britannica.com/topic/opium-trade/The-Opium-Wars.

190   **the breakfast beverage of choice:** Tasha Marks, "The Tea-Rific History of Victorian Afternoon Tea," *British Museum Blog*, https://blog.british museum.org/the-tea-rific-history-of-victorian-afternoon-tea/.

191   **To address this darker side of art history:** Jeanne Goswami, "Every Eleven Minutes," *Peabody Essex Museum Blog*, October 9, 2019, https://www.pem.org/blog/every-eleven-minutes.

191   **The typical American opiate addict:** Erick Trickey, "Inside the Story of America's 19th-Century Opiate Addiction," *Smithsonian*, January 4, 2018.

192   **Germans loved their porcelain:** Suzanne L. Marchand, *Porcelain: A History from the Heart of Europe* (Princeton, NJ: Princeton University Press, 2020).

194   **much of it is likely fake:** Marchand, *Porcelain*, 366.

194   **Jen Graves:** Jen Graves, "Charles Krafft Is a White Nationalist Who Believes the Holocaust Is a Deliberately Exaggerated Myth," *The Stranger*, February 13, 2013.

195   **"what cred":** David Lewis, "We Snuck into Seattle's Super Secret White Nationalist Convention," *The Stranger*, October 4, 2017.

195   **Edmund de Waal argues:** Edmund de Waal, *The White Road: Journey into an Obsession* (New York: Farrar, Straus and Giroux, 2015).

195   **"It feels clean":** de Waal, *White Road*, 5.

197   **Hitler's partner, Eva Braun:** Paul Bedard, "Hitler's Gal Pal Eva Braun's Pink Lingerie Sells for $2,250," *Washington Examiner*, December 18, 2015.

10. THE EXHALATIONS OF THE EARTH

206   **A member of the Romantic movement:** "Curator Andrew Eschelbacher Explains the Romantic Ideal of a 'Beautiful Death,'" PMA Guide, https://pmaguide.stqry.app/en/story/95098.

208   **The color of marble:** Fabio Barry, *Painting in Stone: Architecture and the Poetics of Marble from Antiquity to the Enlightenment* (New Haven, CT: Yale University Press, 2020).

211 **"I will replace":** Graham Lanktree, "Donald Trump's History of Bashing the U.N. and What It Tells Us About His Speech," *Newsweek*, September 18, 2017.

211 **the building stood 70 percent empty:** John Malathronas, "See Nicolae Ceaușescu's Grandiose and Bloody Legacy in Bucharest," CNN Travel, December 5, 2014.

212 **When reporter Stanislav Volkov was a little boy:** Stanislav Volkov, "'People are afraid to say a word': Inside the Closed City of Ashgabat," *The Guardian*, October 16, 2017.

212 **Footage of the city from the 1980s:** Username: Demirgazyk, "Best Turkmen Song," uploaded on July 15, 2017, YouTube, https://www.youtube.com/watch?v=1xoXGv9JvgE.

212 **"It felt like entering":** Alan Taylor, "The City of White Marble: Ashgabat, Turkmenistan," *The Atlantic*, June 5, 2013.

214 **Silica dust is toxic:** Imran Butt et al., "Pulmonary Function Parameters Among Marble Industry Workers in Lahore, Pakistan," *F1000Research* 10 no. 938 (September 2021), doi:10.12688/f1000research.52749.1.

214 **"exploitation by employers":** Butt, "Pulmonary Function Parameters."

216 **Not Jose Martinez, though:** Nell Greenfieldboyce, "Workers Are Falling Ill, Even Dying, After Making Kitchen Countertops," NPR, December 6, 2019, https://www.kcur.org/2019-12-06/workers-are-falling-ill-even-dying-after-making-kitchen-countertops.

218 **You might imagine that people:** Rebecca Greenfield, "Our First Public Parks: The Forgotten History of Cemeteries," *The Atlantic*, March 16, 2011.

221 **In *The Book of Unconformities*:** Hugh Raffles, *The Book of Unconformities: Speculations on Lost Time* (Portland, OR: Verse Chorus Press, 2022).

INDEX

INDEX

atomic weapons, 181
Atropa belladonna, 107–9. *See also*
    belladonna
attraction-repulsion dynamic, 2
"augmented reality," 113
Augustus the Strong, 192
authenticity, 74–75
autoimmune disorders, 214
Aztec, 70

Babylon, 124–25
Bacchantae, 108
The Bachelor, 38, 40, 41
Bailey-Matthews National Shell Museum,
    93, 158–59
ballroom culture, 102
Barber, Aja, 163
Barents Sea, 91–92
Barney's, 146
Barnum, P. T., 180
basalt, 222
Bath & Body Works, 122
Bauck, Whitney, 163
beachcombing, 93, 227
beadmaking, 167–71
beauty
    appreciation of, 9–10, 199–200
    capitalism and, 217–18
    consumerism and, 99–100
    darkness and, 123–24
    death and, 110–11, 119–20, 124, 223
    depression and, 1–2
    desire and, 228
    digital, 113–15
    estrangement from, 204
    "ideal," 119–20
    importance of, 1–2
    jouissance and, 227–28
    mortality and, 223, 228
    in nature, 225–27, 229
    replication and, 79–80
    success and, 8
    sustainability and, 225–26
    tragedy and, 205–6
    transience and, 228
    ugliness and, 2, 3
    unexpected, 227, 229
    waste and, 165
    women and, 99–100

"beauty-game" archetype, 119
beauty industry, 100, 102–3, 118
beauty standards, 107, 119, 196
bedrock, 222
beetle shells, 103, 117
Bell, Quentin, 166
belladonna, 107–10, 112–13
benzodiazepines, 73–74
bergamot, 125
Berger, John, 20
Berry, Christopher J., 155–56
beryls, 66
Beyoncé, 89
Black Is King, 89
black trumpet mushroom, 143
Bleeding Nun, 179
Blood Diamond, 63
blue lace agate, 51
blue lotus, 28
Blunt, John, "The Orchid Horror," 36
blush, 117
Bolin, Alice, 111–12
Bombyx mori, 149–50
bonded labor, 59–60, 162, 163
"bone china," 186, 188
Book of Revelation, 177
books of secrets, 109
boronia, 131
Botox, 103, 112–13, 116, 120
Botticelli, Sandro, 108
    The Birth of Venus, 80
Bourges Cathedral, 178
Braun, Eva, 197–98, 199
Brazil, 58, 59
bread baking, 200
Breast Cancer Prevention Partners, 127
British East India Company, 190
Bronzino, Agnolo, 109
Bucharest, Romania, 211
Buddhism, 29
building materials, 207, 210
byssus, 158
Byzantine Empire, 155

calamus, 124–25
calcite, 207, 208
California, 90
Callava, Trini, *Silk Through the Ages*, 155,
    156

250

INDEX

INDEX

smell. *See* perfumery
Smith, Adam, 54–55
smoke, 141, 142
snail mucin, 103
social media, 21, 97, 113–14, 116, 120.
   See also filters
soft power, 157
"solastalgia," 91
Solomon, 37
Sophie Hallette lace, 165–66
Soubirous, Bernadette, 110
South Africa, 59–60
Spain, 188
Spanish colonialism, 70
species extinction, 92
spectacles, 178–79, 180
spice, 139, 144
spiders, 159
spider silk, 159–60
spirals, 77–96
Sri Lanka, 86
stained glass, 170, 172, 176–78
statues, 203–24. *See also* figurines;
   sculpture
St. Clair, Kassia, *The Golden Thread*,
   153
St. Elizabeth of Hungary Parish, Acton,
   Massachusetts, 171
Stewart, Amy, *Flower Confidential*, 43–44
Stewart, Susan, *Painted Faces: A Colorful
   History of Cosmetics*, 101
still lifes, 228
Stoker, Bram, *Dracula*, 110
stone, 203–24. *See also specific kinds of
   stone*
   engineered, 216–17
   gravestones, 219–21
   white, 196
stonecutters, 216
St. Paul's Monastery, Jarrow, England,
   176–77
The Stranger, 194
strongmen, 211
sumptuary laws, 155
superiority, 209–11
surveillance capitalism, 114
Susini, Clemente, 110–11
sustainability, 225–26
Swans Island, 220

Sweden, 31
sweet fern, 143

talismans, 88
Tapputi-Belatekallim, 124–25
Tartt, Donna, *The Secret History*,
   167–68
taste, 7, 208–9, 211. *See also* aesthetic
   preferences
tattoos, 100
tea, 190
technology, 178, 180–82
telescope, 178
temperance movement, 190
Tennyson, Alfred, Lord, 27
   "The Lotos-Eaters," 27
Teresa, Saint, 228
terpenoid, 141
textiles, women and, 153–55
Theophilus, 177
thyroid disease, 118
timber, 207
time, 223. *See also* decay; impermanence;
   mortality
tin, 59
tincture, 125
tinted moisturizer, 115
Titanic, 102
Titian (Tiziano Vecelli), 20
tobacco, 142
Tolentino, Jia, 113–14, 119
topaz, 74
tourmaline, 50
Town & Country, 53
toxins, 104–10, 112, 117–18, 159, 214–15.
   See also poison
tradition, 199–200
traditional Chinese medicine, 128
traditional Korean medicine, 128
tragedy, beauty and, 205–6
Transmit, 203–4, 205
trans people, 102
transubstantiation, 175–76
Troubelot, Étienne Léopold, 157
Trucco, Terry, 156
Trump, Donald, 211
tuberculosis, 110, 206, 215
tumblers, 199
Turkmenistan, 211–13